BUSINESS STATUS

MONEY-MAKING MACHINE

ARVIND UPADHYAY

ISBN 979-888546695-0

You have comfort. You don't have luxury. And don't tell me that money plays a part. The luxury I advocate has nothing to do with money. It cannot be bought. It is the reward of those who have no fear of discomfort.

Whenever you find yourself on the side of the majority, it is time to pause and reflect. —MARK TWAIN

Anyone who lives within their means suffers from a lack of imagination. —OSCAR WILDE, Irish dramatist and novelist

Business activity affects the daily lives of all people, as they work, spend, save, invest, travel, and play. Business influences jobs, incomes, and opportunities for personal enterprise and development. Business has a significant effect not only on the standard of living and quality of life, but also on the environment in which people live.

At some point in their lives, all students will encounter the world of business. They, therefore, must be prepared to engage in business activity with confidence and competence, by understanding how businesses function and the role it plays in our society. Students should familiarise themselves with the skills that are required in the business environment and the impact these skills can have on their own lives and on society.

Studying business involves not only involves studying individuals, communities, and organizations, it involves assessing their needs and problems, as well as generating solutions. This subject will build a strong foundation for those students who wish to move on to further study and training in specialised areas such as management, international business, marketing, accounting, information and communication technology, or entrepreneurship. It will also provide practical skills for those who wish to move directly into the workplace.

Business studies also provides students with a new, practical context for many of the subjects they have studied, including mathematics, science and technology, language, and social studies. It will help students to recognise the relevance of these subjects as they are applied in the world of business – for example, in helping people with their needs, challenges, and problems; and in creating products and services that help to improve the quality of life.

Business studies demonstrates how a variety of areas of study can be combined in productive activity. It provides an increased understanding of mutual dependence through business system, as people becoming increasingly dependent on others. Finally, as the business environment is dynamic and ever-changing, it can be an important tool to develop skills to cope with change.

For any country's economy, setting up and establishing business units is important for them. When any country has lots of business ventures at its end, then it becomes easy for that nation to offer employment opportunities, goods, and services to its citizens.

It is only by setting up businesses, firms, industries, and organizations that we can boost the economy of our country.

First of all, the presence of business units ensures and guarantees the non-stop supply of goods and services.

Moreover, different business units make and manufacture different products and services, and then they are supplied to people living in that country.

They create and develop new utilities that bring benefits and pros to the people and residents living in that society.

Local businesses make their society in a position to supply and manufacture locally produced goods and services instead of importing it from other countries.

Thus, the presence of businesses ensures and claims to give constant supply as well as the delivery of goods and services.

It is seen and observed that business units harness capital and also other kinds of resources while they enter in the production zone. Besides, they borrow loans from financial institutions and employ those funds and loans in their productive activities.

That is why you can say that business units harness capital and invest them in these economic activities and meanwhile make use of natural resources so that value addition factors can be created for citizens.

In any country, when lots of business units and industries are there, it means that country will never and ever run short of providing employment opportunities.

These business units offer and generate a variable number of job choices and options for their residents.

Business is important and significant to society because it preserves natural resources. In other words, it is these business units that manage to create new utilities for your natural resources.

This whole concept and phenomenon are done with the help of value addition as well as preservation.

This phenomenon of research development can only be carried out in any country and society if they have business units at their end. So, the presence of businesses ensures and guarantees the promotion of innovation and too research development.

We all know that all kinds of businesses continuously and constantly do researches and they make use of alternative resources for the sake of developing new products and services.

Businesses generate income on the highest notes

This factor of income generation plays an important role in any society and it is possible if you have business units and varied firms working in your country.

These businesses generate enough income for residents and individuals. They make use of land and labor and also the capital and are able to generate sufficient income for their country.

Businesses socially develop a country

For the sake of social development, setting up businesses matters a lot. They heavily and immensely contribute to social development.

These business units increase and boost your social national income. At the same time, they make your economy profitable and help the government to carry out different numbers of development activities.

Develop the sector of education, technology, and also science

You need to understand that businesses help in developing the sector of education, science, and too technology.

The income-generating from these business platforms establishes and innovates your technology and science sector.

More benefits of setting up businesses and how they are productive to society?

We all know that businesses generate and develop new jobs. No doubt, they are marked and recognized as one of the valuable assets for your country,

Businesses give identity to your community

Most importantly, businesses give immense and wide identity to your community. It gives a unique character as well as charm to your society.

It transforms your country to keep on gaining and getting more advantages in the form of constant profits, growth, and development.

Businesses heavily involve your community

On the other hand, it is all through the establishment of businesses that your community gets involved and submerges in a profitable manner.

Business owners tend to develop and generate a sense of community among their residents. They build relationships with their customers and come out as a key tool to foster their country's growth!

Business units offer environmental benefits

All those business units that are located and present near to any of the residential zones, they manage to reduce the traffic congestion aspect and also bring down automobile use.

In addition, the presence of business units results and leads to better air quality and too less amount of urban sprawl.

It is studied that all those businesses that are located in smart growth places, they protect and secure environmental resources. At the same time, they reduce air pollution and encourage people to walk and cycle.

Hence, we can say that businesses offer significant and immense numbers of economic advantages to society. Besides, society experiences increased productivity and increased innovation at its end.

That country witnessed the improved ability and stronger retail sales.

The establishment of businesses increases the tax base

If you want to see an increased tax base in your country, then it is important for you to keep on setting up business units and private firms.

With the presence of an increased tax base, your local economy starts to get improved and stronger too.

It improves and develops your community and pumps more profits for your society.

Increases the number of local jobs in your country

You should get this understanding that the presence of businesses increases the number of local jobs in your country.

It is these small and local businesses that turn out to be job creators. It is time that each country and each society should support these local businesses.

With its promotion, you can help out your local members to keep on growing. Moreover, the development of business units gives ample growth and success-gaining opportunities to local members of your society.

Business enhances and promotes the concept of entrepreneurship

Most importantly, businesses immensely and widely promote the concept of entrepreneurship in any country.

If you want to boost and enhance entrepreneurial spirit in your country, then make sure to set up industries and businesses over there so that other people also get motivated to initiate such entrepreneurial skills.

Furthermore, it is just because of this entrepreneurship skill that a country witnesses and experiences economic innovation.

Your country starts to move on to the prosperity state. Now, you know why business is so important to society.

Brings the spirit of competition as well as innovation

The significance and importance of businesses to any society is increasing day by day. We have seen and this is a proven fact that business units promote and encourage the spirit of competition and innovation.

If any society has multiple numbers of businesses, then this becomes a unique and innovative factor for them.

Any country that has a business-oriented approach, no one can stop that country or society to develop and grow itself.

Business units need low maintenance

For each society, setting up business units is a preferable choice because they need less infrastructure and also low maintenance as compared to setting up shopping malls and to chain stores.

Apart from that, business units bolster and promote the factor of tourism. At the same time, they manage to contribute heavily to the local vibe zone of your society.

It is the need of the hour that one should support this aspect of local businesses and keep on growing your country's economy. We have provided you enough details that describe and convey to you the importance of large and small businesses.

It is all because of these establishments that your local economy will be able to get lots of benefits. Your community builds upon the best and high notes.

Without businesses, your economy cannot grow and gain success. You have to take and move your economy targets, goals, and milestones by keeping in mind this business-oriented mindset.

Thus, we can now say that businesses are significant and crucial because they give goods and services and offer job avenues.

If no business units are operating in your country, then there is a heavy chance that your economy will become immensely weak.

Contents

Foreword

A business is any activity that provides goods or services to consumers for the purpose of making a profit. When Steve Jobs and Steve Wozniak created Apple Computer in Jobs's family garage, they started a business. The product was the Apple I, and the company's founders hoped to sell their computers to customers for more than it cost to make and market them. If they were successful (which they were), they'd make a profit2 . Before we go on, let's make a couple of important distinctions concerning the terms in our definitions. First, whereas Apple produces and sells goods (iPhone, iPod, Mac), many businesses provide services. Your bank is a service company, as is your Internet provider. Airlines, law firms, movie theaters, and hospitals are also service companies. Many companies provide both goods and services. For example, your local car dealership sells goods (cars) and also provides services (automobile repairs). Second, some organizations are not set up to make profits. Many are established to provide social or educational services. Such not-for-profit (or nonprofit) organizations include the United Way of America, Habitat for Humanity, the Boys and Girls Clubs, the Sierra Club, the American Red Cross, and many colleges and universities. Most of these organizations, however, function in much the same way as a business. They establish goals and work to meet them in an effective, efficient manner. Thus, most of the business principles introduced in this text also apply to nonprofits.Every business must have one or more owners whose primary role is to invest money in the business. When a business is being started, it's generally the owners who polish the business idea and bring together the resources (money and people) needed to turn the idea into a business. The owners also hire employees to work for the company and help it reach its goals. Owners and employees depend on a third group of participants—customers. Ultimately, the goal of any business is to satisfy the needs of its customers.

The activities needed to operate a business can be divided into a number of functional areas: management, operations, marketing, accounting, and finance. Let's briefly explore each of these areas.

Managers are responsible for the work performance of other people. Management involves planning for, organizing, staffing, directing, and controlling a company's resources so that it can achieve its goals. Managers plan by setting goals and developing strategies for achieving them. They organize activities and resources to ensure that company goals are met. They staff the organization with qualified employees and direct them to accomplish organizational goals. Finally, managers design controls for assessing the success of plans and decisions and take corrective action when needed.All companies must convert resources (labor, materials, money, information, and so forth) into goods or services. Some companies, such as Apple, convert resources into tangible products—iPhones, iPods, Macs. Others, such as hospitals, convert resources into intangible products—health care. The person who designs and oversees the transformation of resources into goods or services is called an operations manager . This individual is also responsible for ensuring that products are of high quality.Marketing consists of everything that a company does to identify customers' needs and design products to meet those needs. Marketers develop the benefits and features of products, including price and quality. They also decide on the best method of delivering products and the best means of promoting them to attract and keep customers. They manage relationships with customers and make them aware of the organization's desire and ability to satisfy their needs.

Managers need accurate, relevant, timely financial information, and accountants provide it. Accountants measure, summarize, and communicate financial and managerial information and advise other managers on financial matters. There are two fields of accounting. Financial accountants prepare financial statements to help users, both inside and outside the organization, assess the financial strength of the company. Managerial accountants prepare information, such as reports on the cost of materials used in the production process, for internal use only.

Finance involves planning for, obtaining, and managing a company's funds. Finance managers address such questions as the following: How much money does the company need? How and where will it get the necessary money? How and when will it pay the money back? What should it do with its funds? What investments should be made in plant and equipment? How much should be spent on research and development? How should excess funds be invested? Good financial management is particularly important when a company is first formed, because new business owners usually need to borrow money to get started.

Apple and other businesses don't operate in a vacuum: they're influenced by a number of external factors. These include the economy, government, consumer trends, and public pressure to act as good corporate citizens.sums up the relationship among the participants in a business, its functional areas, and the external forces that influence its activities. One industry that's clearly affected by all these factors is the fast food industry. A strong economy means people have more money to eat out at places where food standards are monitored by a government agency, the Food and Drug Administration.

Preface

Motivating yourself is hard. In fact, I often compare it to one of the exploits of the fictional German hero Baron Munchausen: Trying to sustain your drive through a task, a project, or even a career can sometimes feel like pulling yourself out of a swamp by your own hair. We seem to have a natural aversion to persistent effort that no amount of caffeine or inspirational posters can fix.

But effective self-motivation is one of the main things that distinguishes high-achieving professionals from everyone else. So how can you keep pushing onward, even when you don't feel like it?

To a certain extent, motivation is personal. What gets you going might not do anything for me. And some individuals do seem to have more stick-to-itiveness than others. However, after 20 years of research into human motivation, my team and I have identified several strategies that seem to work for most people—whether they're trying to lose weight, save for retirement, or implement a long, difficult initiative at work. If you've ever failed to reach an attainable goal because of procrastination or lack of commitment—and who of us hasn't?—I encourage you to read on. These four sets of tactics can help propel you forward.

Design Goals, Not Chores

Ample research has documented the importance of goal setting. Studies have shown, for example, that when salespeople have targets, they close more deals, and that when individuals make daily exercise commitments, they're more likely to increase their fitness levels. Abstract ambitions—such as "doing your best"—are usually much less effective than something concrete, such as bringing in 10 new customers a month or walking 10,000 steps a day. As a first general rule, then, any objectives you set for yourself or agree to should be specific.

Goals should also, whenever possible, trigger intrinsic, rather than extrinsic, motivation. An activity is intrinsically motivated when it's seen as its own end; it's extrinsically motivated when it's seen as serving a separate, ulterior purpose—earning you a reward or allowing you to avoid punishment. My research shows that intrinsic motives predict achievement and success better than extrinsic ones do.

The trick is to focus on the elements of the work that you do find enjoyable.

Take New Year's resolutions. We found that people who made resolutions at the start of January that were more pleasant to pursue—say, taking on a yoga class or phone-free Saturdays—were more likely to still be following through on them in March than people who chose more-important but less enjoyable goals. This is despite the obvious fact that aspirations for the New Year are usually tough to achieve; if they weren't, they wouldn't require a resolution!

Of course, if the external reward is great enough, we'll keep at even the most unpleasant tasks. Undergoing chemotherapy is an extreme example. In a work context, many people stay in their jobs for the money, feeling like "wage slaves." But in such situations they usually do the minimum required to meet the goal. Extrinsic motivation alone is unlikely to help us truly excel.

In an ideal world we would all seek out work roles and environments that we enjoy and thus keep our engagement high. Unfortunately, people often fail to do this. For example, my research shows that when asked whether positive relationships with colleagues and managers are critical in their current position, most people say yes. But they don't remember that office morale was key to success in past jobs, nor do they predict it will be important for them in the future. So simply remembering to consider intrinsic motivation when choosing jobs and taking on projects can go a long way toward helping sustain success.

In cases where that's impractical—we don't all find jobs and get assignments we love—the trick is to focus on the elements of the work that you do find enjoyable. Think expansively about how accomplishing the task might be satisfying—by, for example, giving you a chance to showcase your skills in front of your company's leaders, build important internal relationships, or create value for customers. Finally, try to offset drudgery with activities that you find rewarding—for instance, listen to music while tackling that big backlog of e-mail in your in-box, or do boring chores with friends, family, or your favorite colleagues.

Find Effective Rewards

Some tasks or even stretches of a career are entirely onerous—in which case it can be helpful to create external motivators for yourself over the short- to-medium term, especially if they complement incentives offered by your organization. You might promise yourself a vacation for finishing a project or buy yourself a gift for losing weight. But be careful to avoid perverse incentives. One mistake is to reward yourself for the quantity of completed tasks or for speed when you actually care about the quality of performance. An accountant who treats herself for finishing her auditing projects quickly might leave herself open to mistakes, while a salesperson focused on maximizing sales rather than repeat business should probably expect some unhappy customers.

Another common trap is to choose incentives that undermine the goal you've reached. If a dieter's prize for losing weight is to eat pizza and cake, he's likely to undo some of his hard work and reestablish bad habits. If the reward for excelling at work one week is to allow yourself to slack off the next, you could diminish the positive impression you've made. Research on what psychologists call balancing shows that goal achievement sometimes licenses people to give in to temptation—which sets them back.

In addition, some external incentives are more effective than others. For instance, in experiments researchers have discovered that most people work harder (investing more effort, time, and money) to qualify for an uncertain reward (such as a 50% chance of getting either $150 or $50) than they do for a certain reward (a 100% chance of getting $100), perhaps because the former is more challenging and exciting. Uncertain rewards are harder to set up at work, but not impossible. You might "gamify" a task by keeping two envelopes at your desk—one containing a treat of greater value—and picking only one, at random, after the job is done.

Finally, loss aversion—people's preference for avoiding losses rather than acquiring equivalent gains—can also be used to design a strong external motivator. In a 2016 study scientists from the University of Pennsylvania asked people to walk 7,000 steps a day for six months. Some participants were paid $1.40 for each day they achieved their goal, while others lost $1.40 if they failed to. The second group hit their daily target 50% more often. Online services such as StickK.com allow users to choose a goal, like "I want to quit smoking," and then commit to a loss if they don't achieve it: They have to donate money to an organization or a political party that they despise, for example.

Sustain Progress

When people are working toward a goal, they typically have a burst of motivation early and then slump in the middle, where they are most likely to stall out. For instance, in one study observant Jews were more likely to light a menorah on the first and last nights of Hanukkah than on the other six nights, even though the religious tradition is to light candles for eight successive days. In another experiment, participants who were working on a paper-shape-cutting task cut more corners in the middle of the project than they did on their initial and final shapes.

Fortunately, research has uncovered several ways to fight this pattern. I refer to the first as "short middles." If you break your goal into smaller subgoals—say, weekly instead of quarterly sales targets—there's less time to succumb to that pesky slump.

Giving advice may be an even more effective way to overcome motivational deficits.

A second strategy is to change the way you think about the progress you've achieved. When we've already made headway, the goal seems within reach, and we tend to increase our effort. For example, consumers in loyalty programs tend to spend more when they're closer to earning a reward. You can take advantage of that tendency by thinking of your starting point as being further back in the past; maybe the project began not the first time you took action but the time it was first proposed.

Another mental trick involves focusing on what you've already done up to the midpoint of a task and then turning your attention to what you have left to do. My research has found that this shift in perspective can increase motivation. For example, in a frequent-buyer promotion, emphasizing finished steps ("you've completed two of 10 purchases") increased customers' purchases at the beginning, and emphasizing missing steps ("you are two purchases away from a free reward") spurred consumption as buyers neared the goal.

This tactic can work for rote tasks (such as sending out 40 thank-you notes) as well as for more-qualitative goals (becoming an expert pianist). The person writing the notes can gain motivation from reminding herself how many she's sent until she passes 20; then she should count down how many she has left to do. In the same way, a novice pianist should focus on all the scales and skills she has acquired in her early stages of development; then, as she improves, focus on the remaining technical challenges (arpeggios, trills and tremolos, and so on) she needs to master.

Harness the Influence of Others

Humans are social creatures. We constantly look around to see what others are doing, and their actions influence our own. Even sitting next to a high-performing employee can increase your output. But when it comes to motivation, this dynamic is more complex. When we witness a colleague speeding through a task that leaves us frustrated, we respond in one of two ways: Either we're inspired and try to copy that behavior, or we lose motivation on the assumption that we could leave the task to our peer.

This is not entirely irrational: Humans have thrived as a species through individual specialization and by making the most of their comparative advantages.

The problem is that, especially at work, we can't always delegate. But we can still use social influence to our advantage. One rule is to never passively watch ambitious, efficient, successful coworkers; there's too much risk that it will be demotivating. Instead, talk to these peers about what they're trying to accomplish with their hard work and why they would recommend doing it. My research shows that when a friend endorses a product, people are more likely to buy it, but they aren't likely to if they simply learn that the friend bought the product. Listening to what your role models say about their goals can help you find extra inspiration and raise your own sights.

Interestingly, giving advice rather than asking for it may be an even more effective way to overcome motivational deficits, because it boosts confidence and thereby spurs action. In a recent study I found that people struggling to achieve a goal like finding a job assumed that they needed tips from experts to succeed. In fact, they were better served by offering their wisdom to other job seekers, because when they did so, they laid out concrete plans they could follow themselves, which have been shown to increase drive and achievement.

A final way to harness positive social influence is to recognize that the people who will best motivate you to accomplish certain tasks are not necessarily those who do the tasks well. Instead, they're folks who share a big-picture goal with you: close friends and family or mentors. Thinking of those people and our desire to succeed on their behalf can help provide the powerful intrinsic incentives we need to reach our goals. A woman may find drudgery at work rewarding if she feels she is providing an example for her daughter; a man may find it easier to stick to his fitness routine if it helps him feel more vibrant when he is with his friends.

To dream of a businessman or a rich man is a good omen. There is a good chance of success in your career in the future. However, if the rich man in the dream is yourself, it is a bad omen.

To dream of an agent means good luck is coming, indicating that you hope that new opportunities will appear in business activities.

Dreaming of a jewelry merchant symbolizes that your career is progressing smoothly, you will get a promotion and raise your salary, gain wealth, or if you are a businessman, it indicates that your business will be prosperous and your wealth will be abundant.

Dreaming of a flower seller represents the feelings between men and women, indicating that you will make great progress in the relationship.

To dream of becoming a businessman is a symbol of pursuing wealth, which means that you are more pursuing the accumulation of wealth, but because there has been no good way, there is no good improvement.

A man dreams of becoming a businessman indicates that you will have some entrepreneurial opportunities, but whether you can grasp it depends on yourself, and the process will be more difficult.

A woman dreams of becoming a businessman indicates that you will be married to a wealthy family, can lead a good life, and will be very happy and envied by others.

The patient dreams of becoming a businessman, reminds you that you may get sick, and treatment of your illness will require a lot of money, and you will be worried about this money.

An employee dreams of becoming a businessman indicates that you have the idea of resigning, don't want to look at people's faces anymore, and want to start your own business as your own boss.

Dream is a merchant. Dreaming as a business man, those who are far away dominate housework and separation of family and family. The dream is a returnee from business, the main body is reunited, the disease is healed, the money is profitable, and everything is auspicious. Those who dream of partnering for business will lead to the worst. Meng, as the person who opened a shop for the Jia, his main career is prosperous, and everything is happy and bright. The dream is for the merchant to receive the goods and benefit the family, and the master is idle. Those who dream of trading goods with merchants, the main disaster is approaching. Dream merchants come home to buy goods, the main wealth is scattered. Women's dreams, the master's tongue dispels. Dreaming of being a great man who is a great fan of the sea, the main family business is drifting; like a dream to the one who trades profitable property, good luck.

CHAPTER ONE

your mba

From the Economist to the cover of the New York Times Style section, from the streets of Dubai to the cafes of Berlin, lifestyle design has cut across cultures to become a worldwide movement. The original ideas of the book have been broken apart, improved, and tested in environments and ways I never could have imagined.One of the beautiful things about learning any subject is the fact that you don't need to know everything—you only need to understand a few critically important concepts that provide most of the value. Once you have a solid scaffold of core principles to work from, building upon your knowledge and making progress becomes much easier. The Personal MBA is a set of foundational business concepts you can use to get things done. Reading this book will give you a firm foundation of business knowledge you can use to make things happen. Once you master the fundamentals, you can accomplish even the most challenging business goals with surprising ease. Over the past five years, I've read thousands of business books, interviewed hundreds of business professionals, worked for a Fortune 50 corporation, started my own businesses, and consulted with businesses ranging from solo operations to multinational corporations with hundreds of thousands of employees and billions of dollars in revenue. Along the way, I've collected, distilled, and refined my findings into the concepts presented in this book. Understanding these fundamental principles will give you the tools you can rely on to make good business decisions. If you invest the time and energy necessary to learn these concepts, you'll easily be in the top 1 percent of the human population when it comes to knowing: � How businesses actually work. � How to start a new business. � How to improve an existing business. � How to use business-related skills to accomplish your personal goals. Think of this book as a filter. Instead of trying to absorb all of the business information that's out there—and there's a lot out there—use this book to help you learn what matters most, so you can focus on what's actually important: making things happen.

People always overestimate how complex business is. This isn't rocket science—we've chosen one of the world's most simple professions. —JACK WELCH, FORMER CEO OF GENERAL ELECTRIC Don't worry if you're a complete beginner. Unlike many other business books, this book does not require any prior business knowledge or experience. I don't assume you're already the CEO of a large company who makes multimillion-dollar decisions on a daily basis. (But this book will still be very useful if you are!) If you do have business experience, take it from many of my clients around the world who have MBAs from top schools—you'll find the information in this book more valuable and practical than anything you learned earning your degree. Together, we'll explore 226 simple concepts that help you think about business in an entirely new way. After reading this book, you'll have a much more comprehensive and accurate understanding of what businesses actually are and what successful businesses actually do.

Education is not the answer to the question. Education is the means to the answer to all questions. —BILL ALLIN, SOCIOLOGIST AND EDUCATION ACTIVIST Most business books attempt to teach you to have more answers: a technique for this, a method for that. This book is diff erent. It won't give you answers—it will help you ask better questions. Knowing what's critically important in every business is the first step in making good business decisions. The more you know about the essential questions to ask in your current situation, the more quickly you'll be able to find the answers you need to move forward. To improve your business skills, you don't need to learn everything there is to know—mastering the fundamentals can take you surprisingly far. I call these foundational business concepts mental models, and together, they create a solid framework you can rely on to make good decisions. Mental models are concepts that represent your understanding of "how things work." Think of driving a car: what do you expect when you press down on the right-side pedal? If the car slows down, you'll be surprised— that pedal is supposed to be the accelerator.That's a mental model—an idea about how something works in the real world. Your brain forms mental models automatically by noticing patterns in what you experience each day. Very often, however, the mental models you form on your own aren't completely accurate—you're only one person, so your knowledge and experiences are limited. Education is a way to make your mental models more accurate by internalizing the knowledge and experiences other people have collected throughout their lives.The best education helps you learn to see the world in a new, more productive way.

I've always been an avid reader, but before I decided to learn everything I could about business, most of what I read was fi ction. I grew up in New London, a small farm town in northern Ohio where the major industries are agriculture and light manufacturing. My mother is a children's librarian, and my father worked as a sixth grade science teacher, then as an elementary school principal. Books were a major part of my life, but business was not. Before getting my first real job, I knew next to nothing about what businesses were or how they functioned, other than that they were places people went every day in order to draw a paycheck. I had no idea that companies like Procter & Gamble even existed until I applied for the job that swept me into the corporate world. Working for P&G was an education in itself. The sheer size and scope of the business—and the complexity required to manage a business of that size—boggled my mind. During my first three years with the company, I participated in decisions across every part of the business process: creating new products, ramping up production, allocating millions of marketing dollars, and securing distribution with major retailers like Walmart,Target, Kroger, and Costco. As an assistant brand manager, I was leading teams of thirty to forty P&G employees, contractors, and agency staff—all of whom had competing projects, plans, and priorities. The stakes were huge and the pressure was intense. To this day, I can't help but marvel at the thousands of manhours, the millions of dollars, and the enormously complex processes necessary to make a simple bottle of dish soap appear on the shelf of the local supermarket. Everything from the shape of the bottle to the scent of the product is optimized—including the text on the cardboard boxes used to ship inventory to the store. My work at P&G, however, wasn't the only thing on my mind. My decision to skip business school in favor of educating myself developed from a side project into a minor obsession. Every day I would spend hour after hour reading and researching, searching for one more tidbit of knowledge that would help me to better understand how the business world worked. Instead of using the summer after graduation to relax and go on vacation, I spent my days haunting the business stacks at the local bookstore, absorbing as much as I possibly could. By the time I offi cially started working full-time for P&G in September 2005, I had read hundreds of books across every discipline that business schools teach, as well as in disciplines that most business schools don't cover, such as psychology, physical science, and systems theory. When my first day at P&G finally arrived, I felt prepared to strategize with the best of them. As it turned out, my self-education served me well—I was doing valuable work, making things happen, and getting good reviews. As time went on, however, I realized three very important things: 1. Large companies move slowly. Good ideas often died on the vine simply because they had to be approved by too many people. 2. Climbing the corporate ladder is an obstacle to doing great work. I wanted to focus on getting things done and making things better, not constantly positioning myself for promotion. Politics and turf wars are an inescapable part of the daily experience of working for a large company. 3. Frustration leads to burnout. I wanted to enjoy the daily experience of work, but instead I felt like I was running a gauntlet each day. It began to affect my health, happiness, and relationships. Th e longer I stayed in the corporate world, the more I realized I wanted out. I desperately wanted to work on my own terms, as an entrepreneur.

In addition to reading books, I was following several hundred business blogs. Some of the best business thinking was being published on the Internet months (or years) before it ever appeared in print, and I wanted to read it all as soon as it was available. One of the bloggers I followed avidly was Seth Godin. A best-selling author (of books like Permission Marketing, Purple Cow, and Linchpin) and one of the earliest successful online marketers, Seth specializes in bold statements of big ideas designed to challenge you to do more, do better, question the status quo, and make a diff erence. One particular morning, Seth was commenting on a recent news story:Harvard was rescinding the admission of 119 previously soon-to-be Harvard MBA students.1 These prospective students had discovered an ethically dubious way to hack into the Harvard admissions Web site to view their application status before the offi cial acceptance letters went out. Th e story quickly became a media frenzy, devolving into a debate about whether MBA students were naturally inclined to lie, cheat, and steal, or if business schools made them that way. Instead of being outraged at the bad behavior of the applicants, Seth (unsurprisingly) had a different perspective: Harvard was giving these students a gift. By rescinding their applications, Harvard was giving these students a significant opportunity: the university was returning $150,000 and two years of their lives, which would otherwise have been spent chasing a mostly worthless piece of paper.

"It's hard for me to understand," he wrote, "why [getting an MBA] is a better use of time and money than actual experience combined with a dedicated reading of 30 or 40 books." "Holy cow," I thought. "That's exactly what I'm doing!" Over the next two days, I created a list of the books and resources I had found most valuable in my studies,2 then published it on my blog with a link to Seth's post, so anyone interested in figuring out how to do what Seth suggested would be able to fi nd it.Then I typed a quick e-mail to Seth and sent him a link to my post. Two minutes later, a post went up on Seth's blog directing people to my reading list, and a flood of readers from around the world started visiting my Web site. Popular personal development and productivity blogs like Lifehacker .com picked up the story, which then spread to social media Web sites like Reddit, Digg, and Delicious. Within the first week of the Personal MBA's existence, thirty thousand people visited my little corner of the Internet to see what I was doing. Better yet, they started talking. Some readers asked questions—where should they start? Others suggested great books they'd read, helping me with my research. A few told me the entire project was naive, and that I was wasting my time.Through it all, I kept reading, researching, and developing the Personal MBA in my spare time, and the business self-education movement began to snowball.

Just as multiple factors shape every system, multiple mental models from a variety of disciplines are necessary to understand that system . . . You have to realize the truth of biologist Julian Huxley's idea that, "Life is just one damn relatedness after another." So you must have all the models, and you must see the relatedness and the effects from the relatedness . . . 7 It's kind of fun to sit here and outthink people who are way smarter than you are because you've trained yourself to be more objective and more multidisciplinary. Furthermore, there is a lot of money in it, as I can testify from my own personal experience.8 By basing their investment decisions on their extensive knowledge of how businesses work, how people work, and how systems work, Buff ett and Munger created a company worth over $195 billion—an astounding track record for a meteorologist-turned-lawyer from Omaha with no formal business education. Discovering Munger's approach to business education was a huge validation. Here was a man who, decades before, had decided to do what I was doing—and it had worked extraordinarily well! Munger's method of identifying and applying fundamental principles made much more sense to me than most of the business books I'd previously read. I resolved to learn everything I could about the "mental models" Charlie used to make decisions. Unfortunately, Charlie has never published a comprehensive collection of his mental models. He's given hints in his speeches and essays—even going so far as to publish a list of the psychological principles he fi nds most useful in Poor Charlie's Almanack, a recent biography—but there was no single text that contained "everything you need to know in order to succeed in business."

Most business books (and business schools) assume that the student already knows what businesses are, what they do, and how they work—as if it were the most obvious thing in the world. It's not. Business is one of the most complex and multidisciplinary areas of human experience, and trying to understand how businesses work can be remarkably intimidating, even though they surround us every day. Businesses are so much a part of daily life that it's easy to take the business world for granted. Day after day, businesses deliver what we want swiftly, efficiently, and with remarkably little fuss. Look around: almost every material good you're surrounded by right now was created and delivered to you by some sort of business. Businesses invisibly create and deliver so many different things in so many different ways that it makes generalizations diffi cult: what do apple cider and airlines have in common? As it turns out, quite a bit—if you know where to look. Here's how I define a business: Every successful business (1) creates or provides something of value that (2) other people want or need (3) at a price they're willing to pay, in a way that (4) satisfies the purchaser's needs and expectations and (5) provides the business sufficient revenue to make it worthwhile for the owners to continue operation. Take away any of these things—value creation, customer demand, transactions, value delivery, or profit sufficiency—and you have something other than a business. Each factor is both essential and universal. As I deconstructed each of those factors, I found additional universal requirements. Value can't be created without understanding what people want (market research). Attracting customers first requires getting their attention, then making them interested (marketing). In order to close a sale, people must first trust your ability to deliver on what's promised (value delivery and operations). Customer satisfaction depends on reliably exceeding the customer's expectations (customer service). Profi t suffi ciency requires bringing in more money than is spent (fi nance). None of these functions is rocket science, but they're always necessary, no matter who you are or what business you're in. Do them well, and your business thrives. Do them poorly, and you won't be in business very long. Every business fundamentally relies on two additional factors: people and systems. Every business is created by people and survives by benefi ting other people in some way. To understand how businesses work, you must have a firm understanding of how people tend to think and behave—how humans make decisions, act on those decisions, and communicate with others. Recent advances in psychology and neuroscience are revealing why people do the things they do, as well as how to improve our own behavior and work more effectively with others. Systems, on the other hand, are the invisible structures that hold every business together. At the core, every business is a collection of processes that can be reliably repeated to produce a particular result. By understanding the essentials of how complex systems work, it's possible to find ways to improve existing systems, whether you're dealing with a marketing campaign or an automotive assembly line.

Every year, millions of individuals determined to make a name for themselves have the following thought: "I want to become a successful businessperson. Where should I get my MBA?" Since you're fl ipping through this book, you've probably wondered the same thing at some point in your life.

I have nothing against people who work in business schools: by and large, business school professors and administrators are lovely people who try their best and want to see their students succeed. Unfortunately, MBA programs around the world have three major systemic issues: 1. MBA programs have become so expensive you must eff ectively mortgage your life to pay the price of admission. "Return on Investment" is always directly related to how much you spend, and after decades of tuition increases, MBA programs are increasingly a burden to their students instead of a benefi t. The primary question is not whether attending a university is a positive experience: it's whether or not the experience is worth the cost.9 2. MBA programs teach many worthless, outdated, even outright damaging concepts and practices—assuming your goal is to actually build a successful business and increase your net worth. Many of my MBAholding readers and clients come to me after spending tens (sometimes hundreds) of thousands of dollars learning the ins and outs of complex financial formulas and statistical models, only to realize that their MBA program didn't teach them how to start or improve a real, operating business. That's a problem—graduating from business school does not guarantee having a useful working knowledge of business when you're done, which is what you actually need to be successful. 3. MBA programs won't guarantee you a high-paying job, let alone make you a skilled manager or leader with a shot at the executive suite. Developing skills such as decision making, management, and leadership takes real practice and experience, which business schools can't provide in the classroom, regardless of how prestigious the program is.

Instead of spending huge sums of money to learn marginally useful information, you can spend your time and resources learning things that actually matter. If you're ready and able to invest in improving your skills and abilities, you can learn everything you need to know about business on your own, without mortgaging your life for the privilege.

It's easy to figure out why business school is attractive: it's sold as a one-way ticket to a permanently prosperous and comfortable life. It's a pleasant daydream: after two years of case studies and happy hour "networking," corporate recruiters will be shamelessly throwing themselves at you, each of them offering a prestigious and high-paying position at a top fi rm. Your rise up the corporate ladder will be swift and sure. You'll be a CAPTAIN OF INDUSTRY, collecting huge bonuses and tabulating the value of your stock options while sitting behind an impressive-looking mahogany desk in the corner office on the top floor of a gigantic glass skyscraper. You'll be the big boss, telling other people what to do until it's time to go play golf or relax on your yacht. You'll be wined and dined all over the world, and the lowly masses will venerate you and your astounding achievements. Everyone will think you're rich, intelligent, and powerful—and they'll be damn right. What price for the promise of riches, power, and glory? A few thousand dollars in application fees, an effortless scribble on a loan document, and you'll be on your way to the top! Not only that, you'll get a two-year vacation from actually working. What a fantastic deal!Top business schools are notoriously hard to get into—the programs can afford to be picky because of their reputations. It's circular.Th e reputation of a business school is built on the success of its graduates, so the top schools only admit those students intelligent and ambitious enough to make it through the rigorous selection process—the ones who are already likely to succeed, MBA or no MBA. Business schools don't create successful people. Th ey simply accept them, then take credit for their success. If you get in, the school will do what it can to help you get a decent job, but making things happen will always be your responsibility. If you're successful in the years after graduation, the school will hold you up as a shining example of the quality of their program and will use the "halo eff ect" of your name to recruit more students. If you lose your job and go broke, you'll get neither publicity nor help, but the loan bills will keep rolling in. Sorry about your luck.If an MBA education is useful training for business, then the following should be true as a matter of logic: (1) having an MBA degree should, other things being equal, be related to various measures of career success and attainment, such as salary; and (2) if what someone learns in business school helps that person be better prepared for the business world and more competent in that domain—in other words, if business schools convey professionally useful knowledge—then a measure of how much one has learned or mastered the material, such as grades in course work, should be at least somewhat predictive of various outcomes that index success in business.Business schools are not very effective: Neither possessing an MBA degree nor grades earned in courses correlate with career success, results that question the eff ectiveness of schools in preparing their students. And, there is little evidence that business school research is influential on management practice, calling into question the professional relevance of management scholarship. According to Pfeffer and Fong's study, it doesn't matter if you graduate at the top of your class with a perfect 4.0 or at the bottom with a barely passing grade—getting an MBA has zero correlation with long-term career success. None. There is scant evidence that the MBA credential, particularly from nonelite schools, or the grades earned in business courses—a measure of the mastery of the material—are related to either salary or the attainment of higher level positions in organizations. These data, at a minimum, suggest that the training or education component of business education is only loosely coupled to the world of managing organizations. That's tough to hear if you've forked over a few hundred thousand dollars to buy a degree whose sole purpose is to make you a more successful businessperson. It gets worse: getting an MBA doesn't even have an impact on your total lifetime earnings. It takes decades of work simply to dig yourself out of the debt you took on to get the degree. Christian Schraga, the Wharton MBA, estimated that the ten-year "net present value" (a financial analysis technique used to estimate whether or not an investment is worthwhile) of a top MBA program is approximately negative $53,000 (that's bad). Th is assumes a pre-MBA base salary of $85,000, a post-MBA salary of $115,000 (a 35 percent increase), marginal tax rate increases (which you'll pay if your job requires moving to a major city), and a discount rate of 7 percent to account for opportunity cost (the opportunities you give up by spending money on business school instead of investing it in something else). In plain English: Schraga used a technique business schools teach to prove that getting an MBA from a top-tier school is a bad fi nancial decision.A large body of evidence suggests that the curriculum taught in business schools has only a small relationship to what is important for succeeding in business . . . If there is, in fact, only a slight connection between the skills needed in business and what is taught in graduate business programs, then the absence of an effect of the MBA or mastery of the subject matter on the careers of graduates is understandable. If you look at the curriculum of any business school, you'll notice a few assumptions about what you'll do after you graduate: you'll either be a C-level executive at a large industrial manufacturing or retail operation, become a consultant, become a corporate accountant, or work as a fi nancier at an investment bank. Accordingly, the coursework is implicitly structured around keeping your massive operation running and/or doing sophisticated quantitative analysis—not doing any of the other critically important things that 99 percent of working businesspeople do in any given day. The disconnect between the classroom and the working world makes sense when you realize that the concepts, principles, and techniques most business schools teach were designed for a very different world. Graduate schools of business started popping up at the end of the nineteenth century during the Industrial Revolution. The intent of early MBA programs was to train managers to be more scientific in an effort to make large operations more efficient. Frederick Winslow Taylor, the pioneer of "scientific management" techniques that now form the foundation of modern management training, used a stopwatch to shave a few seconds off the average time a workman took to load iron ingots into a train car. That should give you a good idea of the underlying mind-set of most business school management programs.Management was thought of mostly as an exercise in getting people to work faster and do exactly what they're told. The philosopher kings behind what passed for management psychology were Ivan Pavlov and, later on, B. F. Skinner, who believed that if you discovered and applied just the right stimulus, people would behave however you wanted. This mentality led to the widespread use of financial incentives to influence behavior: salary, bonuses, stock options, and so on, in an effort to encourage business professionals and managers to act in the best interest of corporate shareholders.Marketing, on the other hand, was originally a way to get additional store distribution for physical products and keep expensive factory production lines busy. With the widespread adoption of the radio and television in the early twentieth century, it became possible to advertise to a large national audience, paving the way for national brands and national retailers. More advertising typically resulted in more distribution, which in turn resulted in more sales and even more money to spend on advertising, continuing the cycle. As decades passed, this self-reinforcing feedback loop resulted in a few dominant behemoths in each industry. Business schools became obsessed with how to capture market share and create gigantic companies quickly via ever-larger mergers, raising the financial stakes with each acquisition. For entrepreneurs, venture capital became a must-have aspect of the business process—how else could you afford to build a factory or a national brand in a few short years? "Economies of scale" in production meant large companies could outcompete smaller rivals by offering similar products at lower prices. Investors wanted to see huge returns on their money quickly,prudence be damned, rewarding speculators who wrote business plans promising a huge exit in a short amount of time. Viable businesses were acquired and gutted in the name of conglomeration and "synergy," all with the blessing of business academia. The sheer enormity of integrating these gigantic, complex business systems was ignored or overlooked, leading most of the companies that attempted huge mergers to ruin.Since 1965, the percentage of graduates of highly ranked business schools who go into consulting and financial services has doubled, from about one-third to about two-thirds. And while some of these consultants and financiers end up in the manufacturing sector, in some respects that's the problem . . . Most of GM's top executives in recent decades hailed from a finance rather than an operations background. (Outgoing GM CEO Fritz Henderson and his failed predecessor, Rick Wagoner, both worked their way up from the company's vaunted Treasurer's offi ce.) But these executives were frequently numb to the sorts of innovations that enable high-quality production at low cost.The world is constantly changing, but business schools aren't changing with it. With the advent of the Internet and the widespread availability of new technologies, successful modern businesses tend to be smaller, require less capital to build, have less overhead, and require fewer employees. According to the U.S. Small Business Administration, small businesses represent 99.7 percent of all employer firms in the United States, employ half of all privatesector workers, have generated 64 percent of net new jobs over the past fifteen years, and create more than 50 percent of U.S. nonfarm gross domestic product (GDP).18 You wouldn't know that from looking at b-school curricula: based on current standards, it seems that most MBA programs believe huge businesses are the only ventures worth managing. Mass-market advertising is no longer able to reliably convert pennies to dollars. Inventories (if they exist at all) tend to be smaller, businesses depend on others for critical functions, and markets change and adapt extremely quickly. Speed, flexibility, and ingenuity are the qualities that successful businesses rely on today—qualities that the corporate giants of the past few decades struggle to acquire and retain, and business school classrooms struggle to teach. The demands of the public market push executives to chase short-term earnings at the expense of long-term stability, creating waves of layoff s and severe budget cuts when times get tight or unexpected events occur. At the same time, more and more employees are looking for a greater sense of autonomy, flexibility, and security from their work—and they're fi nding these things outside of the confines of the traditional corporate job. How do you manage someone who doesn't really want to work for you in the fi rst place? MBA programs are trying to cope, but they're still teaching theories that are outdated, misguided, and even outright wrong. Even so, don't expect them to start doing things differently. Why bother, when MBA programs are profitable status symbols for the colleges and in such high demand? As long as students are still signing up, don't expect the hallowed halls of business schools to change their tune.one signifi cant benefit that business schools do provide is better access to Fortune 50 recruiters, consulting firms, large accounting firms, and investment banks via on-campus recruiting and alumni networks. Upon graduating from a top-tier business school, you'll find it much easier to get an interview with a corporate recruiter who works for a Fortune 50, investment bank, or consulting fi rm. Th e effect is strongest immediately after graduation, then largely wears out within three to fi ve years. After that, you're on your own: hiring managers no longer care so much about where you went to school—they care more about what you've accomplished since then. Hiring managers typically use MBA programs as a filter when deciding whom to bring in for an interview. HR managers are busy, and since each student in the program has been prescreened, there's less of a chance the manager will be wasting precious time. Hiring directly from MBA programs also provides plausible deniability for the recruiter if the hire doesn't work out: "I'm not sure what the issue was—she graduated from Harvard Business School!" Th e filtering aspect of MBA programs is very real, and diffi cult to overcome on your own. If you have your heart set on becoming a management .consultant, international fi nancier, or Fortune 50 fast-track management candidate, you may have to buy yourself a $150,000 interview.If you're more interested in working for yourself or holding down an enjoyable job while having a life, getting an MBA is a waste of time and money. As Dr. Pfeffer says,"If you are good enough to get in, you obviously have enough talent to do well, regardless."Every successful business creates something of value. The world is full of opportunities to make other people's lives better in some way, and your job as a businessperson is to identify things that people don't have enough of, then find a way to provide them. The value you create can take on one of several different forms, but the purpose is always the same: to make someone else's life a little bit better. Without value creation, a business can't exist—you can't transact with others unless you have something valuable to trade. The best businesses in the world are the ones that create the most value for other people. Some businesses thrive by providing a little value to many, and others focus on providing a lot of value to only a few people. Regardless, the more real value you create for other people, the better your business will be and the more prosperous you'll become.Roughly defined, a business is a repeatable process that: 1. Creates and delivers something of value . . . 2. That other people want or need . . . 3. At a price they're willing to pay . . . 4. In a way that satisfies the customer's needs and expectations . . . 5. So that the business brings in enough profit to make it worthwhile for the owners to continue operation.It doesn't matter if you're running a solo venture or a billion-dollar brand. Take any one of these five factors away, and you don't have a business—you have something else. A venture that doesn't create value for others is a hobby. A venture that doesn't attract attention is a flop. A venture that doesn't sell the value it creates is a nonprofit. A venture that doesn't deliver what it promises is a scam. A venture that doesn't bring in enough money to keep operating will inevitably close. At the core, every business is fundamentally a collection of fi ve Interdependent (discussed later) processes, each of which flows into the next:

1. Value Creation. Discovering what people need or want, then creating it.

2. Marketing. Attracting attention and building demand for what you've created.

3. Sales. Turning prospective customers into paying customers.

4. Value Delivery. Giving your customers what you've promised and ensuring that they're satisfi ed.

5. Finance. Bringing in enough money to keep going and make your eff ort worthwhile.

If these five things sound simple, it's because they are. Business is not (and has never been) rocket science—it's simply a process of identifying a problem and finding a way to solve it that benefits both parties. Anyone who tries to make business sound more complicated than this is either trying to impress you or trying to sell you something you don't need. Th e Five Parts of Every Business are the basis of every good business idea and business plan. If you can clearly defi ne each of these fi ve processes for any business, you'll have a complete understanding of how it works. If you're thinking about starting a new business, defining what these processes might look like is the best place to start. If you can't describe or diagram your business idea in terms of these core processes, you don't understand it well enough to make it work.Not every skill or area of knowledge is Economically Valuable, and that's okay—there are many things worth pursuing for the sake of relaxation or enjoyment alone. You may enjoy whitewater rafting, but it's very unlikely anyone will pay you to shoot the rapids unless you apply your skills for the benefit of others. Make the leap from personal enjoyment to Products and Services (discussed later), however, and you'll find yourself getting paid—plenty of adventurous souls are willing to pay for rafting equipment and guides. As Michael Masterson suggests in Ready, Fire, Aim, don't expect skills that aren't related to the Five Parts of Every Business to be economically rewarded. Find a way to use them to create Economic Value, and you'll inevitably find a way to get paid. Any skill or knowledge that helps you create value, market, sell, deliver .

Th e Ten Ways to Evaluate a Market provide a back-of-the-napkin method you can use to identify the attractiveness of any potential market. Rate each of the ten factors below on a scale of 0 to 10, where 0 is extremely unattractive and 10 is extremely attractive. When in doubt, be conservative in your estimate: 1. Urgency—How badly do people want or need this right now? (Renting an old movie is typically low urgency; seeing the fi rst showing of a new movie on opening night is high urgency, since it only happens once.) 2. Market Size—How many people are actively purchasing things like this? (The market for underwater basket weaving courses is very small; the market for cancer cures is massive.) 3. Pricing Potential—What is the highest price a typical purchaser would be willing to spend for a solution? (Lollipops sell for $0.05; aircraft carriers sell for billions.) 4. Cost of Customer Acquisition—How easy is it to acquire a new customer? On average, how much will it cost to generate a sale, in both money and effort? (Restaurants built on high-traffi c interstate highways spend little to bring in new customers. Government contractors can spend millions landing major procurement deals.) 5. Cost of Value Delivery—How much would it cost to create and deliver the value offered, both in money and effort? (Delivering fi les via the Internet is almost free; inventing a product and building a factory costs millions.) 6. Uniqueness of Off er—How unique is your offer versus competing offerings in the market, and how easy is it for potential competitors to copy you? (There are many hair salons, but very few companies that offer private space travel.) 7. Speed to Market—How quickly can you create something to sell? (You can offer to mow a neighbor's lawn in minutes; opening a bank can take years.) 8. Up-Front Investment—How much will you have to invest before you're ready to sell? (To be a housekeeper, all you need is a set of inexpensive cleaning products. To mine for gold, you need millions to purchase land and excavating equipment.) 9. Upsell Potential—Are there related secondary offers that you could also present to purchasing customers? (Customers who purchase razors need shaving cream and extra blades as well; buy a Frisbee, and you won't need another unless you lose it.) 10. Evergreen Potential—Once the initial offer has been created, how much additional work will you have to put into it in order to continue selling? (Business consulting requires ongoing work to get paid; a book can be produced once, then sold over and over as is.)

When any two markets are equally attractive in other respects, you're better off choosing to enter the one with competition. Here's why: it means you know from the start there's a market of paying customers for this idea, eliminating your biggest risk.The existence of a market means you're already on the right side of the Iron Law of the Market, so you can spend more time developing your off er instead of proving a market exists. If there are several successful businesses serving a market, you don't have to worry so much about investing in a dead end, since you already know that people are buying. The best way to observe what your potential competitors are doing is to become a customer. Buy as much as you can of what they off er. Observing your competition from the inside can teach you an enormous amount about the market: what value the competitor provides, how they attract attention, what they charge, how they close sales, how they make customers happy, how they deal with issues, and what needs they aren't yet serving.Becoming a Mercenary doesn't pay: don't start a business for the money alone. Here's why: starting and running a business always takes more eff ort than you fi rst expect. Even if you identify a business that will largely run itself, setting up the Systems (discussed later) necessary to run the business requires persistence and dedication. If the only thing that interests you about an opportunity is the money, you'll probably quit well before you fi nd the pot of gold at the bottom of the landfi ll. Pay very close attention to the things you find yourself coming back to over and over again. Building or finishing anything is mostly a matter of starting over and over again; don't ignore what pulls you.The trick is to fi nd an attractive market that interests you enough to keep you improving your offering every single day. Finding that market is mostly a matter of patience and active exploration.That said, don't ignore "boring" businesses until you investigate them; if you can find some aspect of the work that interests you and keeps you engaged, mundane markets can be quite attractive. "Dirty" businesses like plumbing and garbage collection certainly aren't sexy, but they can be quite lucrative because there's a significant ongoing need combined with relatively few people willing to step up and meet the demand. If you find a way to make a necessary but dull market interesting enough to pursue, you may have discovered a hidden vein of gold waiting to be mined.Being a Crusader doesn't pay either. Every once in a while, you'll find an idea so fascinating it becomes hard to think about it objectively.The stars align, heavenly trumpets blare, and suddenly you have the unmistakable impression that you've found your calling. In all the excitement, it's easy to forget that there's often a huge diff erence between an interesting idea and a solid business. In your optimism, forget ye not prudence: changing the world is difficult if you can't pay the bills. Some ideas don't have enough of a market behind them to support a business, and that's perfectly okay. That doesn't mean you should ignore them: side projects can help you expand your knowledge, improve your skills, and experiment with new methods and techniques. I'm a huge advocate of pursuing side projects as long as you don't count on them to reliably produce income. Once you have your financial bases covered, crusade all you want.

In order to successfully provide value to another person, it must take on a form they're willing to pay for. Fortunately, there's no need to reinvent the wheel—Economic Value usually takes on one of twelve standard forms: 1. Product. Create a single tangible item or entity, then sell and deliver it for more than what it cost to make. 2. Service. Provide help or assistance, then charge a fee for the benefi ts rendered. 3. Shared Resource. Create a durable asset that can be used by many people, then charge for access. 4. Subscription. Offer a benefit on an ongoing basis, and charge a recurring fee. 5. Resale. Acquire an asset from a wholesaler, then sell that asset to a retail buyer at a higher price. 6. Lease. Acquire an asset, then allow another person to use that asset for a predefined amount of time in exchange for a fee. 7. Agency. Market and sell an asset or service you don't own on behalf of a third party, then collect a percentage of the transaction price as a fee. 8. Audience Aggregation. Get the attention of a group of people with certain characteristics, then sell access in the form of advertising to another business looking to reach that audience.9. Loan. Lend a certain amount of money, then collect payments over a predefined period of time equal to the original loan plus a predefined interest rate. 10. Option. Offer the ability to take a predefined action for a fi xed period of time in exchange for a fee. 11. Insurance. Take on the risk of some specific bad thing happening to the policy holder in exchange for a predefined series of payments, then pay out claims only when the bad thing actually happens. 12. Capital. Purchase an ownership stake in a business, then collect a corresponding portion of the profit as a one-time payout or ongoing dividend.

A Product is a tangible form of value. To run a Product-oriented business, you must: 1. Create some sort of tangible item that people want. 2. Produce that item as inexpensively as possible while maintaining an acceptable level of quality. 3. Sell as many units as possible for as high a price as the market will bear. 4. Keep enough inventory of finished product available to fulfi ll orders as they come in. The book you're holding right now is a good example of a Product. It had to be written, edited, typeset, printed, bound, and shipped to bookstores in suffi cient quantities before reaching your hands. Leave out any of these steps and you wouldn't be reading this right now. To make money, a book must be sold for more than it cost to create, print, and distribute. Products can be durable, like cars, computers, and vacuum cleaners. They can also be consumable: goods like apples, donuts, and prescription medications are products as well. Products don't have to be physical—even though things like software, e-books, and MP3s don't have a distinct physical form, they are entities that can be sold.

A Service involves helping or assisting someone in exchange for a fee. To create value via Services, you must be able to provide some type of benefi t to the user. In order to create a successful Service, your business must: 1. Have employees capable of a skill or ability other people require but can't, won't, or don't want to use themselves. 2. Ensure that the Service is provided with consistently high quality. 3. Attract and retain paying customers. A good example of a Service business is a barbershop. A haircut is not a Product: you can't purchase one from a shelf. The Service is the series of actions the stylist uses to transform your current hairstyle into the one you want. In this sense, doctors, freelance designers, massage therapists, lawn care providers, and consultants are all Service providers. Services can be lucrative, particularly if the skills required to provide ficult to duplicate. Services typically depend on the Service provider's investment of time and energy, both of which are finite. A heart surgeon can only complete so many four-hour operations on any given day. If you're developing a Service, be sure to charge enough to compensate for the time you'll be investing on a daily basis in providing the Service to your customers. Otherwise, you'll discover that you're working too hard for too little a reward.A Shared Resource is a durable asset that can be used by many people. Shared Resources allow you to create the asset once, then charge your customers for its use. In order to create a successful Shared Resource, you must: 1. Create an asset people want to have access to. 2. Serve as many users as you can without affecting the quality of each user's experience. 3. Charge enough to maintain and improve the Shared Resource over time. Gyms and fitness clubs are a classic example of a Shared Resource. A fitness club may purchase forty treadmills, thirty exercise bikes, six sets of free weights, a set of kettlebells, and other useful but expensive equipment that lasts a long time. The club's members benefit by being able to access this equipment without having to purchase it themselves—instead, they pay an access fee, which is much easier for an individual to aff ord. (Most gyms combine access to their Shared Resource with Services and Subscriptions, a common example of Bundling—discussed later.) Businesses like museums and amusement parks work in much the sameway. Whether it means studying a Monet or riding a roller coaster, Shared Resources allow many people to take advantage of experiences that would otherwise be too expensive. The tricky part about offering a Shared Resource is carefully monitoring usage levels. If you don't have enough users, you won't be able to spread out the cost of the asset enough to cover up-front costs and ongoing maintenance. If you have too many users, overcrowding will diminish the experience so much that they'll become frustrated, stop using the resource, and advise others not to patronize your business, diminishing your Reputation (discussed later). Finding the sweet spot between too few members and too many is the key to making a Shared Resource work.A Subscription program provides predefi ned benefits on an ongoing basis in exchange for a recurring fee. The actual benefits provided can be tangible or intangible—the key differences are (a) the expectation of additional value to be provided in the future and (b) that fees will be collected until the Subscription is canceled. In order to create a successful Subscription, you must: 1. Provide significant value to each subscriber on a regular basis. 2. Build a subscriber base and continually attract new subscribers to compensate for attrition. 3. Bill customers on a recurring basis. 4. Retain each subscriber as long as possible. Cable or satellite television service is a great example of a Subscription. After you sign up, the company will continue to provide television service as long as you make the payments. You don't have to call up the company every month to buy another thirty days' worth—the service continues as long as the invoice is paid. Subscription is an attractive form of value because it provides more predictable revenue. Instead of having to resell to your existing customers every day, Subscriptions allow you to build a steady base of loyal customers over time. This model ensures a certain level of revenue coming in each billing period. The key to Subscription offers is doing everything you can to keep customer attrition as low as possible. As long as you continue to make your customers happy, only a small percentage of your customer base will cancel each period, giving you the ability to plan your finances with more certainty. Any subscriber attrition you experience can be overcome by enrolling more customers.Resale is the acquisition of an asset from a wholesale seller, followed by the sale of that asset to a retail buyer at a higher price. Resale is how most of the retailers you're familiar with work: they purchase what they sell from other businesses, then resell each purchase for more than it cost. In order to provide value as a reseller, you must: 1. Purchase a product as inexpensively as possible, usually in bulk. 2. Keep the product in good condition until sale—damaged goods can't be sold. 3. Find potential purchasers of the product as quickly as possible to keep inventory costs low. 4. Sell the product for as high a markup as possible, preferably a multiple of the purchase price.Resellers are valuable because they help wholesalers sell products without having to find individual purchasers.To a farmer, selling apples to millions of individuals would be time-intensive and inefficient: it's far better to sell them all to a grocery chain and focus on growing more apples. Th e grocery then takes the apples into inventory and sells them to individual consumers at a higher price. Major retailers like Walmart and Tesco, book retailers like Barnes &

Noble, and catalog operations like Lands' End work in fundamentally the same way: purchase products at low prices directly from manufacturers, then sell them for a higher price as quickly as possible. Sourcing good products at low prices and managing inventory levels are the keys to reselling. Without a steady supply of sellable product at a low enough price to turn a profit, a reseller will have a hard time bringing in enough revenue to keep going. Accordingly, most successful resellers establish close relationships with the businesses that supply their stock to ensure they continue to get a reliable supply of good assets at low prices.

A Lease involves acquiring an asset, followed by allowing another person to use that asset for a predefined amount of time in exchange for a fee. Th e asset can be pretty much anything: cars, boats, houses, DVDs. As long as an asset is durable enough to survive rental to another person and return ready for reuse, you can Lease it. In order to provide value via a Lease, you must: 1. Acquire an asset people want to use. 2. Lease the asset to a paying customer on favorable terms. 3. Protect yourself from unexpected or adverse events, including the loss or damage of the leased asset. Leasing benefits the customer by allowing the use of an asset for less than the outright purchase price. You may not be able to afford to spend tens of thousands of dollars to purchase a luxury car or a speedboat, but for a few hundred dollars a month, you can certainly lease or rent one. Th e same principle applies to housing: leasing makes it possible to live in an expensive building for much less than it would cost to purchase or build it yourself. After your lease is up, the asset can be leased by the owner to someone else. To successfully provide value via Leases, you must ensure that the revenue from the Lease covers the purchase price of the asset before it wears out or is lost. Most assets have a limited useful life, so you must charge enough to bring in more revenue than the purchase price before the asset loses its value. In addition, be sure to plan for repair and replacement costs to ensure you're charging enough money to cover you in the event your asset is lost or damaged in use.

Agency involves the marketing and sale of an asset you don't own. Instead of producing value by yourself, you team up with someone else who has value to offer, then work to find a purchaser. In exchange for establishing a new relationship between your source and a buyer, you earn a commission or fee. In order to provide value via Agency, you must: 1. Find a seller who has a valuable asset. 2. Establish contact and trust with potential buyers of that asset.3. Negotiate until an agreement is reached on the terms of sale. 4. Collect the agreed-upon fee or commission from the seller. Sellers benefit from an Agency relationship because it generates sales that might not otherwise happen. Literary agents are a classic example: a potential author may have an idea for a book, but may not know anyone in publishing. By working with an agent who has preexisting connections in the publishing industry, it's far more likely the author will land a publishing contract. In exchange for finding a publisher and negotiating the deal, the agent gets a percentage of the book's advance and royalties. Buyers also benefit from an Agency relationship—good agents can help them find great assets to purchase. Agents often act as a filter for buyers, who trust that the agent will bring their attention to assets worth purchasing and keep them away from bad deals. Residential real estate is a great example: working with an experienced buyer's agent who knows the area often makes purchasing a home in a new town much easier. The key to Agency is to ensure that your fee or commission is high enough to make the effort worth it. Since most Agency relationships are dependent upon closing a sale, spend your time on activities that will result in a completed transaction, and ensure that the commission or fee from that transaction compensates you for the time and effort you put into closing the deal.

Audience Aggregation revolves around collecting the attention of a group of people with similar characteristics, then selling access to that audience to a third party. Since attention is limited and valuable, gathering a group of people in a certain demographic is quite valuable to businesses or groups that are interested in getting the attention of those people.In order to provide value via Audience Aggregation, you must: 1. Identify a group of people with common characteristics or interests. 2. Create and maintain some way of consistently attracting that group's attention. 3. Find third parties who are interested in buying the attention of that audience. 4. Sell access to that audience without alienating the audience itself. Audience Aggregation benefits the audience because it provides something worthy of their attention. Magazines and advertising-supported Web sites are great examples: readers benefit from the information and entertainment these sources provide in exchange for being exposed to some level of advertising. If the advertising becomes obnoxious, they'll leave, but most people are willing to be exposed to a certain amount of advertising if the content is good. Audience Aggregation benefits the advertiser because it gets attention, which leads to sales. Think of a conference or trade show: buying a booth in the center of a building full of people interested in what you have to off er can be a smart decision. Done well, advertising attracts attention, attention brings prospects, and prospects lead to sales. As long as the sales bring in more money than the cost of the advertising plus the business's Overhead (discussed later), the advertising can be a valuable tool to bring in new customers, which means the advertiser can continue to support the aggregator by purchasing more advertising.

A Loan involves an agreement to let the borrower use a certain amount of resources for a certain period of time. In exchange, the borrower must pay the lender a series of payments over a predefi ned period of time, which is equal to the original loan plus a predefined interest rate. In order to provide value via Loans, you must: 1. Have some amount of money to lend. 2. Find people who want to borrow that money. 3. Set an interest rate that compensates you adequately for the Loan. 4. Estimate and protect against the possibility that the Loan won't be repaid. Used responsibly, Loans allow people to benefit from immediate access to products or services that would otherwise be too expensive to purchase outright. Mortgages allow people to live in houses without having hundreds of thousands of dollars in the bank. Auto Loans allow people to drive new vehicles in exchange for a monthly payment instead of a 100 percent down payment. Credit cards allow people to purchase goods and services immediately, then pay for them over the course of several months. Loans are beneficial to the lender because they provide a way to benefi t from excess capital. The addition of compound interest on top of the original loan (the "principal") means that the lender will collect much more than the original loan—in the case of long-term Loans like mortgages, often two to three times more. After the Loan is made, little additional work is required on the part of the lender aside from collecting payments—unless the borrower stops making payments. Accordingly, the process of identifying how risky a particular Loan is—a process called "underwriting"—is critically important for lenders, who often require some sort of asset as collateral to protect against the risks of a Loan gone sour. If the Loan is not repaid, ownership of the collateral is transferred to the borrower, then sold to recoup any funds lost in the transaction.

A n Option is the ability to take a predefined action for a fixed period of time in exchange for a fee. Most people think of Options as fi nancial securities, but they're all around us: movie or concert tickets, coupons, retainers, and licensing rights are all examples of Options. In exchange for a fee, the purchaser has the right to take some specific action—attend the show, purchase an asset, or buy a fi nancial security at a particular price—before the deadline. In order to provide value via Options, you must: 1. Identify some action people might want to take in the future. 2. Offer potential buyers the right to take that action before a specifi ed deadline. 3. Convince potential buyers that the Option is worth the asking price. 4. Enforce the specified deadline on taking action. Options are valuable because they allow the purchaser the ability to take a specific action without requiring them to take that action. For example, if you purchase a movie ticket, you have the ability to occupy a seat in the theater, but you don't have to if a better opportunity presents itself. When you purchase the ticket, all you're purchasing is the right to exercise the Option to see the movie at the time specifi ed—nothing more. Options are often used to keep specific courses of action open for a certain period of time before another transaction takes place. For example, in moving to Colorado from New York, my wife, Kelsey, and I put a deposit down on an apartment we hadn't seen in person. The deposit ensured that the landlord wouldn't rent the apartment to someone else before we moved. Once we signed the official rental agreement, the deposit became a standard rental security deposit. If we had decided not to move forward, the landlord would have kept the deposit in compensation for holding the apartment for us and would have been free to find another tenant. Th us, the Option was beneficial for both of us.

Insurance involves the transfer of risk from the purchaser to the seller. In exchange for taking on the risk of some specific bad thing happening to the policy holder, the policy holder agrees to give the insurer a predefi ned series of payments. If the bad thing actually happens, the insurer is responsible for footing the bill. If it doesn't, the insurer gets to keep the money. In order to provide value via Insurance, you must: 1. Create a binding legal agreement that transfers the risk of a specific bad thing (a "loss") happening from the policy holder to you. 2. Estimate the risk of that bad thing actually happening, using available data. 3. Collect the agreed-upon series of payments (called "premiums") over time. 4. Pay out legitimate claims upon the policy. Insurance provides value to the purchaser by protecting them from downside risk. For example, a house can catch fire in any number of ways, and most homeowners don't have enough cash to purchase another if their home burns to the ground. Homeowners' Insurance transfers this risk to the insurer. If the home is destroyed by fire, the Insurance will compensate the homeowner and allow them to purchase a new home. If it isn't, the insurer gets to keep the premium payments. Insurance works because it spreads risk over a large number of individuals. If an insurer writes policies for thousands or millions of homes, it's highly unlikely that every single one will burn to the ground at once—only a certain number of claims will have to be paid. As long as the insurer brings in more premium payments than it pays in claims, the insurer makes money. Car insurance, health insurance, and warranty coverage for consumer goods work the same way. The more premiums an insurer collects and the fewer claims the insurer pays, the more money it makes. Insurers have a vested interest in avoiding "bad risks," maximizing premiums, and minimizing payments on claims. Accordingly, insurers must be constantly vigilant to avoid fraudulent activity, both by preventing fraudulent claims and by refraining from defrauding purchasers by collecting premium payments without paying legitimate claims. If an insurer fails to pay legitimate claims, they're likely to find themselves in court as policy holders use the legal system to uphold their Insurance contract.

Capital is the purchase of an ownership stake in a business. For parties that have resources to allocate, providing Capital is a way to help owners of new or existing businesses expand or enter new markets. Angel investing, venture capital, and purchasing stock in publicly traded companies are all examples of providing value via Capital, which we'll discuss in detail later in the Hierarchy of Funding. In order to provide value via Capital, you must: 1. Have a pool of resources available to invest. 2. Find a promising business in which you'd be willing to invest. 3. Estimate how much that business is currently worth, how much it may be worth in the future, and the probability that the business will go under, which would result in the loss of your Capital.

4. Negotiate the amount of ownership you'd receive in exchange for the amount of Capital you're investing. Businesses benefit from Capital investment because it enables them to gather the resources necessary to expand or enter new industries. Some industries, like manufacturing and financial services, require huge amounts of funding to start or expand. By taking on investors, business owners can secure enough funding to move forward quickly. Investors benefit by acquiring a certain percentage of that company's ownership, which allows them to benefit from the business's activities without active involvement. Instead of leaving their money in a bank account, investors can allocate it to companies that are involved in promising ventures, which may provide a higher rate of return. If the

business brings in a lot of cash, investors may benefit from a regular dividend. If it's acquired by another company or is listed on a public stock exchange, investors may receive a percentage of the purchase price as a lumpsum payment or sell their shares of the company on the open market for a profit.

A ll forms of value are not created equal. Perceived Value determines how much your customers will be willing to pay for what you're off ering.The higher the perceived value of your off ering, the more you'll be able to charge for it, which signifi cantly improves your chances of succeeding. As a rule of thumb, the less attractive the End Result (discussed later) and the more end-user involvement it takes to get the benefit, the lower the value your customers will place on the offer.

The benefit of making your offers small and Modular is that it allows you to take advantage of a strategy called Bundling. Bundling allows you to repurpose value that you have already created to create even more value. Bundling occurs when you combine multiple smaller offers into a single large offer. An example of Bundling occurs in the mobile phone industry, where a mobile phone (a physical Product) is bundled with a monthly service plan (a Subscription) for a single price. Similarly, buy-one-get-one-free off ers at the grocery store are a form of Bundling. Typically, the more offers contained in the bundle, the higher the Perceived Value of the off er, and the more the business can charge. Th at's why mobile phone providers add things like more minutes, unlimited text messaging, and Internet service onto the basic service plan. The more benefi ts provided, the more a customer is typically willing to pay on a monthly basis for the entire package. Unbundling is the opposite of Bundling: it's taking one offer and splitting it up into multiple offers. A good example of Unbundling is selling MP3 downloads of a single album instead of the CD. Customers may not be willing to pay $10 for an entire album, but they may be willing to pay a dollar or two for the songs they particularly like. Unbundling the album into individual units opens the way to sales that wouldn't otherwise happen. Bundling and Unbundling can help you create value for diff erent types of customers without requiring the creation of something new. By combining offers and forms in various configurations, you can offer your customers exactly what they want.Nobody—no matter how smart or talented they are—gets it right the fi rst time. For proof, consider any artistic masterpiece. Beneath the fi nished surface of the Mona Lisa, you'll fi nd layer upon layer of draft sketches, false starts, and major alterations. The ceiling of the Sistine Chapel is covered with hundreds of millions of very small brushstrokes, each of which brought the resulting masterpiece one step closer to completion. It took Michelangelo millions of hammer strokes to turn a crude block of marble into the David. Th e Iteration Cycle is a process you can use to make anything better over time. There's nothing wasteful about the inevitable changes and revisions that these artists made to their creations: every iteration brought the project one step closer to completion. Iteration has six major steps, which I call the WIGWAM method: 1. Watch—What's happening? What's working and what's not? 2. Ideate—What could you improve? What are your options? 3. Guess—Based on what you've learned so far, which of your ideas do you think will make the biggest impact?4. Which?—Decide which change to make. 5. Act—Actually make the change. 6. Measure—What happened? Was the change positive or negative? Should you keep the change, or go back to how things were before this iteration? Iteration is a cycle—once you measure the results of the change and decide whether or not to keep it, you go back to the beginning to observe what's happening, and the cycle repeats. For best results, clearly define what you're trying to accomplish with each iteration. Are you trying to make the offering more attractive or appealing? Are you trying to add a new feature people will value? Are you trying to make the offering cost less without detracting from its value? Th e more clearly you can define what you're after, the easier it'll be to understand the Feedback (discussed later) you're receiving and the more value you'll extract from each Iteration Cycle.

Until one is committed, there is hesitancy, the chance to draw back, always ineffectiveness. Concerning all acts of initiative and creation, there is one elementary truth the ignorance of which kills countless ideas and splendid plans: that the moment one defi nitely commits oneself, the providence moves too. —W. H. MURRAY, MOUNTAINEER AND WRITER It's Friday night. You're hungry, and you're thinking about going out to eat. You've already decided that you value having food prepared for you enough to justify the extra expense. Where should you go for dinner? If you go to the neighborhood diner, you'll have access to a large variety of decent food at a reasonable price. The place may not be very fancy, but you know you'll be served a pretty good meal quickly and without a lot of fuss or expense. If you go to a swanky hot spot, you'll be treated to attractive décor, impeccable service, and sophisticated cuisine. You'll have an impressive story to tell your friends, as well as the anticipation and excitement of a big night on the town. You'll also have a heftier tab at the end of the evening. Unless you're really hungry, you won't patronize both restaurants on the same evening—it's an either/or decision. At the same time, there's no "right" decision—in fact, you may choose to go to the diner one evening and the trendy restaurant the next. It all depends on what you value most at the moment you decide where to eat. Now let's flip the situation. You're the owner of the diner, and you're looking for ways to serve your customers better and bring new people into the restaurant. What should you focus on improving? Would expanding your entrée selection, reducing the time it takes to serve customers, or remodeling the restaurant make the biggest difference to the bottom line? In a perfect world, it would be best to do all of these things, but business has been lackluster recently, and you don't have an unlimited budget to work with. You know you need to do something, but it's not clear which improvements—if any—would make the cash register ring more often. What do you do? As you develop your offering, you can't avoid making choices between competing Alternatives. Should you add a particular feature, or not? Should you optimize for market A, optimize for market B, or attempt to please both? If you invest more in the offering, will your customers be willing to pay more to defray the expense? Examining the possible Alternatives and considering the customer's perspective results in better choices. As you make decisions about what to include and what to leave out, it's essential to appreciate the Alternatives that your potential customers face when they decide whether or not to purchase your offering. Once you're aware of the options, you can examine the combinations and permutations of those Alternatives to present an attractive offer.

Every time your customers purchase from you, they're deciding that they value what you have to offer more than they value anything else their money could buy at that moment. As you develop your offering, one of your first priorities should be to find out what your potential customers value more than the buying power of the dollars in their wallets. Everyone has slightly different values at any given time, but there are a few common patterns that appear when people evaluate a potential purchase. Assuming the promised benefits of the offering are appealing, there are nine common Economic Values that people typically consider when evaluating a potential purchase. Th ey are: 1. Efficacy—How well does it work? 2. Speed—How quickly does it work? 3. Reliability—Can I depend on it to do what I want?4. Ease of Use—How much effort does it require? 5. Flexibility—How many things does it do? 6. Status—How does this affect the way others perceive me? 7. Aesthetic Appeal—How attractive or otherwise aesthetically pleasing is it? 8. Emotion—How does it make me feel? 9. Cost—How much do I have to give up to get this? In the book Trade-Off : Why Some Things Catch On, and Others Don't, Kevin Maney discusses these common values in terms of two primary characteristics: convenience and fi delity.Things that are quick, reliable, easy, and flexible are convenient.Things that offer quality, status, aesthetic appeal, or emotional impact are high-fi delity. Almost every improvement you make to an offer can be thought of in terms of improving either convenience or fidelity. It's incredibly diffi cult to optimize for both fidelity and convenience at the same time, so the most successful offerings try to provide the most convenience or fi delity among all competing offerings. If you're craving pizza, a table at the original Pizzeria Uno in Chicago is high-fidelity; Domino's home delivery is convenient. Accordingly, Pizzeria Uno benefits more from making the dining experience remarkable, while Domino's benefi ts more from delivering decent pizza as quickly as possible. Th e Trade-offs that are made in the development of new off erings are what give each option its unique identity. Here's an example from the apparel business: Old Navy, Banana Republic, and Gap are owned by the same company, Gap Inc. All three lines make the same types of clothing— shirts, pants, and so on—but off er diff erent Trade-off s. Instead of attempting to make a single clothing line that's designed to appeal to everyone (which is impossible, since everyone wants something diff erent), the company focused each line around a specifi c Trade-off . Old Navy emphasizes functionality and low cost. Gap emphasizes style and fashion at a moderate cost. Banana Republic emphasizes aesthetics and status at a premium cost. Each line has its own identity and appeals to a diff erent type of potential customer, even though the clothes may be manufacturedusing the same processes and the revenues end up in the coffers of the same company.

The tricky thing about trying to figure out what people want is that people want everything. Here's proof: bring together a group of potential customers for a focus group. Ask each participant to rate the importance of each of the nine Economic Values for your offering on a scale of 0 to 10. What will the results look like? Regardless of your product or service, the results will be the same: your customers want products that provide exceptional results instantly, every time, with absolutely no effort. Simultaneously, they want the offer to make them rich, famous, attractive, and eternally blissful. They also want it to be free. If you ask them what they'd be willing to give up, they'll answer that everything is critically important, and they won't be happy with less. The reality outside of the focus group is always quite diff erent. Shortly after the group adjourns, each of those participants will go out and purchase something that's not free and not perfect, and they'll be happy with their decision. Why? As a rule, people never accept Trade-offs unless they're forced to make a Decision. If the perfect option existed, they'd buy it. Since there's no such thing as the perfect offering, people are happy to settle for the Next Best Alternative (discussed later). The best way to discover what people actually value is to ask them to make explicit Trade-offs during the research process. The problem with the hypothetical focus group was that it didn't ask the participants to make any real Decisions—the participants could have everything, so they wanted everything.

Relative Importance Testing—a set of analysis techniques pioneered by statistician Jordan Louviere in the 1980s3 —gives you a way to determine what people actually want by asking them a series of simple questions designed to simulate real-life Trade-offs. Here's how it works. Let's assume we're conducting a Relative Importance Test for the diner previously mentioned. Instead of asking the participant to rank each benefit from 0 to 10, we show the participant something like the following: A. Orders delivered to table in five minutes or less. B. Most entrée prices under $20. C. Appealing restaurant décor. D. Large variety of menu options. After this set is shown, the participant is asked the following questions: 1. Which of these items is most important? 2. Which of these items is least important? Once the participant answers the questions, another set is shown: E. Unique entrées I can't get anywhere else. F. Knowing I can always order my favorite dishes. G. People are impressed that I dine here. H. Large portions. Random question sets containing four or five criteria are provided until there are no more possible combinations or the participant's attention wanders, which will typically occur around the five- to ten-minute mark. It won't take the participant long to provide a response to each of these simple questions, but the results are quite revealing. By asking the participant to make an actual choice, you're collecting more accurate information about how the participant would respond when faced with a similar choice in the real world. When the results are aggregated and statistically analyzed, the relative importance of each benefit becomes very clear.Th e more sets each participant completes, the more clearly you'll be able to judge the relative importance of each benefit.

n order to conduct a Shadow Test, you need something to sell. Fortunately, you don't have to create the entire offer before you start selling. A Minimum Economically Viable Offer (MEVO) is an offer that promises and /or provides the smallest number of benefits necessary to produce an actual sale. A MEVO is essentially a Prototype that's been developed to the point that someone will actually pull out their wallet and commit to making a purchase. It doesn't have to be complicated: Fitbit's MEVO was a Prototype, a description, and a few computer renderings. All you need to do is convey enough information to convince a real potential customer to buy. Creating a MEVO is useful because it's impossible to predict 100 percent accurately what will work in advance. You don't want to invest a ton of time and money in something that has no chance of working, and the faster you can figure out if your idea will work or not, the better off you'll be. Since Feedback from prospective customers and paid-in-full orders are very different things, creating a MEVO allows you to start collecting data from real customers as quickly as possible, directly testing the idea's Critically Important Assumptions and reducing the risk of making a business-ending investment decision. Here's how the hypothetical yoga studio we discussed earlier could use a MEVO and Shadow Testing to evaluate their CIAs: Step 1: Create a simple Web site describing the studio in detail, including location, tentative schedule, teaching staff, sketches of the space, and membership fees. The site includes a sign-up form for visitors to preorder memberships by submitting their credit card information. By signing up, members commit to a twelve-month membership when the studio opens, but they have the opportunity to cancel within the first month if they don't like it. If the studio doesn't open, all preorders are canceled without charge. Total cost: a few hundred dollars. Step 2: Direct prospective customers to the Web site. This can be done inexpensively in any number of ways: fl yers, door-to-door inquiry, direct mail, and local search engine advertising. Total cost: a few hundred dollars. Step 3: Track how many individuals sign up for preopening memberships at the full rate via the Web site or request additional information. Total cost: a few hours of analysis. This simple process can be done quickly and cheaply, and will reveal a great deal about the real-world accuracy of the business's CIAs. Spending a few hundred dollars to pretest critical assumptions is a very good use of money, particularly if the findings prevent the investment of larger sums of money in a business idea that's doomed to fail from the start. The purpose of starting with a MEVO is to minimize your risk. By keeping the investments small, incremental, and learning oriented, you'll be able to quickly discover what works and what doesn't. If the idea is promising, you're in a great position to make it happen. If your assumptions don't hold true, you're able to cut your losses without losing your shirt or your dignity.

Once your MEVO is selling and you've proven that your CIAs are valid, you're in good shape, but you're not finished. If you're committed to making your offer as good as it can be, you'll need to keep making small changes that improve the offer if you want to stay competitive and attract more customers. Incremental Augmentation is the process of using the Iteration Cycle to add new benefits to an existing off er. The process is simple: keep making and testing additions to the core offer, continue doing what works, and stop doing what doesn't. The process of customizing cars is an example of Incremental Augmentation. Starting with a stock car, the "tuner" steadily replaces and upgrades parts: a better engine, spoiler, tinted windows, and chrome hubcaps. Th e intent of every change is to make the car just a little bit better, until it's the best it can be. When the car is finished, it's a diff erent machine. Incremental Augmentation helps you improve your offering while minimizing the risk that any single iteration will fail catastrophically. If you're not careful, drastic changes after launch can eliminate the qualities that made your offer attractive or break the systems you use to create the value you're providing to your customers. By making and testing changes quickly and incrementally, you can continually improve your offer without betting the farm, helping you create even more value for your customers over time. Keep in mind that Incremental Augmentation can only take you so far. In order to enter a new market or change the game, you may need to create something completely new. If that's the case, start over with a new Prototype and work your way through the value creation process from the beginning. When it's ready, get Feedback and use Testing (discussed later) to compare the new version with the old version to make sure it's actually better before you launch it.

Offering value is not enough. If no one knows (or cares) about what you have to offer, it doesn't matter how much value you create. Without Marketing, no business can survive—people who don't know you exist can't purchase what you have to offer, and people who aren't interested in what you have to offer won't become paying customers. Every successful business finds a way to attract the attention of the right people and make them interested in what's being off ered. Without prospects, you won't sell anything, and without completing profi table transactions, your business will fail. Marketing is the art and science of finding "prospects"—people who are actively interested in what you have to off er. The best businesses in the world fi nd ways to attract the attention of qualifi ed prospects quickly and inexpensively. The more prospects you entice, the better off your business will be. Marketing is not the same thing as selling. While "direct marketing" strategies often try to minimize the time between attracting attention and asking for the sale, Marketing and selling are two diff erent things. Marketing is about getting noticed; Sales, which we'll discuss in chapter 4, is about closing the deal.

Modern life is overloaded with demands on your Attention. Think of all of the things that are competing for your attention right now: there's work to be done, people to call, e-mail to check,TV to watch, music to listen to, and countless Web sites to visit. Everyone has too many things to do, and too little time to do them all. Rule #1 of Marketing is that your potential customer's available attention is limited. Keeping up with everything in your world would require way more attention than you actually have to work with. To compensate, you filter: you ration your attention, allocating more to things you care about and less to things you don't. So does everyone else, including your potential prospects. To get someone's attention, you have to find a way around their fi lters. High-quality attention must be earned. When you're seeking someone's attention, it's useful to take a moment to remember that you're competing against everything else in their world. In order to be noticed, you need to fi nd a way to earn that attention by being more interesting or useful than the competing alternatives. Attention doesn't matter if people don't care about what you're doing. If all you're looking for is attention, don't bother with all of this business stuff : skipping down the street in a pink bunny suit while yelling at the top of your lungs will get you all the attention you'll ever want. When it comes to business, however, some kinds of attention aren't worth having. You want the attention of prospects who will ultimately purchase from you—otherwise, you're wasting your time. It's nice to be the center of attention, but business is about making profitable sales, not winning a popularity contest. Being featured on national television or on a huge Web site is a wonderful thing, but very often this kind of broad publicity fails to deliver actual sales. Spending time and energy acting like a socialite reduces the amount of resources you can devote to creating real value for your customers, which doesn't help anyone. Earn the attention of the people who are likely to buy from you, and you'll inevitably build your business.

People ignore what they don't care about. One of the primary functions of the human brain is perceptual filtering: determining what to pay attention to and what to ignore. The fastest way to be ignored by anyone is to start talking about something they don't care about. Receptivity is a measure of how open a person is to your message. Rabid fans of hit novels like Stephenie Meyer's Twilight books are paragons of Receptivity: they're interested in almost anything they can find about their obsession as soon as it's available. From a business perspective, that's ideal— it's diffi cult to offer something that this audience won't want immediately. On the other hand, a committed ethical vegan isn't likely to be interested in hearing about the benefits of red meat consumption, regardless of how much disconfirming evidence there is or how compelling the presentation. The worldview mismatch is just too big, and even the largest publicity campaign won't be able to overcome the overwhelming urge to ignore. Receptivity has two primary components: what and when. People tend to be receptive only to certain categories of things at certain times. I love hearing about great new business books, but I never want to be on the receiving end of a 3:00 a.m. phone call from a publicist. If you want your message to be heard, the medium matters. Th e form of your message has a big influence on how receptive people are to the information that message contains. If the form of your message suggests that it was created just for them, you're far more likely to get your prospect's attention. Here's an example: Almost everyone will ignore postal junk mail—if it looks blatantly commercial or mass-produced, there's a 99 percent chance the recipient will throw it away without a second thought. Change the form, however, and Receptivity changes as well. Most people will at least open a hand-addressed envelope, since it's clear someone spent time and effort sending it to them. Taken to an extreme, almost everyone (including busy executives) will open and look through the contents of a large overnight hand-addressed FedEx envelope—it's big, expensive, and clearly requires effort to send. Even then, if the contents don't match what they're interested in, you'll lose their attention immediately.Assuming that everyone in the world cares about what you have to off er is a huge marketing mistake. You may think that what you have to offer is the greatest thing since sliced bread—in fact, I hope you do! Th at doesn't change the fact that it's not right for everyone.Whatever you're offering, I can guarantee you that most of the people in this world don't—and will never—care about what you're doing. Harsh but true. Fortunately, you don't have to appeal to everyone in order to succeed.You just have to attract enough Attention to close enough sales to produce enough profit to keep going. To do that, it's best to focus on attracting the attention of the people who will actually care about what you're doing. Skilled marketers don't try to get everyone's attention—they focus on getting the attention of the right people at the right time. If you're marketing Harley-Davidson motorcycles, trying to land an appearance on Oprah to show off this year's new models probably isn't the best strategy. Likewise, Oprah's core audience is not likely to include burly men in leather jackets with handlebar mustaches and tattoos, so don't expect her to pay for a marketing booth at a motorcycle trade show any time soon. Your Probable Purchaser is the type of person who is perfectly suited to what you're offering. Harley's most profitable customer is the "weekend warrior"—middle-aged men with disposable income who want to feel powerful and dangerous while cruising around in their spare time. Oprah's Probable Purchasers are middle-aged women who want to improve themselves and enjoy listening to intimate confessions and emotional stories. Harley doesn't try to appeal to Oprah's Probable Purchasers, and vice versa—they each focus on appealing to their specific core audience, to great eff ect. Attempting to appeal to everyone is a waste of time and money: focus your marketing efforts on your Probable Purchaser. By spending your limited resources reaching out to people who are already interested in the types of things you offer, you'll maximize the effectiveness of your attentiongrabbing activities.

Believe it or not, it's often wise to turn away paying customers. Not every customer is a good customer: customers who require more time, energy, attention, or risk than they're worth to your bottom line aren't worth attracting in the first place.

Qualifi cation is the process of determining whether or not a prospect is a good customer before they purchase from you. By evaluating a prospect before they buy, you can minimize the chance of wasting your time dealing with a customer who's not a good fit for your business. Progressive Insurance has turned Qualification into a profi table business strategy.To see Qualification in action, go to the Progressive Insurance Web site (www.progressive.com) and request a quote for car insurance. When you request a quote, Progressive asks you a set of basic questions: 1. What type of car do you have? 2. Do you own or lease it? If you own it, are you still making payments? 3. What's your ZIP code? 4. Are you married? 5. Did you go to college? 6. Have you had any at-fault accidents in the past fi ve years? Progressive then uses your answers to gather data from a series of databases to answer two questions: (A) Are you the type of person Progressive wants to insure? (B) If so, how much should they charge to insure you? If you're the type of person Progressive wants as a customer, they'll quote you a price and encourage you to purchase an insurance policy immediately. If you're not, Progressive will tell you that you can get a better price elsewhere and actively encourage you to purchase insurance from one of their competitors. Why in the world would a business encourage a hot prospect to purchase from the competition? As you recall from our previous discussion of Insurance, the profitability of an insurer depends on collecting as much money as possible in premiums while paying out as little money as possible in claims. Progressive doesn't want to maximize its total client base: it wants to insure only people who are likely to drive safely and have few accidents, which means attracting customers who will pay premiums for a long time without making claims. Qualification allows Progressive to maximize the number of highly profi table customers it insures while funneling the "bad risks" directly to their competitors. It's good for customers as well—if they're "good risks," they get lower rates on their car insurance. Screening your customers can help you filter out the bad customers before they do business with you. The more clearly you define your ideal customer, the better you can screen out the prospects who don't fi t that description, and the more you'll be able to focus on serving your best customers well.

Assuming you don't have a small child and aren't expecting one any time soon, you probably don't care about diapers, strollers, cribs, infant toys, day care, and Baby Einstein DVDs. Any information you're exposed to about these things is likely to be filtered away by your brain, since it's not relevant to your life at the moment. But once you're expecting a little bundle of joy to enter your life, you suddenly care a great deal about these things, and will probably start actively searching for information about them. Before hearing the news, you had no reason to care; now you do. Certain markets have clearly defi ned entry and exit points. Learning a newborn is on the way is an example of a Point of Market Entry. Once you know you're expecting, you're suddenly much more receptive to information about products and services that will help you take care of a child. Attempting to attract the Attention of people who don't care about what you do is a waste of time, money, and energy, so it's best to fi nd out when people are interested in hearing from you before you reach out. Attracting your

Probable Purchaser's Attention immediately after they've reached the Point of Market Entry is hugely valuable. Companies like Procter & Gamble, Kimberly-Clark, Johnson & Johnson, and Fisher-Price pay an enormous amount of attention to Points of Market Entry, since they have a huge.impact on the effectiveness of every baby-product-related marketing activity. It's not uncommon for new moms and dads to come home from the hospital with a complimentary "care package" from one or more of these companies containing samples of diapers, diaper rash ointment, formula, and other newborn-care basics. If you can get a prospective customer's attention as soon as they become interested in what you're offering, you become the standard by which competing offers are evaluated. That's a remarkably powerful position that increases the likelihood the prospect will ultimately purchase from you. Discovering where Probable Purchasers start looking for information after crossing the interest threshold is extremely valuable. Before the advent of the Internet, most expecting parents immediately started devouring books and talking to more experienced family and friends. Today, newly minted moms and dads hit the Web first, which is why organic and paid search engine marketing is often so valuable. By optimizing for key words your prospective customers are likely to search for, you can ensure that they find you first.

CHAPTER TWO

Apples and Oranges: A Comparison

So, what makes the difference? What separates the New Rich, characterized by options, from the Deferrers (D), those who save it all for the end only to find that life has passed them by? It begins at the beginning. The New Rich can be separated from the crowd based on their goals, which reflect very distinct priorities and life philosophies. Note how subtle differences in wording completely change the necessary actions for fulfilling what at a glance appear to be similar goals. These are not limited to business owners. Even the first, as I will show later, applies to employees. D: To work for yourself. NR: To have others work for you. D: To work when you want to. NR: To prevent work for work's sake, and to do the minimum necessary for maximum effect ("minimum effective load"). D: To retire early or young. NR: To distribute recovery periods and adventures (mini-retirements) throughout life on a regular basis and recognize that inactivity is not the goal. Doing that which excites you is. D: To buy all the things you want to have. NR: To do all the things you want to do, and be all the things you want to be. If this includes some tools and gadgets, so be it, but they are either means to an end or bonuses, not the focus. D: To be the boss instead of the employee; to be in charge. NR: To be neither the boss nor the employee, but the owner. To own the trains and have someone else ensure they run on time. D: To make a ton of money. NR: To make a ton of money with specific reasons and defined dreams to chase, timelines and steps included. What are you working for? D: To have more. NR: To have more quality and less clutter. To have huge financial reserves but recognize that most material wants are justifications for spending time on the things that don't really matter, including buying things and preparing to buy things. You spent two weeks negotiating your new Infiniti with the dealership and got $10,000 off? That's great. Does your life have a purpose? Are you contributing anything useful to this world, or just shuffling papers, banging on a keyboard, and coming home to a drunken existence on the weekends? D: To reach the big pay-off, whether IPO, acquisition, retirement, or other pot of gold. NR: To think big but ensure payday comes every day: cash flow first, big payday second. D: To have freedom from doing that which you dislike. NR: To have freedom from doing that which you dislike, but also the freedom and resolve to pursue your dreams without reverting to work for work's sake (W4W). After years of repetitive work, you will often need to dig hard to find your passions, redefine your dreams, and revive hobbies that you let atrophy to near extinction. The goal is not to simply eliminate the bad, which does nothing more than leave you with a vacuum, but to pursue and experience the best in the world. Getting Off the Wrong Train The first principle is that you must not fool yourself, and you are the easiest person to fool. —RICHARD P. FEYNMAN, Nobel Prize–winning physicist Enough is enough. Lemmings no more. The blind quest for cash is a fool's errand. I've chartered private planes over the Andes, enjoyed many of the best wines in the world in between world-class ski runs, and lived like a king, lounging by the infinity pool of a private villa. Here's the little secret I rarely tell: It all cost less than rent in the U.S. If you can free your time and location, your money is automatically worth 3– 10 times as much. This has nothing to do with currency rates. Being financially rich and having the ability to live like a millionaire are fundamentally two very different things. Money is multiplied in practical value depending on the number of W's you control in your life: what you do, when you do it, where you do it, and with whom you do it. I call this the "freedom multiplier." Using this as our criterion, the 80-hour-per-week, $500,000-per-year investment banker is less "powerful" than the employed NR who works ¼ the hours for $40,000, but has complete freedom of when, where, and how to live. The former's $500,000 may be worth less than $40,000 and the latter's $40,000 worth more than $500,000 when we run the numbers and look at the lifestyle output of their money. Options—the ability to choose—is real power. This book is all about how to see and create those options with the least effort and cost. It just so happens, paradoxically, that you can make more money—a lot more money—by doing half of what you are doing now. So, Who Are the NR? ? The employee who rearranges his schedule and negotiates a remote work agreement to achieve 90% of the results in one-tenth of the time, which frees him to practice cross-country skiing and take road trips with his family two weeks per month. ? The business owner who eliminates the least profitable customers and projects, outsources all operations entirely, and travels the world collecting rare documents, all while working remotely on a website to showcase her own illustration work. ? The student who elects to risk it all—which is nothing—to establish an online video rental service that delivers $5,000 per month in income from a small niche of Blu-ray aficionados, a two-hour-perweek side project that allows him to work full-time as an animal rights lobbyist. The options are limitless, but each path begins with the same first step: replacing assumptions. To join the movement, you will need to learn a new lexicon and recalibrate direction using a compass for an unusual world. From inverting responsibility to jettisoning the entire concept of "success," we need to change the rules.

As he rotated 360 degrees through the air, the deafening noise turned to silence. Dale Begg-Smith executed the backflip perfectly—skis crossed in an X over his head—and landed in the record books as he slid across the finish. It was February 16, 2006, and he was now a mogul-skiing gold medalist at the Turin Winter Olympics. Unlike other full-time athletes, he will never have to return to a dead-end job after his moment of glory, nor will he look back at this day as the climax of his only passion. After all, he was only 21 years old and drove a black Lamborghini. Born a Canadian and something of a late bloomer, Dale found his calling, an Internet-based IT company, at the age of 13. Fortunately, he had a more-experienced mentor and partner to guide him: his 15-year-old brother, Jason. Created to fund their dreams of standing atop the Olympic podium, it would, only two years later, become the third-largest company of its kind in the world. While Dale's teammates were hitting the slopes for extra sessions, he was often buying sake for clients in Tokyo. In a world of "work harder, not smarter," it came to pass that his coaches felt he was spending too much time on his business and not enough time in training, despite his results. Rather than choose between his business or his dream, Dale chose to move laterally with both, from either/or to both/and. He wasn't spending too much time on his business; he and his brother were spending too much time with Canucks. In 2002, they moved to the ski capital of the world, Australia, where the team was smaller, more flexible, and coached by a legend. Three short years later, he received citizenship, went head-to-head against former teammates, and became the third "Aussie" in history to win winter gold. In the land of wallabies and big surf, Dale has since gone postal. Literally. Right next to the

Elvis Presley commemorative edition, you can buy stamps with his face on them. Fame has its perks, as does looking outside the choices presented to you. There are always lateral options. NEW CALEDOINA, SOUTH PACIFIC OCEAN Once you say you're going to settle for second, that's what happens to you in life. —JOHN F. KENNEDY Some people remain convinced that just a bit more money will make things right. Their goals are arbitrary moving targets: $300,000 in the bank, $1,000,000 in the portfolio, $100,000 a year instead of $50,000, etc. Julie's goal made intrinsic sense: come back with the same number of children she had left with. She reclined in her seat and glanced across the aisle past her sleeping husband, Marc, counting as she had done thousands of times—one, two, three. So far so good. In 12 hours, they would all be back in Paris, safe and sound. That was assuming the plane from New Caledonia held together, of course. New Caledonia? Nestled in the tropics of the Coral Sea, New Caledonia was a French territory and where Julie and Marc had just sold the sailboat that took them 15,000 miles around the world. Of course, recouping their initial investment had been part of the plan. All said and done, their 15-month exploration of the globe, from the gondola-rich waterways of Venice to the tribal shores of Polynesia, had cost between $18,000 and $19,000. Less than rent and baguettes in Paris. Most people would consider this impossible. Then again, most people don't know that more than 300 families set sail from France each year to do the same. The trip had been a dream for almost two decades, relegated to the back of the line behind an ever-growing list of responsibilities. Each passing moment brought a new list of reasons for putting it off. One day, Julie realized that if she didn't do it now, she would never do it. The rationalizations, legitimate or not, would just continue to add up and make it harder to convince herself that escape was possible. One year of preparation and one 30-day trial run with her husband later, they set sail on the trip of a lifetime. Julie realized almost as soon as the anchor lifted that, far from being a reason not to travel and seek adventure, children are perhaps the best reason of all to do both. Pre-trip, her three little boys had fought like banshees at the drop of a hat. In the process of learning to coexist in a floating bedroom, they learned patience, as much for themselves as for the sanity of their parents. Pre-trip, books were about as appealing as eating sand. Given the alternative of staring at a wall on the open sea, all three learned to love books. Pulling them out of school for one academic year and exposing them to new environments had proven to be the best investment in their education to date. Now sitting in the plane, Julie looked out at the clouds as the wing cut past them, already thinking of their next plans: to find a place in the mountains and ski all year long, using income from a sail-rigging workshop to fund the slopes and more travel. Now that she had done it once, she had the itch. LIFESTYLE DESIGN IN ACTION I was done with driving across town to collect my son from child- care only to slide across icy highways trying to get back to work with him in tow to finish my work. My mini-retirement brought us both to live at an alternative boarding school full of creative lifestyle redesigning children and staff in a gorgeous Florida forest with a spring-fed pond and plenty of sunshine. You can easily search for alternative schools or traditional schools that might accept your children during your stay. Alternative schools often see themselves as supportive communities and are exceptionally welcoming. You might even find an opportunity to work at a school where you could experience a new environment with your child. —DEB Tim, Your book and blog have inspired me to quit my job, write two e-books, sky dive, backpack through South America, sell all the clutter in my life, and host an annual convention of the world's top dating instructors (my primary business venture, third year running). The best part? I can't even buy a drink yet. Thank you so much, bro! —ANTHONY

EVERYTHING POPULAR IS WRONG I can't give you a surefire formula for success, but I can give you a formula for failure: try to please everybody all the time. —HERBERT BAYARD SWOPE, American editor and journalist; first recipient of the Pulitzer Prize Everything popular is wrong. —OSCAR WILDE, The Importance of Being Earnest Beating the Game, Not Playing the Game In 1999, sometime after quitting my second unfulfilling job and eating peanut-butter sandwiches for comfort, I won the gold medal at the Chinese Kickboxing (Sanshou) National Championships. It wasn't because I was good at punching and kicking. God forbid. That seemed a bit dangerous, considering I did it on a dare and had four weeks of preparation. Besides, I have a watermelon head—it's a big target. I won by reading the rules and looking for unexploited opportunities, of which there were two: 1. Weigh-ins were the day prior to competition: Using dehydration techniques commonly practiced by elite powerlifters and Olympic wrestlers, I lost 28 pounds in 18 hours, weighed in at 165 pounds, and then hyperhydrated back to 193 pounds.2 It's hard to fight someone from three weight classes above you. Poor little guys. 2. There was a technicality in the fine print: If one combatant fell off the elevated platform three times in a single round, his opponent won by default. I decided to use this technicality as my principal technique and push people off. As you might imagine, this did not make the judges the happiest Chinese I've ever seen. The result? I won all of my matches by technical knock-out (TKO) and went home national champion, something 99% of those with 5–10 years of experience had been unable to do. But, isn't pushing people out of the ring pushing the boundaries of ethics? Not at all—it's no more than doing the uncommon within the rules. The important distinction is that between official rules and self-imposed rules. Consider the following example, from the official website of the Olympic movement (www.olympic.org). The 1968 Mexico City Olympics marked the international debut of Dick Fosbury and his celebrated "Fosbury flop," which would soon revolutionize high-jumping. At the time, jumpers... swung their outside foot up and over the bar [called the "straddle," much like a hurdle jump, it allowed you to land on your feet]. Fosbury's technique began by racing up to the bar at great speed and taking off from his right (or outside) foot. Then he twisted his body so that he went over the bar head-first with his back to the bar. While the coaches of the world shook their heads in disbelief, the Mexico City audience was absolutely captivated by Fosbury and shouted, "Olé!" as he cleared the bar. Fosbury cleared every height through 2.22 metres without a miss and then achieved a personal record of 2.24 metres to win the gold medal. By 1980, 13 of the 16 Olympic finalists were using the Fosbury flop. The weight-cutting techniques and off-platform throwing I used are now standard features of Sanshou competition. I didn't cause it, I just foresaw it as inevitable, as did others who tested this superior approach. Now it's par for the course. Sports evolve when sacred cows are killed, when basic assumptions are tested. The same is true in life and in lifestyles.

Most people walk down the street on their legs. Does that mean I walk down the street on my hands? Do I wear my underwear outside of my pants in the name of being different? Not usually, no. Then again, walking on my legs and keeping my thong on the inside have worked just fine thus far. I don't fix it if it isn't broken. Different is better when it is more effective or more fun. If everyone is defining a problem or solving it one way and the results are subpar, this is the time to ask, What if I did the opposite? Don't follow a model that doesn't work. If the recipe sucks, it doesn't matter how good a cook you are. When I was in data storage sales, my first gig out of college, I realized that most cold calls didn't get to the intended person for one reason: gatekeepers. If I simply made all my calls from 8:00–8:30 A.M. and 6:00–6:30 P.M., for a total of one hour, I was able to avoid secretaries and book more than twice as many meetings as the senior sales executives who called from 9–5. In other words, I got twice the results for 1/8 the time. From Japan to Monaco, from globetrotting single mothers to multimillionaire racecar drivers, the basic rules of successful NR are surprisingly uniform and predictably divergent from what the rest of the world is doing. The following rules are the fundamental differentiators to keep in mind throughout this book. 1. Retirement Is Worst-Case-Scenario Insurance. Retirement planning is like life insurance. It should be viewed as nothing more than a hedge against the absolute worst-case scenario: in this case, becoming physically incapable of working and needing a reservoir of capital to survive. Retirement as a goal or final redemption is flawed for at least three solid reasons: 1. It is predicated on the assumption that you dislike what you are doing during the most physically capable years of your life. This is a nonstarter— nothing can justify that sacrifice. 2. Most people will never be able to retire and maintain even a hotdogs-fordinner standard of living. Even one million is chump change in a world where traditional retirement could span 30 years and inflation lowers your purchasing power 2–4% per year. The math doesn't work.3 The golden years become lower-middle-class life revisited. That's a bittersweet ending. 3. If the math does work, it means that you are one ambitious, hardworking machine. If that's the case, guess what? One week into retirement, you'll be so damn bored that you'll want to stick bicycle spokes in your eyes. You'll probably opt to look for a new job or start another company. Kinda defeats the purpose of waiting, doesn't it? I'm not saying don't plan for the worst case—I have maxed out 401(k)s and IRAs I use primarily for tax purposes—but don't mistake retirement for the goal. 2. Interest and Energy Are Cyclical. If I offered you $10,000,000 to work 24 hours a day for 15 years and then retire, would you do it? Of course not—you couldn't. It is unsustainable, just as what most define as a career: doing the same thing for 8+ hours per day until you break down or have enough cash to permanently stop. How else can my 30-year-old friends all look like a cross between Donald Trump and Joan Rivers? It's horrendous—premature aging fueled by triple bypass frappuccinos and impossible workloads. Alternating periods of activity and rest is necessary to survive, let alone thrive. Capacity, interest, and mental endurance all wax and wane. Plan accordingly. The NR aims to distribute "mini-retirements" throughout life instead of hoarding the recovery and enjoyment for the fool's gold of retirement. By working only when you are most effective, life is both more productive and more enjoyable. It's the perfect example of having your cake and eating it, too. Personally, I now aim for one month of overseas relocation or high-intensity learning (tango, fighting, whatever) for every two months of work projects. 3. Less Is Not Laziness. Doing less meaningless work, so that you can focus on things of greater personal importance, is NOT laziness. This is hard for most to accept, because our culture tends to reward personal sacrifice instead of personal productivity. Few people choose to (or are able to) measure the results of their actions and thus measure their contribution in time. More time equals more self-worth and more reinforcement from those above and around them. The NR, despite fewer hours in the office, produce more meaningful results than the next dozen non-NR combined. Let's define "laziness" anew—to endure a non-ideal existence, to let circumstance or others decide life for you, or to amass a fortune while passing through life like a spectator from an office window. The size of your bank account doesn't change this, nor does the number of hours you log in handling unimportant e-mail or minutiae. Focus on being productive instead of busy. 4. The Timing Is Never Right. I once asked my mom how she decided when to have her first child, little ol' me. The answer was simple: "It was something we wanted, and we decided there was no point in putting it off. The timing is never right to have a baby." And so it is. For all of the most important things, the timing always sucks. Waiting for a good time to quit your job? The stars will never align and the traffic lights of life will never all be green at the same time. The universe doesn't conspire against you, but it doesn't go out of its way to line up all the pins either. Conditions are never perfect. "Someday" is a disease that will take your dreams to the grave with you. Pro and con lists are just as bad. If it's important to you and you want to do it "eventually," just do it and correct course along the way. 5. Ask for Forgiveness, Not Permission. If it isn't going to devastate those around you, try it and then justify it. People— whether parents, partners, or bosses—deny things on an emotional basis that they can learn to accept after the fact. If the potential damage is moderate or in any way reversible, don't give people the chance to say no. Most people are fast to stop you before you get started but hesitant to get in the way if you're moving. Get good at being a troublemaker and saying sorry when you really screw up. 6. Emphasize Strengths, Don't Fix Weaknesses. Most people are good at a handful of things and utterly miserable at most. I am great at product creation and marketing but terrible at most of the things that follow. My body is designed to lift heavy objects and throw them, and that's it. I ignored this for a long time. I tried swimming and looked like a drowning monkey. I tried basketball and looked like a caveman. Then I became a fighter and took off. It is far more lucrative and fun to leverage your strengths instead of attempting to fix all the chinks in your armor. The choice is between multiplication of results using strengths or incremental improvement fixing weaknesses that will, at best, become mediocre. Focus on better use of your best weapons instead of constant repair. 7. Things in Excess Become Their Opposite. It is possible to have too much of a good thing. In excess, most endeavors and possessions take on the characteristics of their opposite. Thus: Pacifists become militants. Freedom fighters become tyrants. Blessings become curses. Help becomes hindrance. More becomes less.4 Too much, too many, and too often of what you want becomes what you don't want. This is true of possessions and even time. Lifestyle Design is thus not interested in creating an excess of idle time, which is poisonous, but the positive use of free time, defined simply as doing what you want as opposed to what you feel obligated to do. 8. Money Alone Is Not the Solution. There is much to be said for the power of money as currency (I'm a fan myself), but adding more of it just isn't the answer as often as we'd like to think. In part, it's laziness. "If only I had more money" is the easiest way to postpone the intense self- examination and decision-making necessary to create a life of enjoyment—now and not later. By using money as the scapegoat and work as our all-consuming routine, we are able to conveniently disallow ourselves the time to do otherwise: "John, I'd love to talk about the gaping void I feel in my life, the hopelessness that hits me like a punch in the eye every time I start my computer in the morning, but I have so much work to do! I've got at least three hours of unimportant e-mail to reply to before calling the prospects who said 'no' yesterday. Gotta run!" Busy yourself with the routine of the money wheel, pretend it's the fix-all, and you artfully create a constant distraction that prevents you from seeing just how pointless it is. Deep down, you know it's all an illusion, but with everyone participating in the same game of make-believe, it's easy to forget. The problem is more than money. 9. Relative Income Is More Important Than Absolute Income. Among dietitians and nutritionists, there is some debate over the value of a calorie. Is a calorie a calorie, much like a rose is a rose? Is fat loss as simple as expending more calories than you consume, or is the source of those calories important? Based on work with top athletes, I know the answer to be the latter. What about income? Is a dollar is a dollar is a dollar? The New Rich don't think so. Let's look at this like a fifth-grade math problem. Two hardworking chaps are headed toward each other. Chap A moving at 80 hours per week and Chap B moving at 10 hours per week. They both make $50,000 per year. Who will be richer when they pass in the middle of the night? If you said B, you would be correct, and this is the difference between absolute and relative income. Absolute income is measured using one holy and inalterable variable: the raw and almighty dollar. Jane Doe makes $100,000 per year and is thus twice as rich as John Doe, who makes $50,000 per year. Relative income uses two variables: the dollar and time, usually hours. The whole "per year" concept is arbitrary and makes it easy to trick yourself. Let's look at the real trade. Jane Doe makes $100,000 per year, $2,000 for each of 50 weeks per year, and works 80 hours per week. Jane Doe thus makes $25 per hour. John Doe makes $50,000 per year, $1,000 for each of 50 weeks per year, but works 10 hours per week and hence makes $100 per hour. In relative income, John is four times richer. Of course, relative income has to add up to the minimum amount necessary to actualize your goals. If I make $100 per hour but only work one hour per week, it's going to be hard for me to run amuck like a superstar. Assuming that the total absolute income is where it needs to be to live my dreams (not an arbitrary point of comparison with the Joneses), relative income is the real measurement of wealth for the New Rich. The top New Rich mavericks make at least $5,000 per hour. Out of college, I started at about $5. I'll get you closer to the former. 10. Distress Is Bad, Eustress Is Good. Unbeknownst to most fun-loving bipeds, not all stress is bad. Indeed, the New Rich don't aim to eliminate all stress. Not in the least. There are two separate types of stress, each as different as euphoria and its seldom-mentioned opposite, dysphoria. Distress refers to harmful stimuli that make you weaker, less confident, and less able. Destructive criticism, abusive bosses, and smashing your face on a curb are examples of this. These are things we want to avoid. Eustress, on the other hand, is a word most of you have probably never heard. Eu-, a Greek prefix for "healthy," is used in the same sense in the word "euphoria." Role models who push us to exceed our limits, physical training that removes our spare tires, and risks that expand our sphere of comfortable action are all examples of eustress—stress that is healthful and the stimulus for growth. People who avoid all criticism fail. It's destructive criticism we need to avoid, not criticism in all forms. Similarly, there is no progress without eustress, and the more eustress we can create or apply to our lives, the sooner we can actualize our dreams. The trick is telling the two apart. The New Rich are equally aggressive in removing distress and finding eustress.

Twenty feet and closing. "Run! Ruuuuuuuuuun!" Hans didn't speak Portuguese, but the meaning was clear enough—haul ass. His sneakers gripped firmly on the jagged rock, and he drove his chest forward toward 3,000 feet of nothing. He held his breath on the final step, and the panic drove him to near unconsciousness. His vision blurred at the edges, closing to a single pinpoint of light, and then ... he floated. The all-consuming celestial blue of the horizon hit his visual field an instant after he realized that the thermal updraft had caught him and the wings of the paraglider. Fear was behind him on the mountaintop, and thousands of feet above the resplendent green rain forest and pristine white beaches of Copacabana, Hans Keeling had seen the light. That was Sunday. On Monday, Hans returned to his law office in Century City, Los Angeles's posh corporate haven, and promptly handed in his three-week notice. For nearly five years, he had faced his alarm clock with the same dread: I have to do this for another 40–45 years? He had once slept under his desk at the office after a punishing half-done project, only to wake up and continue on it the next morning. That same morning, he had made himself a promise: two more times and I'm out of here. Strike number three came the day before he left for his Brazilian vacation. We all make these promises to ourselves, and Hans had done it before as well, but things were now somehow different. He was different. He had realized something while arcing in slow circles toward the earth—risks weren't that scary once you took them. His colleagues told him what he expected to hear: He was throwing it all away. He was an attorney on his way to the top—what the hell did he want? Hans didn't know exactly what he wanted, but he had tasted it. On the other hand, he did know what bored him to tears, and he was done with it. No more passing days as the living dead, no more dinners where his colleagues compared cars, riding on the sugar high of a new BMW purchase until someone bought a more expensive Mercedes. It was over. Immediately, a strange shift began—Hans felt, for the first time in a long time, at peace with himself and what he was doing. He had always been terrified of plane turbulence, as if he might die with the best inside of him, but now he could fly through a violent storm sleeping like a baby. Strange indeed. More than a year later, he was still getting unsolicited job offers from law firms, but by then had started Nexus Surf,5 a premier surf-adventure company based in the tropical paradise of Florianopolis, Brazil. He had met his dream girl, a Carioca with caramel-colored skin named Tatiana, and spent most of his time relaxing under palm trees or treating clients to the best times of their lives. Is this what he had been so afraid of? These days, he often sees his former self in the underjoyed and overworked professionals he takes out on the waves. Waiting for the swell, the true emotions come out: "God, I wish I could do what you do." His reply is always the same: "You can." The setting sun reflects off the surface of the water, providing a Zen-like setting for a message he knows is true: It's not giving up to put your current path on indefinite pause. He could pick up his law career exactly where he left off if he wanted to, but that is the furthest thing from his mind. As they paddle back to shore after an awesome session, his clients get ahold of themselves and regain their composure. They set foot on shore, and reality sinks its fangs in: "I would, but I can't really throw it all away." He has to laugh.

Action may not always bring happiness, but there is no happiness without action. —BENJAMIN DISRAELI, former British Prime Minister To door not to do? To try or not to try? Most people will vote no, whether they consider themselves brave or not. Uncertainty and the prospect of failure can be very scary noises in the shadows. Most people will choose unhappiness over uncertainty. For years, I set goals, made resolutions to change direction, and nothing came of either. I was just as insecure and scared as the rest of the world. The simple solution came to me accidentally four years ago. At that time, I had more money than I knew what to do with—I was making $70K or so per month—and I was completely miserable, worse than ever. I had no time and was working myself to death. I had started my own company, only to realize it would be nearly impossible to sell.6 Oops. I felt trapped and stupid at the same time. I should be able to figure this out, I thought. Why am I such an idiot? Why can't I make this work?! Buckle up and stop being such a (insert expletive)! What's wrong with me? The truth was, nothing was wrong with me. I hadn't reached my limit; I'd reached the limit of my business model at the time. It wasn't the driver, it was the vehicle.

Critical mistakes in its infancy would never let me sell it. I could hire magic elves and connect my brain to a supercomputer—it didn't matter. My little baby had some serious birth defects. The question then became, How do I free myself from this Frankenstein while making it self-sustaining? How do I pry myself from the tentacles of workaholism and the fear that it would fall to pieces without my 15-hour days? How do I escape this self-made prison? A trip, I decided. A sabbatical year around the world. So I took the trip, right? Well, I'll get to that. First, I felt it prudent to dance around with my shame, embarrassment, and anger for six months, all the while playing an endless loop of reasons why my cop-out fantasy trip could never work. One of my more productive periods, for sure. Then, one day, in my bliss of envisioning how bad my future suffering would be, I hit upon a gem of an idea. It was surely a highlight of my "don't happy, be worry" phase: Why don't I decide exactly what my nightmare would be—the worst thing that could possibly happen as a result of my trip? Well, my business could fail while I'm overseas, for sure. Probably would. A legal warning letter would accidentally not get forwarded and I would get sued. My business would be shut down, and inventory would spoil on the shelves while I'm picking my toes in solitary misery on some cold shore in Ireland. Crying in the rain, I imagine. My bank account would crater by 80% and certainly my car and motorcycle in storage would be stolen. I suppose someone would probably spit on my head from a high-rise balcony while I'm feeding food scraps to a stray dog, which would then spook and bite me squarely on the face. God, life is a cruel, hard bitch. Conquering Fear = Defining Fear Set aside a certain number of days, during which you shall be content with the scantiest and cheapest fare, with course and rough dress, saying to yourself the while: "Is this the condition that I feared?" —SENECA Then a funny thing happened. In my undying quest to make myself miserable, I accidentally began to backpedal. As soon as I cut through the vague unease and ambiguous anxiety by defining my nightmare, the worst-case scenario, I wasn't as worried about taking a trip. Suddenly, I started thinking of simple steps I could take to salvage my remaining resources and get back on track if all hell struck at once. I could always take a temporary bartending job to pay the rent if I had to. I could sell some furniture and cut back on eating out. I could steal lunch money from the kindergarteners who passed by my apartment every morning. The options were many. I realized it wouldn't be that hard to get back to where I was, let alone survive. None of these things would be fatal—not even close. Mere panty pinches on the journey of life. I realized that on a scale of 1–10, 1 being nothing and 10 being permanently lifechanging, my so-called worst-case scenario might have a temporary impact of 3 or 4. I believe this is true of most people and most would-be "holy sh*t, my life is over" disasters. Keep in mind that this is the one-in-a-million disaster nightmare. On the other hand, if I realized my best-case scenario, or even a probable-case scenario, it would easily have a permanent 9 or 10 positive life-changing effect. In other words, I was risking an unlikely and temporary 3 or 4 for a probable and permanent 9 or

10, and I could easily recover my baseline workaholic prison with a bit of extra work if I wanted to. This all equated to a significant realization: There was practically no risk, only huge life-changing upside potential, and I could resume my previous course without any more effort than I was already putting forth. That is when I made the decision to take the trip and bought a one-way ticket to Europe. I started planning my adventures and eliminating my physical and psychological baggage. None of my disasters came to pass, and my life has been a near fairy tale since. The business did better than ever, and I practically forgot about it as it financed my travels around the world in style for 15 months.

Sometimes timing is perfect. There are hundreds of cars circling a parking lot, and someone pulls out of a spot 10 feet from the entrance just as you reach his or her bumper. Another Christmas miracle! Other times, the timing could be better. The phone rings during sex and seems to ring for a half hour. The UPS guy shows up 10 minutes later. Bad timing can spoil the fun. Jean-Marc Hachey landed in West Africa as a volunteer, with high hopes of lending a helping hand. In that sense, his timing was great. He arrived in Ghana in the early 1980s, in the middle of a coup d'état, at the peak of hyperinflation, and just in time for the worst drought in a decade. For these same reasons, some people would consider his timing quite poor from a more selfish survival standpoint. He had also missed the memo. The national menu had changed, and they were out of luxuries like bread and clean water. He would be surviving for four months on a slushlike concoction of corn meal and spinach. Not what most of us would order at the movie theater. "WOW, I CAN SURVIVE." Jean-Marc had passed the point of no return, but it didn't matter. After two weeks of adjusting to the breakfast, lunch, and dinner (Mush à la Ghana), he had no desire to escape. The most basic of foods and good friends proved to be the only real necessities, and what would seem like a disaster from the outside was the most lifeaffirming epiphany he'd ever experienced: The worst really wasn't that bad. To enjoy life, you don't need fancy nonsense, but you do need to control your time and realize that most things just aren't as serious as you make them out to be. Now 48, Jean-Marc lives in a nice home in Ontario, but could live without it. He has cash, but could fall into poverty tomorrow and it wouldn't matter. Some of his fondest memories still include nothing but friends and gruel. He is dedicated to creating special moments for himself and his family and is utterly unconcerned with retirement. He's already lived 20 years of partial retirement in perfect health. Don't save it all for the end. There is every reason not to. Q&A: QUESTIONS AND ACTIONS I am an old man and have known a great many troubles, but most of them never happened. —MARK TWAIN If you are nervous about making the jump or simply putting it off out of fear of the unknown, here is your antidote. Write down your answers, and keep in mind that thinking a lot will not prove as fruitful or as prolific as simply brain vomiting on the page. Write and do not edit—aim for volume. Spend a few minutes on each answer. 1. Define your nightmare, the absolute worst that could happen if you did what you are considering. What doubt, fears, and "what-ifs" pop up as you consider the big changes you can—or need—to make? Envision them in painstaking detail. Would it be the end of your life? What would be the permanent impact, if any, on a scale of 1–10? Are these things really permanent? How likely do you think it is that they would actually happen? 2. What steps could you take to repair the damage or get things back on the upswing, even if temporarily? Chances are, it's easier than you imagine. How could you get things back under control? 3. What are the outcomes or benefits, both temporary and permanent, of more probable scenarios? Now that you've defined the nightmare, what are the more probable or definite positive outcomes, whether internal (confidence, self-esteem, etc.) or external? What would the impact of these more-likely outcomes be on a scale of 1–10? How likely is it that you could produce at least a moderately good outcome? Have less intelligent people done this before and pulled it off? 4. If you were fired from your job today, what would you do to get things under financial control? Imagine this scenario and run through questions 1–3 above. If you quit your job to test other options, how could you later get back on the same career track if you absolutely had to? 5. What are you putting off out of fear? Usually, what we most fear doing is what we most need to do. That phone call, that conversation, whatever the action might be—it is fear of unknown outcomes that prevents us from doing what we need to do. Define the worst case, accept it, and do it. I'll repeat something you might consider tattooing on your forehead: What we fear doing most is usually what we most need to do. As I have heard said, a person's success in life can usually be measured by the number of uncomfortable conversations he or she is willing to have. Resolve to do one thing every day that you fear. I got into this habit by attempting to contact celebrities and famous businesspeople for advice. 6. What is it costing you—financially, emotionally, and physically—to postpone action? Don't only evaluate the potential downside of action. It is equally important to measure the atrocious cost of inaction. If you don't pursue those things that excite you, where will you be in one year, five years, and ten years? How will you feel having allowed circumstance to impose itself upon you and having allowed ten more years of your finite life to pass doing what you know will not fulfill you? If you telescope out 10 years and know with 100% certainty that it is a path of disappointment and regret, and if we define risk as "the likelihood of an irreversible negative outcome," inaction is the greatest risk of all. 7. What are you waiting for? If you cannot answer this without resorting to the previously rejected concept of good timing, the answer is simple: You're afraid, just like the rest of the world. Measure the cost of inaction, realize the unlikelihood and re-pairability of most missteps, and develop the most important habit of those who excel and enjoy doing so: action.

Doing the Unrealistic Is Easier Than Doing the Realistic From contacting billionaires to rubbing elbows with celebrities—the second group of students did both—it's as easy as believing it can be done. It's lonely at the top. Ninety-nine percent of people in the world are convinced they are incapable of achieving great things, so they aim for the mediocre. The level of competition is thus fiercest for "realistic" goals, paradoxically making them the most time-and energy-consuming. It is easier to raise $1,000,000 than it is $100,000. It is easier to pick up the one perfect 10 in the bar than the five 8s. If you are insecure, guess what? The rest of the world is, too. Do not overestimate the competition and underestimate yourself. You are better than you think. Unreasonable and unrealistic goals are easier to achieve for yet another reason. Having an unusually large goal is an adrenaline infusion that provides the endurance to overcome the inevitable trials and tribulations that go along with any goal. Realistic goals, goals restricted to the average ambition level, are uninspiring and will only fuel you through the first or second problem, at which point you throw in the towel. If the potential payoff is mediocre or average, so is your effort. I'll run through walls to get a catamaran trip through the Greek islands, but I might not change my brand of cereal for a weekend trip through Columbus, Ohio. If I choose the latter because it is "realistic," I won't have the enthusiasm to jump even the smallest hurdle to accomplish it. With beautiful, crystal-clear Greek waters and delicious wine on the brain, I'm prepared to do battle for a dream that is worth dreaming. Even though their difficulty of achievement on a scale of 1–10 appears to be a 10 and a 2 respectively, Columbus is more likely to fall through. The fishing is best where the fewest go, and the collective insecurity of the world makes it easy for people to hit home runs while everyone else is aiming for base hits. There is just less competition for bigger goals. Doing big things begins with asking for them properly. What Do You Want? A Better Question, First of All Most people will never know what they want. I don't know what I want. If you ask me what I want to do in the next five months for language learning, on the other hand, I do know. It's a matter of specificity. "What do you want?" is too imprecise to produce a meaningful and actionable answer. Forget about it. "What are your goals?" is similarly fated for confusion and guesswork. To rephrase the question, we need to take a step back and look at the bigger picture. Let's assume we have 10 goals and we achieve them—what is the desired outcome that makes all the effort worthwhile? The most common response is what I also would have suggested five years ago: happiness. I no longer believe this is a good answer. Happiness can be bought with a bottle of wine and has become ambiguous through overuse. There is a more precise alternative that reflects what I believe the actual objective is. Bear with me. What is the opposite of happiness? Sadness? No. Just as love and hate are two sides of the same coin, so are happiness and sadness. Crying out of happiness is a perfect illustration of this. The opposite of love is indifference, and the opposite of happiness is—here's the clincher—boredom. Excitement is the more practical synonym for happiness, and it is precisely what you should strive to chase. It is the cure-all. When people suggest you follow your "passion" or your "bliss," I propose that they are, in fact, referring to the same singular concept: excitement. This brings us full circle. The question you should be asking isn't, "What do I want?" or "What are my goals?" but "What would excite me?" Adult-Onset ADD: Adventure Deficit Disorder Somewhere between college graduation and your second job, a chorus enters your internal dialogue: Be realistic and stop pretending. Life isn't like the movies. If you're five years old and say you want to be an astronaut, your parents tell you that you can be anything you want to be. It's harmless, like telling a child that Santa Claus exists. If you're 25 and announce you want to start a new circus, the response is different: Be realistic; become a lawyer or an accountant or a doctor, have babies, and raise them to repeat the cycle. If you do manage to ignore the doubters and start your own business, for example, ADD doesn't disappear. It just takes a different form. When I started BrainQUICKEN LLC in 2001, it was with a clear goal in mind: Make $1,000 per day whether I was banging my head on a laptop or cutting my toenails on the beach. It was to be an automated source of cash flow. If you look at my chronology, it is obvious that this didn't happen until a meltdown forced it, despite the requisite income. Why? The goal wasn't specific enough. I hadn't defined alternate activities that would replace the initial workload. Therefore, I just continued working, even though there was no financial need. I needed to feel productive and had no other vehicles. This is how most people work until death: "I'll just work until I have X dollars and then do what I want." If you don't define the "what I want" alternate activities, the X figure will increase indefinitely to avoid the fear-inducing uncertainty of this void. This is when both employees and entrepreneurs become fat men in red BMWs. The Fat Man in the Red BMW Convertible There have been several points in my life—among them, just before I was fired from TrueSAN and just before I escaped the U.S. to avoid taking an Uzi into McDonald's—at which I saw my future as another fat man in a midlife-crisis BMW. I simply looked at those who were 15–20 years ahead of me on the same track, whether a director of sales or an entrepreneur in the same industry, and it scared the hell out of me. It was such an acute phobia, and such a perfect metaphor for the sum of all fears, that it became a pattern interrupt between myself and fellow lifestyle designer and entrepreneur Douglas Price. Doug and I traveled parallel paths for nearly five years, facing the same challenges and self-doubt and thus keeping a close psychological eye on each other. Our down periods seem to alternate, making us a good team. Whenever one of us began to set our sights lower, lose faith, or "accept reality," the other would chime in via phone or e-mail like an A A sponsor: "Dude, are you turning into the bald fat man in the red BMW convertible?" The prospect was terrifying enough that we always got our asses and priorities back on track immediately. The worst that could happen wasn't crashing and burning, it was accepting terminal boredom as a tolerable status quo. Remember—boredom is the enemy, not some abstract "failure." Correcting Course: Get Unrealistic There is a process that I have used, and still use, to reignite life or correct course when the Fat Man in the BMW rears his ugly head. In some form or another, it is the same process used by the most impressive NR I have met around the world: dreamlining. Dreamlining is so named because it applies timelines to what most would consider dreams. It is much like goal-setting but differs in several fundamental respects: 1. The goals shift from ambiguous wants to defined steps. 2. The goals have to be unrealistic to be effective. 3. It focuses on activities that will fill the vacuum created when work is removed. Living like a millionaire requires doing interesting things and not just owning enviable things. Now it's your turn to think big. How to Get George Bush Sr. or the CEO of Google on the Phone The article below, titled "Fail Better" and written by Adam Gottesfeld, explores how I teach Princeton students to connect with luminary-level business mentors and celebrities of various types. I've edited it for length in a few places. People are fond of using the "it's not what you know, it's who you know" adage as an excuse for inaction, as if all successful people are born with powerful friends. Nonsense. Here's how normal people build supernormal networks. Fail Better BY ADAM GOTTESFELD MOST PRINCETON students love to procrastinate in writing their dean's date [term] papers. Ryan Marrinan '07, from Los Angeles, was no exception. But while the majority of undergraduates fill their time by updating their Facebook profiles or watching videos on YouTube, Marrinan was discussing Soto Zen Buddhism via email with Randy Komisar, a partner at the venture capital firm Kleiner Perkins Caufield and Byers, and asking Google CEO Eric Schmidt via e-mail when he had been happiest in his life. (Schmidt's answer: "Tomorrow.") Prior to his e-mail, Marrinan had never contacted Komisar. He had met Schmidt, a Princeton University trustee, only briefly at an academic affairs meeting of the trustees in November. A self-described "naturally shy kid," Marrinan said he would never have dared to randomly e-mail two of the most powerful men in Silicon Valley if it weren't for Tim Ferriss, who offered a guest lecture in Professor Ed Zschau's "HighTech Entrepreneurship" class. Ferriss challenged Marrinan and his fellow seniors to contact high-profile celebrities and CEOs and get their answers to questions they have always wanted to ask. For extra incentive, Ferriss promised the student who could contact the most hardto-reach name and ask the most intriguing question a round-trip plane ticket anywhere in the world. "I believe that success can be measured in the number of uncomfortable conversations you're willing to have. I felt that if I could help students overcome the fear of rejection with cold-calling and cold e-mail, it would serve them forever," Ferriss said. "It's easy to sell yourself short, but when you see classmates getting responses from people like [former president] George Bush, the CEOs of Disney, Comcast, Google, and HP, and dozens of other impossible-to-reach people, it forces you to reconsider your self-set limitations." ... Ferriss lectures to the students of "High-Tech Entrepreneurship" each semester about creating a startup and designing the ideal lifestyle. "I participate in this contest every day," said Ferriss. "I do what I always do: find a personal e-mail if possible, often through their little-known personal blogs, send a two- to three-paragraph e-mail which explains that I am familiar with their work, and ask one simple-to-answer but thought-provoking question in that e-mail related to their work or life philosophies. The goal is to start a dialogue so they take the time to answer future e-mails—not to ask for help. That can only come after at least three or four genuine e-mail exchanges." With "textbook execution of the Tim Ferriss Technique," as he put it, Marrinan was able to strike up a bond with Komisar. In his initial e-mail, he talked about reading one of Komisar's Harvard Business Review articles and feeling inspired to ask him, "When were you happiest in your life?" After Komisar replied with references to Tibetan Buddhism, Marrinan responded, "Just as words are inadequate to explain true happiness, so too are words inadequate to express my thanks." His e-mail included his personal translation of a French poem by Taisen Deshimaru, the former European head of Soto Zen. An e-mail relationship was formed, and Komisar even e-mailed Marrinan a few days later with a link to a New York Times article on happiness. Contacting Schmidt proved more challenging. For Marrinan, the toughest part was getting Schmidt's personal e-mail address. He e-mailed a Princeton dean asking for it. No response. Two weeks later, he e-mailed the same dean again, defending his request by reminding her that he had previously met Schmidt. The dean said no, but Marrinan refused to give up. He e-mailed her a third time. "Have you ever made an exception?" he asked. The dean finally gave in, he said, and provided him with Schmidt's e-mail. "I know some of my classmates pursued the alternative scattershot technique with some success, but that's not my bag," Marrinan said, explaining his perseverance. "I deal with rejection by persisting, not by taking my business elsewhere. My maxim comes from Samuel Beckett, a personal hero of mine: 'Ever tried. Ever failed. No matter. Try again. Fail again. Fail better.' You won't believe what you can accomplish by attempting the impossible with the courage to repeatedly fail better." Nathan Kaplan, another participant in the contest, was most proud of the way that he was able to contact former Newark mayor Sharpe James. Because James had made a campaign contribution to Al Sharpton, the website www.fundrace.org listed James's home address. Kaplan then input James's address into an online serach-by-address phone directory, through which he received the former mayor's phone number. Kaplan left a message for James, and a few days later finally got to ask him about childhood education. Ferriss is proud of the effort students have put into his contest. "Most people can do absolutely awe-inspiring things," he said. "Sometimes they just need a little nudge." Q&A: QUESTIONS AND ACTIONS The existential vacuum manifests itself mainly in a state of boredom. —VIKTOR FRANKL, Auschwitz survivor and founder of Logotherapy, Man's Search for Meaning Life is too short to be small. —BENJAMIN DISRAELI

When I was younger ... I [didn't] want to be pigeonholed ... Basically, now you want to be pigeonholed. It's your niche. —JOAN CHEN, actress; appeared in The Last Emperor and Twin Peaks Creating demand is hard. Filling demand is much easier. Don't create a product, then seek someone to sell it to. Find a market—define your customers—then find or develop a product for them. I have been a student and an athlete, so I developed products for those markets, focusing on the male demographic whenever possible. The audiobook I created for college guidance counselors failed because I have never been a guidance counselor. I developed the subsequent speed-reading seminar after realizing that I had free access to students, and the business succeeded because—being a student myself—I understood their needs and spending habits. Be a member of your target market and don't speculate what others need or will be willing to buy Danny Black rents dwarfs as entertainment for $149 per hour. How is that for a niche market? It is said that if everyone is your customer, then no one is your customer. If you start off aiming to sell a product to dog- or car-lovers, stop. It's expensive to advertise to such a broad market, and you are competing with too many products and too much free information. If you focus on how to train German shepherds or a restoration product for antique Fords, on the other hand, the market and competition shrink, making it less expensive to reach your customers and easier to charge premium pricing. BrainQUICKEN was initially designed for students, but the market proved too scattered and difficult to reach. Based on positive feedback from student-athletes, I relaunched the product as BodyQUICK and tested advertising in magazines specific to martial artists and powerlifters. These are minuscule markets compared to the massive student market, but not small. Low media cost and lack of competition enabled me to dominate with the first "neural accelerator"26 in these niches. It is more profitable to be a big fish in a small pond than a small undefined fish in a big pond. How do you know if it's big enough to meet your TMI? For a detailed real-life example of how I determined the market size of a recent product, see "Muse Math" on this book's companion site. Ask yourself the following questions to find profitable niches. 1. Which social, industry, and professional groups do you belong to, have you belonged to, or do you understand, whether dentists, engineers, rock climbers, recreational cyclists, car restoration aficionados, dancers, or other? Look creatively at your resume, work experience, physical habits, and hobbies and compile a list of all the groups, past and present, that you can associate yourself with. Look at products and books you own, include online and offline subscriptions, and ask yourself, "What groups of people purchase the same?" Which magazines, websites, and newsletters do you read on a regular basis?2. Which of the groups you identified have their own magazines? Visit a large bookstore such as Barnes & Noble and browse the magazine rack for smaller specialty magazines to brainstorm additional niches. There are literally thousands of occupation- and interest/hobby-specific magazines to choose from. Use Writer's Market to identify magazine options outside the bookstores. Narrow the groups from question 1 above to those that are reachable through one or two small magazines. It's not important that these groups all have a lot of money (e.g., golfers)—only that they spend money (amateur athletes, bass fishermen, etc.) on products of some type. Call these magazines, speak to the advertising directors, and tell them that you are considering advertising; ask them to e-mail their current advertising rate card and include both readership numbers and magazine back-issue samples. Search the back issues for repeat advertisers who sell direct-to-consumer via 800 numbers or websites—the more repeat advertisers, and the more frequent their ads, the more profitable a magazine is for them ... and will be for us. Step Two: Brainstorm (Do Not Invest In) Products Genius is only a superior power of seeing. —JOHN RUSKIN, famed art and social critic Pick the two markets that you are most familiar with that have their own magazines with full-page advertising that costs less than $5,000. There should be no fewer than 15,000 readers. This is the fun part. Now we get to brainstorm or find products with these two markets in mind. The goal is come up with well-formed product ideas and spend nothing; in Step 3, we will create advertising for them and test responses from real customers before investing in manufacturing. There are several criteria that ensure the end product will fit into an automated architecture. The Main Benefit Should Be Encapsulated in One Sentence. People can dislike you—and you often sell more by offending some—but they should never misunderstand you. The main benefit of your product should be explainable in one sentence or phrase. How is it different and why should I buy it? ONE sentence or phrase, folks. Apple did an excellent job of this with the iPod. Instead of using the usual industry jargon with GB, bandwidth, and so forth, they simply said, "1,000 songs in your pocket." Done deal. Keep it simple and do not move ahead with a product until you can do this without confusing people. It Should Cost the Customer $50–200. The bulk of companies set prices in the midrange, and that is where the most competition is. Pricing low is shortsighted, because someone else is always willing to sacrifice more profit margin and drive you both bankrupt. Besides perceived value, there are three main benefits to creating a premium, high-end image and charging more than the competition. 1. Higher pricing means that we can sell fewer units—and thus manage fewer customers—and fulfill our dreamlines. It's faster. 2. Higher pricing attracts lower-maintenance customers (better credit, fewer complaints/questions, fewer returns, etc.). It's less headache. This is HUGE. 3. Higher pricing also creates higher profit margins. It's safer. I personally aim for an 8–10x markup, which means a $100 product can't cost me more than $10–12.50.27 If I had used the commonly recommended 5 x markup with BrainQUICKEN, it would have gone bankrupt within 6 months due to a dishonest supplier and late magazine. The profit margin saved it, and within 12 months it was generating up to $80,000 per month. High has its limits, however. If the per-unit price is above a certain point, prospects need to speak to someone on the phone before they are comfortable enough to make the purchase. This is contraindicated on our low-information diet. I have found that a price range of $50–200 per sale provides the most profit for the least customer service hassle. Price high and then justify. It Should Take No More Than 3 to 4 Weeks to Manufacture. This is critically important for keeping costs low and adapting to sales demand without stockpiling product in advance. I will not pursue any product that takes more than three to four weeks to manufacture, and I recommend aiming for one to two weeks from order placement to shippable product.

Option One: Resell a Product Purchasing an existing product at wholesale and reselling it is the easiest route but also the least profitable. It is the fastest to set up but the fastest to die off due to price competition with other resellers. The profitable life span of each product is short unless an exclusivity agreement prevents others from selling it. Reselling is, however, an excellent option for secondary back-end28 products that can be sold to existing customers or cross-sold29 to new customers online or on the phone. To purchase at wholesale, use these steps. 1. Contact the manufacturer and request a "wholesale pricelist" (generally 40% off retail) and terms. 2. If a business tax ID number is needed, print out the proper forms from your state's Secretary of State website and file for an LLC (which I prefer) or similar protective business structure for $100–200. Do NOT purchase product until you have completed Step 3 in the next chapter. It is enough at this point to confirm the profit margin and have product photos and sales literature. That's reselling. Not much more to it. Option Two: License a Product I not only use all the brains that I have, but all that I can borrow. —WOODROW WILSON Some of the world's best-known brands and products have been borrowed from someone or somewhere else. The basis for the energy drink Red Bull came from a tonic in Thailand, and the Smurfs were brought from Belgium. Pokémon came from the land of Honda. The band KISS made millions in record and concert sales, but the real profit has been in licensing—granting others the right to produce hundreds of products with their name and image in exchange for a percentage of sales. There are two parties involved in a licensing deal, and a member of the New Rich could be either. First, there is the inventor of the product,30 called the "licensor," who can sell others the right to manufacture, use, or sell his or her product, usually for 3– 10% of the wholesale price (usually around 40% off retail) for each unit sold. Invent, let someone else do the rest, and cash checks. Not a bad model. The other side of the equation is the person interested in manufacturing and selling the inventor's product for 90–97% of the profit: the licensee. This is, for me and most NR, more interesting. Licensing is, however, dealmaking-intensive on both sides and a science unto itself. Creative contract negotiation is essential and most readers will run into problems if it's their first product. For real-world case studies on both sides, ranging from Teddy Ruxpin to Tae-Bo, and full agreements with actual dollar amounts From how to sell inventions without prototypes or patents to how to secure rights to products as a no-name beginner, it's all there. The economics are fascinating and the profits can be astounding. In the meantime, we will focus on the least complicated and most profitable option open to the most people: product creation. Option Three: Create a Product Creation is a better means of self-expression than possession; it is through creating, not possessing, that life is revealed. —VIDA D. SCUDDER, The Life of the Spirit in the Modern English Poets Creating a product is not complicated. "Create" sounds more involved than it actually is. If the idea is a hard product—an invention—it is possible to hire mechanical engineers or industrial designers on www.elance.com to develop a prototype based on your description of its function and appearance, which is then taken to a contract manufacturer. If you find a generic or stock product made by a contract manufacturer that can be re-purposed or positioned for a special market, it's even easier: Have them manufacture it, stick a custom label on it for you, and presto— new product. This latter example is often referred to as "private labeling." Have you ever seen a massage therapist's office with its own line of vitamin products or the Kirkland brand at Costco? Private labeling in action. It is true that we'll be testing market response without manufacturing, but if the test is successful, manufacturing is the next step. This means we need to keep in mind setup costs, per-unit costs, and order minimums. Innovative gadgets and devices are great but often require special tooling, which makes the manufacturing start-up costs too expensive to meet our criteria. Putting mechanical devices aside and forgetting about welding and engineering, there is one class of product that meets all of our criteria, has a manufacturing lead time of less than a week in small quantities, and often permits not just an 8–10 x markup, but a 20–50 x markup. No, not heroin or slave labor. Too much bribing and human interaction required. Information. Information products are low-cost, fast to manufacture, and time-consuming for competitors to duplicate. Consider that the top-selling non-information infomercial products—whether exercise equipment or supplements—have a useful life span of two to four months before imitators flood the market. I studied economics in Beijing for six months and observed firsthand how the latest Nike sneaker or Callaway golf club could be duplicated and on eBay within a week of first appearing on shelves in the U.S. This is not an exaggeration, and I am not talking about a look-alike product— I mean an exact duplicate for 1/20 the cost. Information, on the other hand, is too time-consuming for most knockoff artists to bother with when there are easier products to replicate. It's easier to circumvent a patent than to paraphrase an entire course to avoid copyright infringement. Three of the most successful television products of all time—all of which have spent more than 300 weeks on the infomercial top-10 bestseller lists—reflect the competitive and profit margin advantage of information products.

I know from conversations with the principal owners of one of the above products that more than $65 million worth of information moved through their doors in 2002. Their infrastructure consisted of fewer than 25 in-house operators, and the rest of the infrastructure, ranging from media purchasing to shipping, was outsourced. Their annual revenue-per-employee is more than $2.7 million. Incredible. On the opposite end of the market size spectrum, I know a man who created a lowbudget how-to DVD for less than $200 and sold it to owners of storage facilities who wanted to install security systems. It's hard to get more niche than that. In 2001, selling DVDs that cost $2 to duplicate for $95 apiece through trade magazines, he made several hundred thousand dollars with no employees. But I'm Not an Expert! If you aren't an expert, don't sweat it. First, "expert" in the context of selling product means that you know more about the topic than the purchaser. No more. It is not necessary to be the best—just better than a small target number of your prospective customers. Let's suppose that your current dreamline—to compete in the 1,150-mile Iditarod dogsledding race in Alaska— requires $5,000 to realize. If there are 15,000 readers and even 50 (0.33%) can be convinced of your superior expertise in skill X and spend $100 for a program that teaches it, that is $5,000. Bring on the Huskies. Those 50 customers are what I call the "minimal customer base"—the minimum number of customers you need to convince of your expertise to fulfill a given dreamline. Second, expert status can be created in less than four weeks if you understand basic credibility indicators. It's important to learn how the PR pros phrase resume points and position their clients. See the boxed text later in this chapter to learn how. The degree to which you personally need expert status also depends on how you obtain your content. There are three main options. 1. Create the content yourself, often via paraphrasing and combining points from several books on a topic. 2. Repurpose content that is in the public domain and not subject to copyright protection, such as government documents and material that predates modern copyright law. 3. License content or compensate an expert to help create content. Fees can be one-time and paid up front or royalty-based (5–10% of net revenue, for example). If you choose option 1 or 2, you need expert status within a limited market. Let's assume you are a real estate broker and have determined that, like yourself, most brokers want a simple but good website to promote themselves and their businesses. If you read and understand the three top-selling books on home-page design, you will know more about that topic than 80% of the readership of a magazine for real estate brokers. If you can summarize the content and make recommendations specific to the needs of the real estate market, a 0.5–1.5% response from an ad you place in the magazine is not unreasonable to expect. Use the following questions to brainstorm potential how-to or informational products that can be sold to your markets using your expertise or borrowed expertise. Aim for a combination of formats that will lend itself to $50–200 pricing, such as a combination of two CDs (30–90 minutes each), a 40-page transcription of the CDs, and a 10-page quickstart guide. Digital delivery is perfectly acceptable—in some cases, ideal—if you can create a high enough perceived value.It's time to obliterate the cult of the expert. Let the PR world scorn me. First and foremost, there is a difference between being perceived as an expert and being one. In the context of business, the former is what sells product and the latter, relative to your "minimal customer base," is what creates good products and prevents returns. It is possible to know all there is to know about a subject—medicine, for example— but if you don't have M.D. at the end of your name, few will listen. The M.D. is what I term a "credibility indicator." The so-called expert with the most credibility indicators, whether acronyms or affiliations, is often the most successful in the marketplace, even if other candidates have more in-depth knowledge. This is a matter of superior positioning, not deception. How, then, do we go about acquiring credibility indicators in the least time possible? Emulating the client-grooming techniques of some of the best PR firms in New York City and Los Angeles isn't a bad place to start. It took a friend of mine just three weeks to become a "top relationship expert who, as featured in Glamour and other national media, has counseled executives at Fortune 500 companies on how to improve their relationships in 24 hours or less." How did she do it? She followed a few simple steps that created a credibility snowball effect. Here's how you can do the same.

Many of these theories have been killed off only when some decisive experiment exposed their incorrectness.... Thus the yeoman work in any science ... is done by the experimentalist, who must keep the theoreticians honest. —MICHIO KAKU, theoretical physicist and cocreator of String Field Theory, Hyperspace Fewer than 5% of the 195,000 books published each year sell more than 5,000 copies. Teams of publishers and editors with decades of combined experience fail more times than not. The founder of Border's Books lost $375 million of investor funding with WebVan,39 a nationwide grocery delivery service. The problem? No one wanted it. The moral is that intuition and experience are poor predictors of which products and businesses will be profitable. Focus groups are equally misleading. Ask ten people if they would buy your product. Then tell those who said "yes" that you have ten units in your car and ask them to buy. The initial positive responses, given by people who want to be liked and aim to please, become polite refusals as soon as real money is at stake.

To get an accurate indicator of commercial viability, don't ask people if they would buy—ask them to buy. The response to the second is the only one that matters. The approach of the NR reflects this.

Micro-testing involves using inexpensive advertisements to test consumer response to a product prior to manufacturing.40 In the pre-Internet era, this was done using small classified ads in newspapers or magazines that led prospects to call a prerecorded sales message. Prospects would leave their contact information, and based on the number of callers or response to a follow-up sales letter, the product would be abandoned or manufactured. In the Internet era, there are better tools that are both cheaper and faster. We'll test the product ideas from the last chapter on Google Adwords—the largest and most sophisticated Pay-Per-Click (PPC) engine—in five days for $500 or less. PPC here refers to the highlighted search results that are listed above and to the right of normal search results on Google. Advertisers pay to have these ads displayed when people search for a certain term related to the advertisers' product, such as "cognitive supplement," and are charged a small fee from $.05 to over $1 each time someone clicks through to their site.

New Rich Revisited: How Doug Did It Remember Doug from ProSoundEffects.com? How did he test the idea and go from $0 to $10,000 per month in the process? He followed these steps. 1. Market Selection He chose music and television producers as his market because he is a musician himself and has used these products. 2. Product Brainstorm He chose the most popular products available for resale from the largest manufacturers of sound libraries and arranged a wholesale purchase and drop-ship agreement with them. Many of these libraries cost well above $300 (up to $7,500), and this is precisely why he needs to answer more customer-service questions than someone with a lower-priced product of $50–200. 3. Micro-Testing He auctioned the products on eBay to test demand (and the highest possible pricing) before purchasing inventory. He ordered product only when people placed orders from him, and product shipped immediately from the manufacturers' warehouses. Based on this demand confirmed on eBay, Doug created a Yahoo Store with these products and began testing Google Adwords and other PPC search engines. 4. Rollout and Automation Following this testing, and upon generating sufficient cash flow, Doug began experimenting with print advertising in trade magazines. Simultaneously, he streamlined and outsourced operations to reduce his time requirements from two hours per day to two hours per week. COMFORT CHALLENGE Rejecting First Offers and Walking Away (3 Days) Before performing this exercise, if possible, read the bonus chapter “How to Get $700,000 of Advertising for $10,000” on our companion site, and then set aside two hours on a consecutive Saturday, Sunday, and Monday. On Saturday and Sunday, go to a farmers’ market or other outdoor event where goods are sold. If this isn’t possible, go to small independent retailers (not chains or mass retail). Set a budget of $100 for your negotiating tuition and look for items to purchase that total at least $150. Your job is to get the sellers down to a total of $100 or less for the lot. It is better to practice on many cheap items rather than a few big items. Be sure to reply to their first offer with, “What type of discount can you offer?” to let them negotiate against themselves. Negotiate near closing time, choose your objective price, bracket, and make a firm offer with cash in hand for that amount.48 Practice walking away if your objective price isn’t met. On Monday, call two magazines (expect the first to be awkward) and use the script on the companion site to negotiate, minus the last firm offer. Get them as low as possible and then call them back later to indicate that your proposal was refused by upper management or otherwise vetoed. This is the negotiating equivalent of paper trading.49 Get used to refusing offers and countering in person and—most importantly—on the phone.The factory of the future will have only two employees, a man and a dog. The man will be there to feed the dog. The dog will be there to keep the man from touching the equipment. —WARREN G. BENNIS, University of Southern California Professor of Business Administration; adviser to Ronald Reagan and John F. Kennedy Most entrepreneurs don’t start out with automation as a goal. This leaves them open to mass confusion in a world where each business guru contradicts the next. Consider the following: A company is stronger if it is bound by love rather than by fear.... If the employees come first, then they’re happy. —HERB KELLEHER, cofounder of Southwest Airlines Look, kiddie. I built this business by being a bastard. I run it by being a bastard. I’ll always be a bastard, and don’t you ever try to change me.50 —CHARLES REVSON, founder of Revlon, to a senior executive within his company Hmm ... Whom to follow? If you are fast on your feet, you’ll notice that I just offered you an either-or option. The good news is that, as usual, there is a third option. The contradictory advice you find in business books and elsewhere usually relates to managing employees—how to handle the human element. Herb tells you to give them a hug, Revson tells you to kick them in the balls, and I tell you to solve the problem by eliminating it altogether: Remove the human element. Once you have a product that sells, it's time to design a self-correcting business architecture that runs itself. The Remote-Control CEO The power of hiding ourselves from one another is mercifully given, for men are wild beasts, and would devour one another but for this protection. —HENRY WARD BEECHER, U.S. abolitionist and clergyman, "Proverbs from Plymouth Pulpit" RURAL PENNSYLVANIA In a 200-year-old stone farmhouse, a quiet "experiment in 21st-century leadership" is proceeding exactly as planned.51Stephen McDonnell is upstairs in his flip-flops looking at a spreadsheet on his computer. His company has increased its annual revenue 30% per year since it all began, and he is able to spend more time with his three daughters than he ever thought possible. The experiment? As CEO of Applegate Farms, he insists on spending just one day per week at the company headquarters in Bridgewater, New Jersey. He's not the only CEO who spends time at home, of course—there are hundreds who have heart attacks or nervous breakdowns and need time to recover—but there is a huge difference. McDonnell has been doing it for more than 17 years. Rarer still, he started doing it just six months after founding the company. This intentional absence has enabled him to create a process-driven instead of founder-driven business. Limiting contact with managers forces the entrepreneur to develop operational rules that enable others to deal with problems themselves instead of calling for help. This isn't just for small operations. Applegate Farms sells more than 120 organic and natural meat products to high-end retailers and generates more than $35 million in revenue per year. It is all possible because McDonnell started with the end in mind. Behind the Scenes: The Muse Architecture Orders are nobody can see the Great Oz! Not nobody, not nohow! —GUARDIAN OF THE EMERALD CITY GATES, The Wizard of Oz Starting with the end in mind—an organizational map of what the eventual business will look like—is not new. Infamous deal-maker Wayne Huizenga copied the org chart of McDonald's to turn Blockbuster into a billion-dollar behemoth, and dozens of titans have done much the same. In our case, it's the "end in mind" that is different. Our goal isn't to create a business that is as large as possible, but rather a business that bothers us as little as possible. The architecture has to place us out of the information flow instead of putting us at the top of it. I didn't get this right the first time I tried. In 2003, I was interviewed in my home office for a documentary called As Seen on TV. We were interrupted every 20–30 seconds with beeping e-mail notifications, IM pings, and ringing phones. I couldn't leave them unanswered, because dozens of decisions depended on me. If I didn't ensure the trains were running on time and put out the fires, no one would. Each outsourcer takes a piece of the revenue pie. Here is what the general profitloss might look like for a hypothetical $80 product sold via phone and developed with the help of an expert, who is paid a royalty. I recommend calculating profit margins using higher-than-anticipated expenses. This will account for unforeseen costs (read: screwups) and miscellaneous fees such as monthly reports, etc.

I set a new goal after that experience, and when I was interviewed six months later as a follow-up, one change was more pronounced than all others: silence. I had redesigned the business from the ground up so that I had no phone calls to answer and no e-mail to respond to. I'm often asked how big my company is—how many people I employ full-time. The answer is one. Most people lose interest at that point. If someone were to ask me how many people run Brain-QUICKEN LLC, on the other hand, the answer is different: between 200 and 300. I am the ghost in the machine.52 From advertisements—print in this example—to a cash deposit in my bank account, the diagram is what a simplified version of my architecture looks like, including some sample costs. If you have developed a product based on the guidelines in the last two chapters, it will plug into this structure hand-in-glove. Where am I in the diagram? Nowhere. I am not a tollbooth through which anything needs to pass. I am more like a police officer on the side of the road who can step in if need be, and I use detailed reports from outsourcers to ensure the cogs are moving as intended. I check reports from fulfillment each Monday and monthly reports from the same the first of each month. The latter reports include orders received from the call center, which I can compare to the call center bills to gauge profit. Otherwise, I just check bank accounts online on the first and fifteenth of each month to look for odd deductions. If I find something, one e-mail will fix it, and if not, it's back to kendo, painting, hiking, or whatever I happen to be doing at the time.

CHAPTER THREE

When and How

The diagram should be your rough blueprint for designing a self-sustaining virtual architecture. There could be differences—more or fewer elements—but the main principles are the same: 1. Contract outsourcing companies53 that specialize in one function vs. freelancers whenever possible so that if someone is fired, quits, or doesn't perform, you can replace them without interrupting your business. Hire trained groups of people who can provide detailed reporting and replace one another as needed. 2. Ensure that all outsourcers are willing to communicate among themselves to solve problems, and give them written permission to make most inexpensive decisions without consulting you first (I started at less than $100 and moved to $400 after two months). How do you get there? It helps to look at where entrepreneurs typically lose their momentum and stall permanently. Most entrepreneurs begin with the cheapest tools available, bootstrapping and doing things themselves to get up and running with little cash. This isn't the problem. In fact, it's necessary so that the entrepreneurs can train outsourcers later. The problem is that these same entrepreneurs don't know when and how to replace themselves or their homemade infrastructure with something more scalable. By "scalable," I mean a business architecture that can handle 10,000 orders per week as easily as it can handle 10 orders per week. Doing this requires minimizing your decision-making responsibilities, which achieves our goal of time freedom while setting the stage for doubling and tripling income with no change in hours worked. Call the companies at the end of the chapter to research costs. Plan and budget accordingly to upgrade infrastructure at the following milestones, which I measure in units of product shipped: Phase I: 0–50 Total Units of Product Shipped Do it all yourself. Put your phone number on the site for both general questions and order-taking—this is important in the beginning—and take customer calls to determine common questions that you will answer later in an online FAQ. This FAQ will also be the main material for training phone operators and developing sales scripts. Is PPC, an offline advertisement, or your website too vague or misleading, thus attracting unqualified and time-consuming consumers? If so, change them to answer common questions and make the product benefits (including what it isn't or doesn't do) clearer. Answer all e-mail and save your responses in one folder called "customer service questions." CC yourself on responses and put the nature of the customers' questions in the subject lines for future indexing. Personally pack and ship all product to determine the cheapest options for both. Investigate opening a merchant account from your local small bank (easier to get than with a larger bank) for later outsourced credit card processing at higher roll-out volumes.

Now you will have the cash flow to afford the setup fees and the monthly minimums that bigger, more sophisticated outsourcers will ask for. Call the end-to-end fulfillment houses that handle it all—from order status to returns and refunds. Interview them about costs and ask them for referrals to call centers and credit card processors they've collaborated with for file transfers and problem solving. Don't assemble an architecture of strangers—there will be programming costs and mistakes, both of which are expensive. Set up an account with the credit card processor first, for which you will need your own merchant account. This is critical, as the fulfillment house can only handle refunds and declined cards for transactions they process themselves through an outsourced credit card processor. Optionally, set up an account with one of the call centers your new fulfillment center recommends. These will often have toll-free numbers you can use instead of purchasing your own. Look at the percentage split of online to phone orders during testing and consider carefully if the extra revenue from the latter is worth the hassle. It often isn't. Those who call to order will generally order online if given no other option. Before signing on with a call center, get several 800 numbers they answer for current clients and make test calls, asking difficult product-related questions and gauging sales abilities. Call each number at least three times (morning, afternoon, and evening) and note the make-or-break factor: wait time. The phone should be answered within three to four rings, and if you are put on hold, the shorter the wait the better. More than 15 seconds will result in too many abandoned calls and waste advertising dollars. The Art of Undecision: Fewer Options = More Revenue Companies go out of business when they make the wrong decisions or, just as important, make too many decisions. The latter creates complexity.

Joseph Sugarman is the marketing genius behind dozens of direct-response and retail successes, including the BluBlocker sunglasses phenomenon. Prior to his string of home runs on television (he sold 20,000 pairs of BluBlockers within 15 minutes of his first QVC appearance), his domain was print media, where he made millions and built an empire called JS&A Group. He was once recruited to design an advertisement for a manufacturer's watch line. The manufacturer wanted to feature nine different watches in the ad, and Joe recommended featuring just one. The client insisted and Joe offered to do both and test them in the same issue of The Wall Street Journal. The result? The one-watch offer outsold the nine-watch offer 6-to-1.55 Henry Ford once said, referring to his Model-T, the bestselling car of all time,56 "The customer can have any color he wants, so long as it's black." He understood something that businesspeople seem to have forgotten: Serving the customer ("customer service") is not becoming a personal concierge and catering to their every whim and want. Customer service is providing an excellent product at an acceptable price and solving legitimate problems (lost packages, replacements, refunds, etc.) in the fastest manner possible. That's it. The more options you offer the customer, the more indecision you create and the fewer orders you receive—it is a disservice all around. Furthermore, the more options you offer the customer, the more manufacturing and customer service burden you create for yourself. The art of "undecision" refers to minimizing the number of decisions your customers can or need to make. Here are a few methods that I and other NR have used to reduce service overhead 20–80%: 1. Offer one or two purchase options ("basic" and "premium," for example) and no more. 2. Do not offer multiple shipping options. Offer one fast method instead and charge a premium. 3. Do not offer overnight or expedited shipping (it is possible to refer them to a reseller who does, as is true with all of these points), as these shipping methods will produce hundreds of anxious phone calls. 4. Eliminate phone orders completely and direct all prospects to online ordering. This seems outrageous until you realize that success stories like Amazon.com have depended on it as a fundamental cost-saver to survive and thrive. 5. Do not offer international shipments. Spending 10 minutes per order filling out customs forms and then dealing with customer complaints when the product costs 20–100% more with tariffs and duties is about as fun as headbutting a curb. It's about as profitable, too. Some of these policies hint at what is perhaps the biggest time-saver of all: customer filtering. Not All Customers Are Created Equal Once you reach Phase III and have some cash flow, it's time to re-evaluate your customers and thin the herd. There are good and bad versions of all things: good food, bad food; good movies, bad movies; good sex, bad sex; and, yes, good customers and bad customers. Decide now to do business with the former and avoid the latter. I recommend looking at the customer as an equal trading partner and not as an infallible blessing of a human being to be pleased at all costs. If you offer an excellent product at an acceptable price, it is an equal trade and not a begging session between subordinate (you) and superior (customer). Be professional but never kowtow to unreasonable people. Instead of dealing with problem customers, I recommend you prevent them from ordering in the first place. I know dozens of NR who don't accept Western Union or checks as payment. Some would respond to this with, "You're giving up 10–15% of your sales!" The NR, in turn, would say, "I am, but I'm also avoiding the 10–15% of the customers who create 40% of the expenses and eat 40% of my time." It's classic 80/20. Those who spend the least and ask for the most before ordering will do the same after the sale. Cutting them out is both a good lifestyle decision and a good financial decision. Low-profit and high-maintenance customers like to call operators and spend up to 30 minutes on the phone asking questions that are unimportant or answered online, costing—in my case—$24.90 (30 x $0.83) per 30-minute incident, eliminating the minuscule profit they contribute in the first place. Those who spend the most complain the least. In addition to our premium $50–200 pricing, here are a few additional policies that attract the high-profit and lowmaintenance customers we want: 1. Do not accept payment via Western Union, checks, or money order. 2. Raise wholesale minimums to 12–100 units and require a tax ID number to qualify resellers who are real businesspeople and not time-intensive novices. Don't run a personal business school. 3. Refer all potential resellers to an online order form that must be printed, filled out, and faxed in. Never negotiate pricing or approve lower pricing for higher-volume orders. Cite "company policy" due to having had problems in the past. 4. Offer low-priced products (à la MRI's NO2 book) instead of free products to capture contact information for follow-up sales. Offering something for free is the best way to attract time-eaters and spend money on those unwilling to return the favor. 5. Offer a lose-win guarantee (see boxed text) instead of free trials.

6. Do not accept orders from common mail fraud countries such as Nigeria. Make your customer base an exclusive club, and treat the members well once they've been accepted. The Lose-Win Guarantee—How to Sell Anything to Anyone If you want a guarantee, buy a toaster. —CLINT EASTWOOD The 30-day money-back guarantee is dead. It just doesn't have the pizzazz it once did. If a product doesn't work, I've been lied to and will have to spend an afternoon at the post office to return it. This costs me more than just the price I paid for the product, both in time and actual postage. Risk elimination just isn't enough. This is where we enter the neglected realm of lose-win guarantees and risk reversal. The NR use what most consider an afterthought—the guarantee—as a cornerstone sales tool. The NR aim to make it profitable for the customer even if the product fails. Losewin guarantees not only remove risk for the consumer but put the company at financial risk. Here are a few examples of putting your money where your mouth is. Delivered in 30 minutes or less or it's free! (Domino's Pizza built its business on this guarantee.) We're so confident you'll like CIALIS, if you don't we'll pay for the brand of your choice. (The "CIALIS® Promise Program" offers a free sample of CIALIS and then offers to pay for competing products if CIALIS doesn't live up to the hype.) If your car is stolen, we'll pay $500 of your insurance deductible. (This guarantee helped THE CLUB become the #1-selling mechanical automobile anti-theft device in the world.) 110% guaranteed to work within 60 minutes of the first dose. (This was for BodyQUICK and a first among sports nutrition products. I offered to not only refund customers the price of the product if it didn't work within 60 minutes of the first dose, but also to send them a check for 10% more.) The lose-win guarantee might seem like a big risk, especially when someone can abuse it for profit like in the BodyQUICK example, but it isn't ... if your product delivers. Most people are honest.

COMFORT CHALLENGE

This is the last Comfort Challenge, placed prior to the chapter that tackles the most uncomfortable turning point for most office dwellers: negotiating remote work agreements. This challenge is intended to be fun while showing—in no uncertain terms—that the rules most follow are nothing more than social conventions. There are no legal boundaries stopping you from creating an ideal life ... or just being selfentertained and causing mass confusion. So, relaxing in public. Sounds easy, right? I'm somewhat famous for relaxing in style to get a laugh out of friends. Here is the deal, and I don't care if you're male or female, 20 or 60, Mongolian or Martian. I call the following a "time-out." Once per day for two days, simply lie down in the middle of a crowded public place at some point. Lunchtime is ideal. It can be a well-trafficked sidewalk, the middle of a popular Starbucks, or a popular bar. There is no real technique involved. Just lie down and remain silent on the ground for about ten seconds, and then get up and continue on with whatever you were doing before. I used to do this at nightclubs to clear space for break-dancing circles. No one responded to pleading, but going catatonic on the ground did the trick. Don't explain it at all. If someone asks about it after the fact (he or she will be too confused to ask you while you're doing it for 10 seconds), just respond, "I just felt like lying down for a second." The less you say, the funnier and more gratifying this will be. Do it on solo missions for the first two days, and then feel free to do it when with a group of friends. It's a riot. It isn't enough to think outside the box. Thinking is passive. Get used to acting outside the box.

There are generally two classes of call centers: order takers and commissioned reps. Interview each provider you consider to understand the options and costs involved. The former is a good option if you give the product price in an advertisement (hard offer), are offering free information (lead generation), or don't need trained salespeople who can overcome objections. In other words, your ad or website is prequalifying prospects. The latter would more appropriately be called "sales centers." Operators are commissioned and trained "closers" whose sole goal is to convert callers to buyers. These calls are often in response to "call for information/ trial/sample" ads that don't feature a price (soft offers). Expect higher costs per sale.

After I read the section on outsourcing, I thought it sounded like a novel idea but would never work for me. However, since the rest of the book was "spot on," I decided to try it. Rather than ship my money overseas, I opted to keep it in the U.S. and use my niece in college, with skills on computers I can't even fathom, to test the theory. Turns out it has been a great experience and timesaver for me, as well as moneymaker for her. It seems I have all of the positives of out sourcing but none of the hassles of language and such.... Being able to mold a young mind for the better ties in well with the rest of your book ... —KEN D.

HOW TO ESCAPE THE OFFICE

By working faithfully eight hours a day, you may eventually get to be a boss and work twelve hours a day. —ROBERT FROST, American poet and winner of four Pulitzer Prizes On this path, it is only the first step that counts. —ST. JEAN–BAPTISTE–MARIE VIANNEY, Catholic saint, "Curé d'Ars" PALO ALTO , CALIFORNIA "We're not going to expense the phone." "I'm not asking you to." Silence. Then a nod, a laugh, and a crooked smile of resignation. "OK, then—it's fine." And that was that, lickity-split. Forty-four-year old Dave Camarillo, lifelong employee, had cracked the code and started his second life. He hadn't been fired; he hadn't been yelled at. His boss seemed to be handling the whole situation quite well. Granted, Dave delivered the goods on the job, and it wasn't like he was doing naked snow angels in client meetings, but still—he had just spent 30 days in China without telling anyone. "It wasn't half as hard as I thought it would be." Dave works among more than 10,000 employees at Hewlett- Packard (HP), and— against all odds—he actually likes it. He has no desire to start his own company and has spent the last seven years doing tech support for customers in 45 states and 22 countries. Six months ago, however, he had a small problem. She measured 5′2″ and weighed 110 pounds. Was he, like most men, afraid of commitment, unwilling to stop running around the house in Spider-Man underoos, or inseparable from the last refuge of any selfrespecting man, the PlayStation? No, he was past all that. In fact, Dave was locked and loaded, ready to pop the big question, but he was short on vacation days and his girlfriend lived out of town. Waaaaay out of town—5,913 miles out of town. He had met her on a client visit to Shenzhen, China, and it was now time to meet the parents, logistics be damned. Dave had only recently begun to take tech calls at home, and, well, isn't home where the heart is? One plane ticket and one T-Mobile GSM tri-band phone later, he was somewhere over the Pacific en route to his first seven-day experiment. Twelve time zones hence, he proposed, she accepted, and no one was the wiser stateside. The second field trip was a 30-day tour of Chinese family and food (pig face, anyone?), ending with Shumei Wu becoming Shumei Camarillo. Back in Palo Alto, HP continued its quest for world domination, neither knowing nor caring where Dave was. He had his calls forwarded to his newly begotten wife's cell phone and all was right in the world. Now back in the U.S. after hoping for the best and preparing for the worst, Dave had earned his Eagle Scout mobility badge. The future looks flexible, indeed. He is going to start by spending two months in China every summer and then move to Australia and Europe to make up for lost time, all with the full support of his boss. The key to cutting the leash was simple—he asked for forgiveness instead of permission. "I didn't travel for 30 years of my life—so why not?" THAT'S PRECISELY THE question everyone should be asking—why the hell not? From Caste to Castaway The old rich, the upper class of yore with castles and ascots and irritating little lapdogs, are characterized as being well-established in one place. The Schwarzes of Nantucket and the McDonnells of Charlottesville. Blech. Summers in the Hamptons is sooooo 1990s. The guard is changing. Being bound to one place will be the new defining feature of middle class. The New Rich are defined by a more elusive power than simple cash—unrestricted mobility. This jet-setting is not limited to start-up owners or freelancers. Employees can pull it off, too.58 Not only can they pull it off, but more and more companies want them to pull it off. BestBuy, the consumer electronics giant, is now sending thousands of employees home from their HQ in Minnesota and claims not only lowered costs, but also a 10– 20% increase in results. The new mantra is this: Work wherever and whenever you want, but get your work done. In Japan, a three-piece zombie who joins the 9–5 grind each morning is called a sarari-man—salaryman—and, in the last few years, a new verb has emerged: datsusara suru, to escape (datsu) the salaryman (sara) lifestyle. It's your turn to learn the datsu-sara dance.59 Trading Bosses for Beer: An Oktoberfest Case Study To create the proper leverage to be unshackled, we'll do two things: demonstrate the business benefit of remote working and make it too expensive or excruciating to refuse a request for it. Remember Sherwood? His French shirts are beginning to move and he is itching to ditch the U.S. for a global walkabout. He has more than enough cash now but needs to escape constant supervision in the office before he can implement all the timesaving tools from Elimination and travel. He is a mechanical engineer and is producing twice as many designs in half the time since erasing 90% of his time-wasters and interruptions. This quantum leap in performance has been noticed by his supervisors and his value to the company has increased, making it more expensive to lose him. More value means more leverage for negotiations. Sherwood has been sure to hold back some of his productivity and efficiency so that he can highlight a sudden jump in both during a remote work trial period.

Step 1: Increase Investment First, he speaks with his boss on July 12 about additional training that might be available to employees. He proposes having the company pay for a four-week industrial design class to help him better interface with clients, being sure to mention the benefit to the boss and business (i.e., he'll decrease intradepartmental back-andforth and increase both client results and billable time). Sherwood wants the company to invest as much as possible in him so that the loss is greater if he quits. Step 2: Prove Increased Output Offsite Second, he calls in sick the next Tuesday and Wednesday, July 18 and 19, to showcase his remote working productivity.60 He decides to call in sick between Tuesday and Thursday for two reasons: It looks less like a lie for a three-day weekend and it also enables him to see how well he functions in social isolation without the imminent reprieve of the weekend. He ensures that he doubles his work output on both days, leaves an e-mail trail of some sort for his boss to notice, and keeps quantifiable records of what he accomplished for reference during later negotiations. Since he uses expensive CAD software that is only licensed on his office desktop, Sherwood installs a free trial of GoToMyPC remote access software so that he can pilot his office computer from home. Step 3: Prepare the Quantifiable Business Benefit Third, Sherwood creates a bullet-point list of how much more he achieved outside the office with explanations. He realizes that he needs to present remote working as a good business decision and not a personal perk. The quantifiable end result was three more designs per day than his usual average and three total hours of additional billable client time. For explanations, he identifies removal of commute and fewer distractions from office noise. Step 4: Propose a Revocable Trial Period Fourth, fresh off completing the comfort challenges from previous chapters, Sherwood confidently proposes an innocent one-day-per-week remote work trial period for two weeks. He plans a script in advance but does not make it a PowerPoint presentation or otherwise give it the appearance of something serious or irreversible.61 Sherwood knocks on his boss's office door around 3 P.M. on a relatively relaxed Thursday, July 27, the week after his absence, and his script looks like the following. Stock phrases are underlined and footnotes explain negotiating points. Sherwood: Hi, Bill. Do you have a quick second? Bill: Sure. What's up? Sherwood: I just wanted to bounce an idea off of you that's been on my mind. Two minutes should be plenty. Bill: OK. Shoot. Sherwood: Last week, as you know, I was sick. Long story short, I decided to work at home despite feeling terrible. So here's the funny part. I thought I would get nothing done, but ended up finishing three more designs than usual on both days. Plus, I put in three more billable hours than usual without the commute, office noise, distractions, etc. OK, so here's where I'm going. Just as a trial, I'd like to propose working from home Mondays and Tuesdays for just two weeks. You can veto it whenever you want, and I'll come in if we need to do meetings, but I'd like to try it for just two weeks and review the results. I'm 100% confident that I'll get twice as much done. Does that seem reasonable? Bill: Hmm ... What if we need to share client designs? Sherwood: There's a program called GoToMyPC that I used to access the office computer when I was sick. I can view everything remotely, and I'll have my cell phone on me 24/7. Sooooo ... What do you think? Test it out starting next Monday and see how much more I get done?62 Bill: Ummm ... OK, fine. But it's just a test. I have a meeting in five and have to run, but let's talk soon. Sherwood: Great. Thanks for the time. I'll keep you posted on it all. I'm sure you'll be pleasantly surprised. Sherwood didn't expect to get two days per week approved. He asked for two so that, in the case his boss refused, he could ask for just one as a fallback position (bracketing). Why didn't Sherwood go for five days remote per week? Two reasons. First, it's a lot for management to accept off the bat. We need to ask for an inch and turn it into a foot without setting off panic alarms. Second, it is a good idea to hone your remote-working abilities—rehearse a bit—before shooting for the big time, as it decreases the likelihood of crises and screwups that will get remote rights revoked. Step 5: Expand Remote Time Sherwood ensures that his days outside of the office are his most productive to date, even minimally dropping in-office production to heighten the contrast. He sets a meeting to discuss the results with his boss on August 15 and prepares a bullet-point page detailing increased results and items completed compared to in-office time. He suggests upping the ante to four days per week remote for a two-week trial, fully prepared to concede to three days if need be. Sherwood: It really turned out even better than I expected. If you look at the numbers, it makes a lot of business sense, and I'm enjoying work a lot more now. So, here we are. I'd like to suggest, if you think it makes sense, that I try four days a week for another two-week trial. I was thinking that coming in Friday63would make sense to prepare for the coming week, but we could do whichever day you prefer. Bill: Sherwood, I'm really not sure we can do that. Sherwood: What's your main concern?64 Bill: It seems like you're on your way out. I mean, are you going to quit on us? Second, what if everyone wants to do the same? Sherwood: Fair enough. Good points. First, to be honest, I was close to quitting before, with all the interruptions and commute and whatnot, but I'm actually feeling great now with the change in routine.I'm doing more and feel relaxed for a change. Second, no one should be allowed to work remotely unless they can show increased productivity, and I'm the perfect experiment. If they can show it, however, why not let them do it on a trial basis? It lowers costs for the office, increases productivity, and makes employees happier. So, what do you say? Can I test it out for two weeks and come in Fridays to take care of the office stuff? I'll still document everything, and you, of course, have the right to change your mind at any point. Bill: Man, you are an insistent one. OK, we'll give it a shot, but don't go blabbing about it. Sherwood: Of course. Thanks, Bill. I appreciate the trust. Talk to you soon. Sherwood continues to be productive at home and maintains his lower in-office performance. He reviews the results with his boss after two weeks and continues with four remote days per week for an additional two weeks until Tuesday, September , when he requests a full-time remote trial of two weeks while he is visiting relatives out of state. Sherwood's team is in the middle of a project that requires his expertise, and he is prepared to quit if his boss refuses. He realizes that, just as you want to negotiate ad pricing close to deadlines, getting what you want often depends more on when you ask for it than how you ask for it. Though he would prefer not to quit, his income from shirts is more than enough to fund his dream-lines of Oktoberfest and beyond. His boss acquiesces and Sherwood doesn't have to use his threat of quitting. He goes home that evening and buys a $524 round-trip ticket, less than one week's shirt sales, to Munich for Oktoberfest. Now he can implement all the time-savers possible and hack out the inessentials. Somewhere between drinking wheat beer and dancing in lederhosen, Sherwood will get his work done in fine form, leaving his company better off than prior to 80/20 and leaving himself all the time in the world. But hold on a second ... What if your boss still refuses? Hmm ... Then they force your hand. If upper management won't see the light, you'll just have to use the next chapter to fire their asses.

It can be effective to take a longer period of absence up front in what some NR have termed the "hourglass" approach, so named because you use a long proof-of-concept up front to get a short remote agreement and then negotiate back up to full-time out of the office. Here's what it looks like. 1. Use a preplanned project or emergency (family issue, personal issue, relocation, home repairs, whatever) that requires you to take one or two weeks out of the office. 2. Say that you recognize you can't just stop working and that you would prefer to work instead of taking vacation days. 3. Propose how you can work remotely and offer, if necessary, to take a pay cut for that period (and that period only) if performance isn't up to par upon returning. 4. Allow the boss to collaborate on how to do it so that he or she is invested in the process. 5. Make the two weeks "off" the most productive period you've ever had at work. 6. Show your boss the quantifiable results upon returning, and tell him or her that—without all the distractions, commute, etc.—you can get twice as much done. Suggest two or three days at home per week as a trial for two weeks. 7. Make those remote days ultraproductive. 8. Suggest only one or two days in the office per week. 9. Make those days the least productive of the week. 10. Suggest complete mobility—the boss will go for it.

To add to your excellent list (we've traveled just like that for several years SWEET!), I'd like to add my modifications as a female traveler and a new mom (16- month-old baby). Personal favorites: (1) Athleta carries excellent, light, quick-dry clothing that hold up well to sports but still look very fashionable. Skorts are a must for looking feminine but being fully covered for hiking and steep pyramid steps—you know what I mean, ladies! Just a note, a slightly longer length will serve you well in a lot of countries, as well as tankini tops and swim skirts for swimming. (2) Fresh & Go toothbrush is simple to use. (3) Marsona sound machine for drowning out unfamiliar noises is a must (regularly use with baby at home too so when they hear the sound they know it's sleep time!). This has been a lifesaver for us on many trips, and we now use it regularly at home for better sleep. No more changing hotels midtrip to avoid noise. AND, I know we have to travel light, but with baby a lot of things are nonnegotiable. These make for smoother sailing: (1) Peanut shell sling in black fleece—it's more comfy than the cotton and you can pop baby in and out wherever you are, from birth to 35 lbs. I never take mine off, it's part of my outfit; (2) Peapod plus portable tent—this is baby's main bed at home and travel so baby has the same sleep place everywhere we go, and the flaps give all travel parties privacy—great from small babies to five-year-olds. I can still jam this onto a little wheeled carry-on and pack mine and baby's minimal clothing around it; (3) Go Go Kidz TravelMate (great for wheeling car seat up to the gate for gate check or use on plane); (4) Britax Diplomat car seat is small but kids can use it from birth to approx. four years old. Make sure the wheeled carry-on bag you get is one size smaller than the allowed carry-on size so you don't get bumped to check the bag in if the plane is full. You can always nicely argue/reason/bat your eyelashes that you will put the bag in your foot space. Also, very helpful to give baby something to sip or munch on during take off and landing so yours isn't the baby screaming from ear pain. Happy travels! —KARYL

Just because something has been a lot of work or consumed a lot of time doesn't make it productive or worthwhile. Just because you are embarrassed to admit that you're still living the consequences of bad decisions made 5, 10, or 20 years ago shouldn't stop you from making good decisions now. If you let pride stop you, you will hate life 5, 10, and 20 years from now for the same reasons. I hate to be wrong and sat in a dead-end trajectory with my own company until I was forced to change directions or face total breakdown—I know how hard it is. Now that we're all on a level playing field: Pride is stupid. Being able to quit things that don't work is integral to being a winner. Going into a project or job without defining when worthwhile becomes wasteful is like going into a casino without a cap on what you will gamble: dangerous and foolish. "But, you don't understand my situation. It's complicated!" But is it really? Don't confuse the complex with the difficult. Most situations are simple—many are just emotionally difficult to act upon. The problem and the solution are usually obvious and simple. It's not that you don't know what to do. Of course you do. You are just terrified that you might end up worse off than you are now. I'll tell you right now: If you're at this point, you won't be worse off. Revisit fearsetting and cut the cord.

CHAPTER FOUR

The Birth of Mini-Retirements and the Death of Vacations

There is more to life than increasing its speed. —MOHANDAS GANDHI In February of 2004, I was miserable and overworked. My travel fantasy began as a plan to visit Costa Rica in March 2004 for four weeks of Spanish and relaxation. I needed a recharge and four weeks seemed "reasonable" by whatever made-up benchmark you can use for such a thing. A friend familiar with Central America dutifully pointed out that it would never work, as Costa Rica was about to enter its rainy season. Torrential downpours weren't the uplifting jolt I needed, so I shifted my focus to four weeks in Spain. It's a long trip over the Atlantic, though, and Spain was close to other countries I'd always wanted to visit. I lost "reasonable" somewhere shortly thereafter and decided that I deserved a full three months to explore my roots in Scandinavia after four weeks in Spain. If there were any real-time bombs or pending disasters, they would certainly crop up in the first four weeks, so there really wasn't any additional risk in extending my trip to three months. Three months would be great. Those three months turned into 15, and I started to ask myself, "Why not take the usual 20–30-year retirement and redistribute it throughout life instead of saving it all for the end?" The Alternative to Binge Traveling Thanks to the Interstate Highway System, it is now possible to travel from coast to coast without seeing anything. —CHARLES KURALT, CBS news reporter If you are accustomed to working 50 weeks per year, the tendency, even after creating the mobility to take extended trips, will be to go nuts and see 10 countries in 14 days and end up a wreck. It's like taking a starving dog to an all-you-can-eat buffet. It will eat itself to death. I did this three months into my 15-month vision quest, visiting seven countries and going through at least 20 check-ins and checkouts with a friend who had negotiated three weeks off. The trip was an adrenaline-packed blast but like watching life on fastforward. It was hard for us to remember what had happened in which countries (except Amsterdam),69 we were both sick most of the time, and we were upset to have to leave some places simply because our pre-purchased flights made it so. I recommend doing the exact opposite. The alternative to binge travel—the mini-retirement—entails relocating to one place for one to six months before going home or moving to another locale. It is the antivacation in the most positive sense. Though it can be relaxing, the mini-retirement is not an escape from your life but a reexamination of it—the creation of a blank slate. Following elimination and automation, what would you be escaping from? Rather than seeking to see the world through photo ops between foreign-but-familiar hotels, we aim to experience it at a speed that lets it change us. This is also different from a sabbatical. Sabbaticals are often viewed much like retirement: as a one-time event. Savor it now while you can. The mini-retirement is defined as recurring—it is a lifestyle. I currently take three or four mini-retirements per year and know dozens who do the same. Sometimes these sojourns take me around the world; oftentimes they take me around the corner—Yosemite, Tahoe, Carmel—but to a different world psychologically, where meetings, e-mail, and phone calls don't exist for a set period of time. Purging the Demons: Emotional Freedom This is the very perfection of a man, to find out his own im perfection. —SAINT AUGUSTINE (354 A.D.–430 A.D.) True freedom is much more than having enough income and time to do what you want. It is quite possible—actually the rule rather than the exception—to have financial and time freedom but still be caught in the throes of the rat race. One cannot be free from the stresses of a speed- and size-obsessed culture until you are free from the materialistic addictions, time-famine mind-set, and comparative impulses that created it in the first place. This takes time. The effect is not cumulative, and no number of two-week (also called "too weak")70 sightseeing trips can replace one good walkabout.71 In the experience of those I've interviewed, it takes two to three months just to unplug from obsolete routines and become aware of just how much we distract ourselves with constant motion. Can you have a two-hour dinner with Spanish friends without getting anxious? Can you get accustomed to a small town where all businesses take a siesta for two hours in the afternoon and then close at 4:00 P.M.? If not, you need to ask, Why? Learn to slow down. Get lost intentionally. Observe how you judge both yourself and those around you. Chances are that it's been a while. Take at least two months to disincorporate old habits and rediscover yourself without the reminder of a looming return flight. The Financial Realities: It Just Gets Better The economic argument for mini-retirements is the icing on the cake. Four days in a decent hotel or a week for two at a nice hostel costs the same as a month in a nice posh apartment. If you relocate, the expenses abroad also begin to replace—often at much lower cost—bills you can then cancel stateside. Here are some actual monthly figures from recent travels. Highlights from both South America and Europe are shown side by side to prove that luxury is limited by your creativity and familiarity with the locale, not gross currency devaluation in third-world countries. It will be obvious that I did not survive on bread and begging—I lived like a rock star—and both experiences could be done for less than 50% of what I spent. My goal was enjoyment and not austere survival.

Most excuses not to travel are exactly that—excuses. I've been there, so this isn't a holier-than-thou sermon. I know too well that it's easier to live with ourselves if we cite an external reason for inaction. I've since met paraplegics and the deaf, senior citizens and single mothers, home owners and the poor, all of whom have sought and found excellent life-changing reasons for extended travel instead of dwelling on the million small reasons against it. Most of the concerns above are addressed in the Q&A, but one in particular requires a bit of preemptive nerve calming. It's 10:00 P.M. Do You Know Where Your Children Are? The prime fear of all parents prior to their first international trip is somehow losing a child in the shuffle. The good news is that if you are comfortable taking your kids to New York, San Francisco, Washington, D.C., or London, you will have even less to worry about in the starting cities I recommend in the Q&A. There are fewer guns and violent crimes in all of them compared to most large U.S. cities. The likelihood of problems is decreased further when travel is less airport and hotel-hopping among strangers and more relocation to a second home: a mini-retirement. But still, what if? Jen Errico, a single mother who took her two children on a five-month world tour, had a more acute fear than most, one that often woke her at 2:00 A.M. in a cold sweat: What if something happens to me? She wanted to prime her kids for worst-case scenario but didn't want to scare them to death, so—like all good mothers—she made it a game: Who can best memorize the itineraries, hotel addresses, and Mom's phone number? She had emergency contacts in each country whose numbers were loaded into the speed dial of her cell phone, which had global roaming. In the end, nothing happened. Now she's planning to move to a ski chalet in Europe and send her kids to school in multilingual France. Success begets success. She was most afraid in Singapore, and in retrospect, it was where she had the least reason to be worried (she took her kids to South Africa, among other places). She was scared because it was the first stop and she was unaccustomed to traveling with her kids. It was perception, not reality. Robin Malinsky-Rummell, who spent a year traveling through South America with her husband and seven-year-old son, was warned by friends and family not to visit Argentina after their devaluation riots in 2001. She did her homework, decided that the fear was unfounded, and proceeded to have the time of her life in Patagonia. When she told locals that she was originally from New York, their eyes widened and jaws dropped: "I saw those buildings blow up on TV! I would never go to such a dangerous place!" Don't assume that places abroad are more dangerous than your hometown. Most aren't. Robin is convinced, as are other NR parents, that people use children as an excuse to stay in their comfort zones. It's an easy excuse not to do something adventurous. How to overcome the fear? Robin recommends two things: 1. Before embarking on a long international trip with your children for the first time, take a trial run for a few weeks. 2. For each stop, arrange a week of language classes that begin upon arrival and take advantage of transportation from the airport if available. The school staff will often handle apartment rentals for you, and you will be able to make friends and learn the area before setting off on your own. But what if your concern isn't so much losing your children but losing your mind because of your children? Several families interviewed for this book recommended the oldest persuasive tool known to man: bribery. Each child is given some amount of virtual cash, 25–50 cents, for each hour of good behavior. The same amount is subtracted from their accounts for breaking the rules. All purchases for fun—whether souvenirs, ice cream, or otherwise—come out of their own individual accounts. No balance, no goodies. This often requires more self-control on the part of the parents than the children. How to Get Airfare at 50–80% Off This is not a book on budget travel. Most of the cost-cutting recommendations found in such guides are designed with the binge traveler in mind. For someone embarking on a mini-retirement, an extra $150 for hassle-free airfare amortized over two months is a better deal than 20 hours of manipulating frequent-flier points on an unknown airline or chasing questionable deals.

Following two weeks of research, I once bought a one-way standby ticket to Europe for $120. I arrived at JFK brimming with enthusiasm and confidence—look at all these schmucks paying retail!—and 90% of the "participating" airlines refused my ticket. Those that didn't were booked for weeks solid. I ended up staying in a hotel for two nights for a $300 tab, filing a complaint with AMEX, and eventually calling 1– 800-FLY-EUROPE from the JFK terminal in frustration. I bought a round-trip ticket to London on Virgin Atlantic for $300 and left an hour later. The same ticket cost more than $700 a week earlier. After 25 countries, I've found a few simple strategies that get you 90% of the possible savings without wasting time or producing migraines. 1. Use credit cards with reward points for large muse-related advertising and manufacturing expenses. I am not spending more money to get pennies on the dollar—these costs are inevitable, so I capitalize on them. This alone gets me a free round-trip international ticket each three months. 2. Purchase tickets far in advance (three months or more) or last minute, and aim for both departure and return between Tues day and Thursday. Long-term travel planning turns me off and can be expensive if plans change, so I opt for purchasing all tickets in the last four or five days prior to target departure. The value of empty seats is $0 as soon as the flight takes off, so true last-minute seats are cheap.

When More Is Less: Cutting the Clutter Human beings have the capacity to learn to want almost any conceivable material object. Given, then, the emergence of a modern industrial culture capable of producing almost anything, the time is ripe for opening the storehouse of infinite need! ... It is the modern Pandora's box, and its plagues are loose upon the world. —JULES HENRY To be free, to be happy and fruitful, can only be attained through sacrifice of many common but overestimated things —ROBERT HENRI I know the son of one deca-millionaire, a personal friend of Bill Gates, who now manages private investments and ranches. He has accumulated an assortment of beautiful homes over the last decade, each with full-time cooks, servants, cleaners, and support staff. How does he feel about having a home in each time zone? It's a pain in the ass! He feels like he's working for his staff, who spend more time in his homes than he does. Extended travel is the perfect excuse to reverse the damage of years of consuming as much as you can afford. It's time to get rid of clutter disguised as necessities before you drag a five-piece Samsonite set around the world. That is hell on earth. I'm not going to tell you to walk around in a robe and sandals scowling at people who have televisions. I hate that kashi-crunching holier-than-thou stuff. Turning you into a possession-less scribe is not my intention. Let's face it, though: There are tons of things in your home and life that you don't use, need, or even particularly want. They just came into your life as impulsive flotsam and jetsam and never found a good exit. Whether you're aware of it or not, this clutter creates indecision and distractions, consuming attention and making unfettered happiness a real chore. It is impossible to realize how distracting all the crap is—whether porcelain dolls, sports cars, or ragged T-shirts—until you get rid of it. Prior to my 15-month trip, I was stressed about how to fit all of my belongings into a 14 x 10-foot rental storage space. Then I realized a few things: I would never reread the business magazines I'd saved, I wore the same five shirts and four pairs of pants 90% of the time, it was about time for new furniture, and I never used the outdoor grill or lawn furniture. Even getting rid of things I never used proved to be like a capitalist short-circuit. It was hard to toss things I had once thought were valuable enough to spend money on. The first ten minutes of sorting through clothing was like choosing which child of mine should live or die. I hadn't exercised my throwing-out muscles in some time. It was a struggle to put nice Christmas clothing I'd never worn into the "go" pile and just as hard to separate myself from worn and ragged clothing I had for sentimental reasons. Once I'd passed through the first few tough decisions, though, the momentum had been built and it was a breeze. I donated all of the seldom-worn clothing to Goodwill. The furniture took less than 10 hours to offload using Craigslist, and though I was paid less than 50% of the retail prices for some and nothing for others, who cared? I'd used and abused them for five years and would get a new set when I landed back in the U.S. I gave the grill and lawn furniture to my friend, who lit up like a kid at Christmas. I had made his month. It felt wonderful and I had an extra $300 in pocket change to cover at least a few weeks of rent abroad. I created 40% more space in my apartment and hadn't even grazed the surface. It wasn't the extra physical space that I felt most. It was the extra mental space. It was as if I had 20 mental applications running simultaneously before, and now I had just one or two. My thinking was clearer and I was much, much happier. I asked every vagabond interviewee in this book what their one recommendation would be for first-time extended travelers. The answer was unanimous: Take less with you. The overpacking impulse is hard to resist. The solution is to set what I call a "settling fund." Rather than pack for all contingencies, I bring the absolute minimum and allocate $100–300 for purchasing things after I arrive and as I travel. I no longer take toiletries or more than a week's worth of clothing. It's a blast. Finding shaving cream or a dress shirt overseas can produce an adventure in and of itself. Pack as if you were coming back in one week. Here are the bare essentials, listed in order of importance: 1. One week of clothing appropriate to the season, including one semiformal shirt and pair of pants or skirt for customs. Think T-shirts, one pair of shorts, and a multipurpose pair of jeans. 2. Backup photocopies or scanned copies of all important documents: health insurance, passport/visa, credit cards, debit cards, etc. 3. Debit cards, credit cards, and $200 worth of small bills in local currency (traveler's checks are not accepted in most places and are a hassle) 4. Small cable bike lock for securing luggage while in transit or in hostels; a small padlock for lockers if needed 5. Electronic dictionaries for target languages (book versions are too slow to be of use in conversation) and small grammar guides or texts 6. One broad-strokes travel guide That's it.73 To laptop or not to laptop? Unless you are a writer, I vote no. It's far too cumbersome and distracting. Using GoToMyPC to access your home computer from Internet cafés encourages the habit we want to develop: making the best use of time instead of killing it. The Bora-Bora Dealmaker BAFFIN ISLAND, NUNAVUT Josh Steinitz74 stood at the edge of the world and stared in amazement. He dug his boots into the six feet of sea ice and the unicorns danced. Ten narwhals—rare cousins of the beluga—came to the surface and pointed their six-foot-plus spiral tusks toward the heavens. The pod of 3,000-pound whales then fell into the depths once again. The narwhals are deep divers—more than 3,000 feet in some cases—so Josh had at least 20 minutes until their reappearance. It seemed appropriate that he was with the narwhals. Their name came from Old Norse and referred to their mottled white and blue skin. Náhvalr—corpse man. He smiled as he had done often in the last few years. Josh himself was a dead man walking. One year after graduating from college, Josh found out that he had oral squamous carcinoma—cancer. He had plans to be a management consultant. He had plans to be lots of things. Suddenly none of it mattered. Less than half of those who suffered from this particular type of cancer survived.75 The reaper didn't discriminate and came without warning. It became clear that the biggest risk in life wasn't making mistakes but regret: missing out on things. He could never go back and recapture years spent doing something he disliked. Two years later and cancer-free, Josh set off on an indefinite global walkabout, covering expenses as a freelance writer. He later became the cofounder of a website that provides customized itineraries to would-be vagabonds. His executive status didn't lessen his mobile addiction. He was as comfortable cutting deals from the overwater bungalows of Bora-Bora as he was in the log cabins of the Swiss Alps. He once took a call from a client while at Camp Muir on Mt. Rainier. The client needed to confirm some sales numbers and asked Josh about all the wind in the background. Josh's answer: "I'm standing at 10,000 feet on a glacier and this afternoon the wind is whipping us down the mountain." The client said he'd let Josh get back to what he was doing. Another client called Josh while he was leaving a Balinese temple and heard the gongs in the background. The client asked Josh if he was in church. Josh wasn't quite sure what to say. All that came out was, "Yes?" Back among the narwhals, Josh had a few minutes before heading to base camp to avoid polar bears. Twenty-four-hour daylight meant that he had much to share with his friends back in the land of cubicles. He sat down on the ice and produced his satellite phone and laptop from a waterproof bag. He began his e-mail in the usual way: "I know you're all sick of seeing me have so much fun, but guess where I am?" Q&A: QUESTIONS AND ACTIONS It is fatal to know too much at the outcome: boredom comes as quickly to the traveler who knows his route as to the novelist who is overcertain of his plot. —PAUL THEROUX, To the Ends of the Earth If this is your first time considering a commitment to the mobile lifestyle and longterm adventuring, I envy you! Making the jump and entering the new worlds that await is like upgrading your role in life from passenger to pilot. The bulk of this Q&A will focus on the precise steps that you should take—and the countdown timeline you can use—when preparing for your first mini-retirement. Most steps can be eliminated or condensed once you get one trip under your belt. Some of the steps are one-time events, after which subsequent mini-retirements will require a maximum of two to three weeks of preparation. It now takes me three afternoons. Grab a pencil and paper—this will be fun. 1. Take an asset and cash-flow snapshot. Set two sheets of paper on a table. Use one to record all assets and corresponding values, including bank accounts, retirement accounts, stocks, bonds, home, and so forth. On the second, draw a line down the middle and write down all incoming cash flow (salary, muse income, investment income, etc.) and outgoing expenses (mortgage, rent, car payments, etc.). What can you eliminate that is either seldom used or that creates stress or distraction without adding a lot of value? 2. Fear-set a one-year mini-retirement in a dream location in Europe. Use the questions from chapter 3 to evaluate your worst-case-scenario fears and evaluate the real potential consequences. Except in rare cases, most will be avoidable and the rest will be reversible. 3. Choose a location for your actual mini-retirement. Where to start? This is the big question. There are two options that I advocate: 1. Choose a starting point and then wander until you find your second home. This is what I did with a one-way ticket to London, vagabonding throughout Europe until I fell in love with Berlin, where I remained for three months. 2. Scout a region and then settle in your favorite spot. This is what I did with a tour of Central and South America, where I spent one to four weeks in each of several cities, after which I returned to my favorite—Buenos Aires—for six months. It is possible to take a mini-retirement in your own country, but the transformative effect is hampered if you are surrounded by people who carry the same socially reinforced baggage. I recommend choosing an overseas location that will seem foreign but that isn't dangerous. I box, race motorcycles, and do all sorts of macho things, but I draw the line at favelas, 76 civilians with machine guns, pedestrians with machetes, and social strife. Cheap is good, but bullet holes are bad. Check the U.S. Department of State for travel warnings before booking tickets (http:// travel.state.gov). Here are just a few of my favorite starting points. Feel free to choose other locations. The most lifestyle for the dollar is underlined: Argentina (Buenos Aires, Córdoba), China (Shanghai, Hong Kong, Taipei), Japan (Tokyo, Osaka), England (London), Ireland (Galway), Thailand (Bangkok, Chiang Mai), Germany (Berlin, Munich), Norway (Oslo), Australia (Sydney), New Zealand (Queenstown), Italy (Rome, Milan, Florence), Spain (Madrid, Valencia, Sevilla), and Holland (Amsterdam). In all of these places, it is possible to live well while spending little. I spend less in Tokyo than in California because I know it well. Hip, recently gentrified artist areas, not unlike the Brooklyn of 10 years ago, can be found in almost all cities. The one place I can't seem to find a decent lunch for less than $20 U.S.? London. Here are a few exotic places I don't recommend for vagabonding virgins, though veterans can make them all work: all countries in Africa, the Middle East, or Central and South America (excepting Costa Rica and Argentina). Mexico City and Mexican border areas are also a bit too kidnap-happy to make it onto my favorites list. 4. Prepare for your trip. Here's the countdown. Three months out—Eliminate Get used to minimalism before the departure. Here are the questions to ask and act upon, even if you never plan to leave: What is the 20% of my belongings that I use 80% of the time? Eliminate the other 80% in clothing, magazines, books, and all else. Be ruthless—you can always repurchase things you can't live without. Which belongings create stress in my life? This could relate to maintenance costs (money and energy), insurance, monthly expenses, time consumption, or simple distraction. Eliminate, eliminate, eliminate. If you sell even a few expensive items, it could finance a good portion of your mini-retirement. Don't rule out the car and home. It's always possible to purchase either upon your return, often losing no money in the process. Check current health insurance coverage for extended overseas travel. Get the wheels in motion to rent, swap, or sell your home—renting out is most recommended by serial vagabonds—or end your apartment lease and move all belongings into storage. In all cases where doubts crop up, ask yourself, "If I had a gun to my head and had to do it, how would I do it?" It's not as hard as you think. Two months out—Automate After eliminating the excess, contact companies (including suppliers) that bill you regularly and set up autopayment with credit cards that have reward points. Telling them that you will be traveling the world for a year often persuades them to accept credit cards rather than chase you around the planet like Carmen Sandiego. For the credit card companies themselves and others that refuse, arrange automatic debit from your checking account. Set up online banking and bill payment. Set up all companies that won't take credit cards or automatic debit as online payees. Set these scheduled checks for $15–20 more than expected when dealing with utilities and other variable expenses. This will cover miscellaneous fees, prevent time-consuming billing problems, and accrue as a credit. Cancel paper bank and credit card statement delivery. Get bank-issued credit cards for all checking accounts—generally one for business and one for personal—and set the cash advances to $0 to minimize abuse potential. Leave these cards at home, as they are just for emergency overdraft protection. Give a trusted member of your family and/or your accountant power of attorney, which gives that person authority to sign documents (tax filings and checks, for example) in your name. Nothing screws up foreign fun faster than having to sign original documents when faxes are unacceptable. One month out— Speak to the manager of your local post office and have all mail forwarded to a friend, family member, or personal assistant,78who will be paid $100–200 per month to email you brief descriptions of all nonjunk mail each Monday. Get all required and recommended immunizations and vaccinations for your target region. Check the Centers for Disease Control . Note that proof of immunizations is sometimes required to pass through foreign customs. Set up a trial account with GoToMyPC or similar remote-access software and take a dry run to ensure that there are no technological glitches. If resellers (or distributors) still send you checks—the fulfillment house should handle customer checks at this point—do one of three things: give the resellers direct bank deposit information (ideal), have the fulfillment house handle these checks (second choice), or have the resellers pay via PayPal or mail checks to one of the people you are trusting with power of attorney (far third). In the last case, give the person with power of attorney deposit slips so he or she can sign or stamp and mail in the checks. It is convenient to become a member of a large bank (Bank of America, Wells Fargo, Washington Mutual, Citibank, etc.) with branches near the person assisting you so that they can drop off the deposits while running other errands. No need to move all accounts to this bank if you don't want to; just open a single new account that is used solely for these deposits. Two weeks out— Scan all identification, health insurance, and credit/debit cards into a computer from which you can print multiple copies, several to be left with family members and several to be taken with you in separate bags. E-mail the scanned file to yourself so that you can access it while abroad if you lose the paper copies. If you are an entrepreneur, downgrade your cell phone to the cheapest plan and set up a voicemail greeting that states, "I am currently overseas on business. Please do not leave a voicemail, as I will not be checking it while gone. Please send me an e-mail at __@__.com if the matter is important. Thank you for your understanding." Then set up e-mail autoresponders that indicate responses could take up to seven days (or whatever you decide for frequency) due to international business travel. If you are an employee, consider getting a quad-band or GSM-compatible cell phone so that the boss can contact you. Get a BlackBerry only if your boss will be checking to see if you are working via e-mail. Be sure to disable the dead giveaway "Sent from a BlackBerry" signature on outgoing e-mail! Other options include using a SkypeIn account that forwards to your foreign cell phone (my preference) or a Vonage IP box that allows you to receive landline calls anywhere in the world via a phone number that begins with your home area code. Find an apartment for your ultimate mini-retirement destination or reserve a hostel or hotel at your starting point for three to four days. Reserving an apartment before you arrive is riskier and will be much more expensive than using the latter three to four days to find an apartment. I recommend hostels for the starting point if possible— not for cost considerations but because the staff and fellow travelers are more knowledgeable and helpful with relocations.

Get foreign medical evacuation insurance if needed for peace of mind. This tends to be redundant if you are in a first-world country and can buy local insurance to augment your own, which I do, and it is useless if you are a 10-hour flight from civilization. I had evacuation insurance in Panama, as it's a 2-hour flight from Miami, but I didn't bother elsewhere. Don't freak out about this; it's just as true if you're in the middle of nowhere in the middle of the U.S. One week out— Decide on a schedule for routine batched tasks such as e-mail, online banking, etc. to eliminate excuses for senseless pseudo-work procrasterbating. I suggest Monday mornings for checking e-mail and online banking. The first and third Mondays of the month can be used for checking credit cards and making other online payments such as affiliates. These promises to yourself will be the hardest to keep, so make a commitment now and expect serious withdrawal cravings. Save important documents—including the scan of your identification, insurance, and credit/debit cards—to a small handheld storage device that plugs into a computer USB port. Move all things out of your home or apartment into storage, pack a single small backpack and carry-on bag for the adventure, and move in briefly with a family member or friend. Two days out— Put remaining automobiles into storage or a friend's garage. Put fuel stabilizer like Sta-Bil in the gas tanks, disconnect the negative leads from batteries to prevent drain, and put the vehicles on jack stands to prevent tire and shock damage. Cancel all auto insurance except for theft coverage.

To be engrossed by something outside ourselves is a powerful antidote for the rational mind, the mind that so frequently has its head up its own ass. —ANNE LAMOTT, Bird by Bird There is not enough time to do all the nothing we want to do. —BILL WATTERSON, creator of the Calvin and Hobbes cartoon strip KING'S CROSS , LONDON

I stumbled into the deli across the cobblestone street and ordered a prosciutto sandwich. It was 10:33 A.M. now, the fifth time I'd checked the time, and the twentieth time I'd asked myself, "What the &%$# am I going to do today?" The best answer I had come up with so far was: get a sandwich. Thirty minutes earlier, I had woken up without an alarm clock for the first time in four years, fresh off arriving from JFK the night before. I had soooo been looking forward to it: awakening to musical birdsong outside, sitting up in bed with a smile, smelling the aroma of freshly brewed coffee, and stretching out overhead like a cat in the shade of a Spanish villa. Magnificent. It turned out more like this: bolt upright as if blasted with a foghorn, grab clock, curse, jump out of bed in underwear to check email, remember that I was forbidden to do so, curse again, look for my host and former classmate, realize that he was off to work like the rest of the world, and proceed to have a panic attack. I spent the rest of the day in a haze, wandering from museum to botanical garden to museum as if on rinse and repeat, avoiding Internet cafés with some vague sense of guilt. I needed a to-do list to feel productive and so put down things like "eat dinner." This was going to be a lot harder than I had thought. Postpartum Depression: It's Normal Man is so made that he can only find relaxation from one kind of labor by taking up another. —ANATOLE FRANCE, author of The Crime of Sylvestre Bonnard I've Got More Money and Time Than I Ever Dreamed Possible ... Why Am I Depressed? It's a good question with a good answer. Just be glad you're figuring this out now and not at the end of life! The retired and ultrarich are often unfulfilled and neurotic for the same reason: too much idle time. But wait a second ... Isn't more time what we're after? Isn't that what this book is all about? No, not at all. Too much free time is no more than fertilizer for self-doubt and assorted mental tail-chasing. Subtracting the bad does not create the good. It leaves a vacuum. Decreasing income-driven work isn't the end goal. Living more—and becoming more—is. In the beginning, the external fantasies will be enough, and there is nothing wrong with this. I cannot overemphasize the importance of this period. Go nuts and live your dreams. This is not superficial or selfish. It is critical to stop repressing yourself and get out of the postponement habit. Let's suppose you decide to dip your toe in dreams like relocating to the Caribbean for island-hopping or taking a safari in the Serengeti. It will be wonderful and unforgettable, and you should do it. There will come a time, however—be it three weeks or three years later—when you won't be able to drink another piña colada or photograph another damn red-assed baboon. Self-criticism and existential panic attacks start around this time. But This Is What I Always Wanted! How Can I Be Bored?! Don't freak out and fuel the fire. This is normal among all high-performers who downshift after working hard for a long time. The smarter and more goal-oriented you are, the tougher these growing pains will be. Learning to replace the perception of time famine with appreciation of time abundance is like going from triple espressos to decaf. But there's more! Retirees get depressed for a second reason, and you will too: social isolation. Offices are good for some things: free bad coffee and complaining thereof, gossip and commiserating, stupid video clips via e-mail with even stupider comments, and meetings that accomplish nothing but kill a few hours with a few laughs. The job itself might be a dead end, but it's the web of human interactions—the social environment—that keeps us there. Once liberated, this automatic tribal unit disappears, which makes the voices in your head louder. Don't be afraid of the existential or social challenges. Freedom is like a new sport. In the beginning, the sheer newness of it is exciting enough to keep things interesting at all times. Once you have learned the basics, though, it becomes clear that to be even a half-decent player requires some serious practice.

Frustrations and Doubts: You're Not Alone People say that what we are seeking is a meaning for life. I don't think this is what we're really seeking. I think what we're seeking is an experience of being alive. —JOSEPH CAMPBELL, The Power of Myth Once you eliminate the 9–5 and the rubber hits the road, it's not all roses and white-sand bliss, though much of it can be. Without the distraction of deadlines and co-workers, the big questions (such as "What does it all mean?") become harder to fend off for a later time. In a sea of infinite options, decisions also become harder— What the hell should I do with my life? It's like senior year in college all over again. Like all innovators ahead of the curve, you will have frightening moments of doubt. Once past the kid-in-a-candy-store phase, the comparative impulse will creep in. The rest of the world will continue with its 9–5 grind, and you'll begin to question your decision to step off the treadmill. Common doubts and self-flagellation include the following: 1. Am I really doing this to be more free and lead a better life, or am I just lazy? 2. Did I quit the rat race because it's bad, or just because I couldn't hack it? Did I just cop out? 3. Is this as good as it gets? Perhaps I was better off when I was following orders and ignorant of the possibilities. It was easier at least. 4. Am I really successful or just kidding myself? 5. Have I lowered my standards to make myself a winner? Are my friends, who are now making twice as much as three years ago, really on the right track? 6. Why am I not happy? I can do anything and I'm still not happy. Do I even deserve it? Most of this can be overcome as soon as we recognize it for what it is: outdated comparisons using the more-is-better and money-as-success mind-sets that got us into trouble to begin with. Even so, there is a more profound observation to be made. These doubts invade the mind when nothing else fills it. Think of a time when you felt 100% alive and undistracted—in the zone. Chances are that it was when you were completely focused in the moment on something external: someone or something else. Sports and sex are two great examples. Lacking an external focus, the mind turns inward on itself and creates problems to solve, even if the problems are undefined or unimportant. If you find a focus, an ambitious goal that seems impossible and forces you to grow,81 these doubts disappear. In the process of searching for a new focus, it is almost inevitable that the "big" questions will creep in. There is pressure from pseudo-philosophers everywhere to cast aside the impertinent and answer the eternal. Two popular examples are "What is the meaning of life?" and "What is the point of it all?" There are many more, ranging from the introspective to the ontological, but I have one answer for almost all of them—I don't answer them at all. I'm no nihilist. In fact, I've spent more than a decade investigating the mind and concept of meaning, a quest that has taken me from the neuroscience laboratories of top universities to the halls of religious institutions worldwide. The conclusion after it all is surprising. I am 100% convinced that most big questions we feel compelled to face—handed down through centuries of overthinking and mistranslation—use terms so undefined as to make attempting to answer them a complete waste of time.82 This isn't depressing. It's liberating. Consider the question of questions: What is the meaning of life? If pressed, I have but one response: It is the characteristic state or condition of a living organism. "But that's just a definition," the questioner will retort, "that's not what I mean at all." What do you mean, then? Until the question is clear—each term in it defined—there is no point in answering it. The "meaning" of "life" question is unanswerable without further elaboration. Before spending time on a stress-inducing question, big or otherwise, ensure that the answer is "yes" to the following two questions: 1. Have I decided on a single meaning for each term in this question? 2. Can an answer to this question be acted upon to improve things? "What is the meaning of life?" fails the first and thus the second. Questions about things beyond your sphere of influence like "What if the train is late tomorrow?" fail the second and should thus be ignored. These are not worthwhile questions. If you can't define it or act upon it, forget it. If you take just this point from this book, it will put you in the top 1% of performers in the world and keep most philosophical distress out of your life. Sharpening your logical and practical mental toolbox is not being an atheist or unspiritual. It's not being crass and it's not being superficial. It's being smart and putting your effort where it can make the biggest difference for yourself and others. The Point of It All: Drumroll, Please What man actually needs is not a tensionless state but rather the striving and struggling for a worthwhile goal, a freely chosen task. —VIKTOR E.

FRANKL, Holocaust survivor; author of Man's Search for Meaning I believe that life exists to be enjoyed and that the most important thing is to feel good about yourself. Each person will have his or her own vehicles for both, and those vehicles will change over time. For some, the answer will be working with orphans, and for others, it will be composing music. I have a personal answer to both—to love, be loved, and never stop learning—but I don't expect that to be universal. Some criticize a focus on self-love and enjoyment as selfish or hedonistic, but it's neither. Enjoying life and helping others—or feeling good about yourself and increasing the greater good—are no more mutually exclusive than being agnostic and leading a moral life. One does not preclude the other. Let's assume we agree on this. It still leaves the question, "What can I do with my time to enjoy life and feel good about myself?" I can't offer a single answer that will fit all people, but, based on the dozens of fulfilled NR I've interviewed, there are two components that are fundamental: continual learning and service. Learning Unlimited: Sharpening the Saw Americans who travel abroad for the first time are often shocked to discover that, despite all the progress that has been made in the last 30 years, many foreign people still speak in foreign languages. —DAVE BARRY To live is to learn. I see no other option. This is why I've felt compelled to quit or be fired from jobs within the first six months or so. The learning curve flattens out and I get bored.

One would expect me to mention service in this chapter, and here it is. Like all before it, the twist is a bit different. Service to me is simple: doing something that improves life besides your own. This is not the same as philanthropy. Philanthropy is the altruistic concern for the well-being of mankind—human life. Human life has long been focused on the exclusion of the environment and the rest of the food chain, hence our current race to imminent extinction. Serves us right. The world does not exist solely for the betterment and multiplication of mankind. Before I start chaining myself to trees and saving the dart frogs, though, I should take my own advice: Do not become a cause snob. How can you help starving children in Africa when there are starving children in Los Angeles? How can you save the whales when homeless people are freezing to death? How does doing volunteer research on coral destruction help those people who need help now? Children, please. Everything out there needs help, so don't get baited into "my cause can beat up your cause" arguments with no right answer. There are no qualitative or quantitative comparisons that make sense. The truth is this: Those thousands of lives you save could contribute to a famine that kills millions, or that one bush in Bolivia that you protect could hold the cure for cancer. The downstream effects are unknown. Do your best and hope for the best. If you're improving the world—however you define that—consider your job well done. Service isn't limited to saving lives or the environment either. It can also improve life. If you are a musician and put a smile on the faces of thousands or millions, I view that as service. If you are a mentor and change the life of one child for the better, the world has been improved. Improving the quality of life in the world is in no fashion inferior to adding more lives. Service is an attitude. Find the cause or vehicle that interests you most and make no apologies. Q&A: QUESTIONS AND ACTIONS Adults are always asking kids what they want to be when they grow up because they are looking for ideas. —PAULA POUNDSTONE The miracle is not to walk on water. The miracle is to walk on the green earth, dwelling deeply in the present moment and feeling truly alive. —THICH NHAT HANH But I can't just travel, learn languages, or fight for one cause for the rest of my life! Of course you can't. That's not my suggestion at all. These are just good "life hubs"— starting points that lead to opportunities and experiences that otherwise wouldn't be found. There is no right answer to the question "What should I do with my life?" Forget "should" altogether. The next step—and that's all it is—is pursuing something, it matters little what, that seems fun or rewarding. Don't be in a rush to jump into a fulltime long-term commitment. Take time to find something that calls to you, not just the first acceptable form of surrogate work. That calling will, in turn, lead you to something else. Here is a good sequence for getting started that dozens of NR have used with success. 1. Revisit ground zero: Do nothing. Before we can escape the goblins of the mind, we need to face them. Principal among them is speed addiction. It is hard to recalibrate your internal clock without taking a break from constant overstimulation. Travel and the impulse to see a million things can exacerbate this.

New Rich Mistakes

If you don't make mistakes, you're not working on hard enough problems. And that's a big mistake. —FRANK WILCZEK, 2004 Nobel Prize winner in physics Ho imparato che niente e impossibile, e anche che quasi niente e facile ... (I've learned that nothing is impossible, and that almost nothing is easy ...) —ARTICOLO 31 (Italian rap group), "Un Urlo" Mistake are the name of the game in lifestyle design. It requires fighting impulse after impulse from the old world of retirement-based life deferral. Here are the slipups you will make. Don't get frustrated. It's all part of the process. 1. Losing sight of dreams and falling into work for work's sake (W4W) Please reread the introduction and next chapter of this book whenever you feel yourself falling into this trap. Everyone does it, but many get stuck and never get out. 2. Micromanaging and e-mailing to fill time Set the responsibilities, problem scenarios and rules, and limits of autonomous decision-making—then stop, for the sanity of everyone involved. 3. Handling problems your outsourcers or co-workers can handle 4. Helping outsourcers or co-workers with the same problem more than once, or with noncrisis problems Give them if-then rules for solving all but the largest problems. Give them the freedom to act without your input, set the limits in writing, and then emphasize in writing that you will not respond to help with problems that are covered by these rules. In my particular case, all outsourcers have at their discretion the ability to fix any problem that will cost less than $400. At the end of each month or quarter, depending on the outsourcer, I review how their decisions have affected profit and adjust the rules accordingly, often adding new rules based on their good decisions and creative solutions. 5. Chasing customers, particularly unqualified or international prospects, when you have sufficient cash flow to finance your nonfinancial pursuits 6. Answering e-mail that will not result in a sale or that can be answered by a FAQ or auto-responder For a good example of an auto-responder that directs people to the appropriate information and outsourcers.

7. Working where you live, sleep, or should relax Separate your environments— designate a single space for work and solely work—or you will never be able to escape it.84 8. Not performing a thorough 80/20 analysis every two to four weeks for your business and personal life 9. Striving for endless perfection rather than great or simply good enough, whether in your personal or professional life Recognize that this is often just another W4W excuse. Most endeavors are like learning to speak a foreign language: to be correct 95% of the time requires six months of concentrated effort, whereas to be correct 98% of the time requires 20–30 years. Focus on great for a few things and good enough for the rest. Perfection is a good ideal and direction to have, but recognize it for what it is: an impossible destination. 10. Blowing minutiae and small problems out of proportion as an excuse to work 11. Making non-time-sensitive issues urgent in order to justify work How many times do I have to say it? Focus

on life outside of your bank accounts, as scary as that void can be in the initial stages. If you cannot find meaning in your life, it is your responsibility as a human being to create it, whether that is fulfilling dreams or finding work that gives you purpose and self-worth—ideally a combination of both. 12. Viewing one product, job, or project as the end-all and be-all of your existence Life is too short to waste, but it is also too long to be a pessimist or nihilist. Whatever you're doing now is just a stepping-stone to the next project or adventure. Any rut you get into is one you can get yourself out of. Doubts are no more than a signal for action of some type. When in doubt or overwhelmed, take a break and 80/20 both business and personal activities and relationships. 13. Ignoring the social rewards of life Surround yourself with smiling, positive people who have absolutely nothing to do with work. Create your muses alone if you must, but do not live your life alone. Happiness shared in the form of friendships and love is happiness multiplied.

There is nothing the busy man is less busied with than living; there is nothing harder to learn. —SENECA For the past 33 years, I have looked in the mirror every morning and asked myself: "If today were the last day of my life, would I want to do what I am about to do today?" And whenever the answer has been "No" for too many days in a row, I know I need to change something ... almost everything—all external expectations, all pride, all fear of embarrassment or failure—these things just fall away in the face of death, leaving only what is truly important. Remembering that you are going to die is the best way I know to avoid the trap of thinking you have something to lose.

If you're confused about life, you're not alone. There are almost seven billion of us. This isn't a problem, of course, once you realize that life is neither a problem to be solved nor a game to be won. If you are too intent on making the pieces of a nonexistent puzzle fit, you miss out on all the real fun. The heaviness of success-chasing can be replaced with a serendipitous lightness when you recognize that the only rules and limits are those we set for ourselves. So be bold and don't worry about what people think. They don't do it that often anyway.

Is it better to have the best outcome but be less satisfied, or have an acceptable outcome and be satisfied? For example, would you rather deliberate for months and get the 1 of 20 houses that's the best investment but second-guess yourself until you sell it five years later, or would you rather get a house that is 80% of the investment potential of the former (still to be sold at a profit) but never second-guess it? Tough call. Schwartz also recommends making nonreturnable purchases. I decided to keep the stupid pooch cartoons. Why? Because it's not just about being satisfied, it's about being practical. Income is renewable, but some other resources—like attention—are not. I've talked before about attention as a currency and how it determines the value of time. For example: Is your weekend really free if you find a crisis in the inbox Saturday morning that you can't address until Monday morning? Even if the inbox scan lasts 30 seconds, the preoccupation and forward projection for the subsequent 48 hours effectively deletes that experience from your life. You had time but you didn't have attention, so the time had no practical value. The choice-minimal lifestyle becomes an attractive tool when we consider two truths. 1. Considering options costs attention that then can't be spent on action or present-state awareness. 2. Attention is necessary for not only productivity but appreciation. Therefore: Too many choices = less or no productivity Too many choices = less or no appreciation Too many choices = sense of overwhelm What to do? There are six basic rules or formulas that can be used: 1. Set rules for yourself so you can automate as much decision making as possible [see the rules I use to outsource my e-mail to Canada, included at the end of this section, as an example of this]. 2. Don't provoke deliberation before you can take action. One simple example: Don't scan the inbox on Friday evening or over the weekend if you might encounter work problems that can't be addressed until Monday. 3. Don't postpone decisions just to avoid uncomfortable conversations. If an acquaintance asks you if you want to come to their house for dinner next week, and you know you won't, don't say, "I'm not sure. I'll let you know next week." Instead, use something soft but conclusive like, "Next week? I'm pretty sure I have another commitment on Thursday, but thank you for the invite. Just so I don't leave you hanging, let's assume I can't make it, but can I let you know if that changes?" Decision made. Move on. 4. Learn to make nonfatal or reversible decisions as quickly as possible. Set time limits (I won't consider options for more than 20 minutes), option limits (I'll consider no more than three options), or finance thresholds (Example: If it costs less than $100 [or the potential damage is less than $100], I'll let a virtual assistant make the judgment call). I wrote most of this post after landing at the monster that is ATL airport in Atlanta. I could have considered half a dozen types of ground transportation in 15 minutes and saved 30–40%, but I grabbed a taxi instead. To use illustrative numbers: I didn't want to sacrifice

10 attention units of my remaining 50 of 100 total potential units, since those 10 units couldn't then be spent on this article. I had about eight hours before bedtime due to time zone differences—plenty of time—but scarce usable attention after an all-nighter of fun and the cross-country flight. Fast decisions preserve usable attention for what matters. 5. Don't strive for variation—and thus increase option consideration—when it's not needed. Routine enables innovation where it's most valuable. In working with athletes, for example, it's clear that those who maintain the lowest bodyfat percentage eat the same foods over and over with little variation. I've eaten the same "slow-carb" breakfast and lunch for nearly two years,88 putting variation only into meals that I focus on for enjoyment: dinner and all meals on Saturdays. This same routine-variation distinction can be found in exercise vs. recreation. For fat loss and muscle gain (even as much as 34 pounds in four weeks), I've followed the same time—minimal exercise protocol with occasional experiments since 1996. For recreation, however, where the focus is enjoyment and not efficacy, I tend to try something new each weekend, whether climbing at Mission Cliffs in San Francisco or mountain biking from tasting to tasting in Napa. Don't confuse what should be results-driven with routine (e.g., exercise) with something enjoyment-driven that benefits from variation (e.g., recreation). 6. Regret is past-tense decision making. Eliminate complaining to minimize regret. Condition yourself to notice complaints and stop making them with a simple program like the "21-day no-complaint experiment" made famous by Will Bowen, where you wear a single bracelet and move it from one wrist to the other each time you complain. The goal is 21 days without complaining and you reset to 0 each time you slip up. This increased awareness helps prevent useless past-tense deliberation and negative emotions that improve nothing but deplete your attention. DECISION-MAKING ISN'T to be avoided—that's not the problem. Look at a good CEO or top corporate performer and you'll see a high volume of decisions. It's deliberation—the time we vacillate over and consider each decision—that's the attention consumer. Total deliberation time, not the number of decisions, determines your attention bank account balance (or debt). Let's assume you pay 10% over time by following the above rules but cut your average "decision cycle" time by an average of 40% (10 minutes reduced to 6 minutes, for example). Not only will you have much more time and attention to spend on revenue-generating activities, but you'll get greater enjoyment from what you have and experience. Consider that 10% additional cost as an investment and part

of your "ideal lifestyle tax," but not as a loss. Embrace the choice-minimal lifestyle. It's a subtle and under-exploited philosophical tool that produces dramatic increases in both output and satisfaction, all with less overwhelm. Make testing a few of the principles the first of many fast and reversible decisions. —FEBRUARY 6, 2008 The Not-to-Do List: 9 Habits to Stop Now "Not-to-do" lists are often more effective than to-do lists for upgrading performance. The reason is simple: What you don't do determines what you can do. Here are nine stressful and common habits that entrepreneurs and office workers should strive to eliminate. The bullets are followed by more detailed descriptions. Focus on one or two at a time, just as you would with high-priority to-do items. 1. Do not answer calls from unrecognized phone numbers. Feel free to surprise others, but don't be surprised. It just results in unwanted interruption or poor negotiating positions. Let it go to voicemail, and consider using a service like GrandCentral (you can listen to people leaving voicemail or receive them as text messages) or Phonetag.com (receive voicemails as e-mail). 2. Do not e-mail first thing in the morning or last thing at night. The former scrambles your priorities and plans for the day, and the latter just gives you insomnia. E-mail can wait until 10 A.M., after you've completed at least one of your critical to-do items. 3. Do not agree to meetings or calls with no clear agenda or end time. If the desired outcome is defined clearly with a stated objective and agenda listing topics/questions to cover, no meeting or call should last more than 30 minutes. Request them in advance so you "can best prepare and make good use of the time together." 4. Do not let people ramble. Forget "How's it going?" when someone calls you. Stick with "What's up?" or "I'm in the middle of getting something out, but what's going on?" A big part of GTD (Getting Things Done) is GTP—Getting To the Point. 5. Do not check e-mail constantly—"batch" and check at set times only. I belabor this point enough. Get off the cocaine pellet dispenser and focus on execution of your top to-do's instead of responding to manufactured emergencies. Set up a strategic autoresponder and check twice or thrice daily. 6. Do not over-communicate with low-profit, high-maintenance customers. There is no sure path to success, but the surest path to failure is trying to please everyone. Do an 80/20 analysis of your customer base in two ways—which 20% are producing 80%+ of my profit, and which 20% are consuming 80%+ of my time? Then put the loudest and least productive on autopilot by citing a change in company policies. Send them an e-mail with new rules as bullet points: number of permissible phone calls, e-mail response time, minimum orders, etc. Offer to point them to another provider if they aren't able to adopt the new policies. 7. Do not work more to fix overwhelmingness—prioritize. If you don't prioritize, everything seems urgent and important. If you define the single most important task for each day, almost nothing seems urgent or important. Oftentimes, it's just a matter of letting little bad things happen (return a phone call late and apologize, pay a small late fee, lose an unreasonable customer, etc.) to get the big important things done. The answer to overwhelmingness is not spinning more plates— or doing more—it's defining the few things that can really fundamentally change your business and life. 8. Do not carry a cell phone or Crackberry 24/7. Take at least one day off of digital leashes per week. Turn them off or, better still, leave them in the garage or in the car. I do this on at least Saturday, and I recommend you leave the phone at home if you go out for dinner. So what if you return a phone call an hour later or the next morning? As one reader put it to a miffed co-worker who worked 24/7 and expected the same: "I'm not the president of the U.S. No one should need me at 8 P.M. at night. OK, you didn't get a hold of me. But what bad happened?" The answer? Nothing. 9. Do not expect work to fill a void that non-work relationships and activities should. Work is not all of life. Your co-workers shouldn't be your only friends. Schedule life and defend it just as you would an important business meeting. Never tell yourself "I'll just get it done this weekend." Review Parkinson's Law and force yourself to cram within tight hours so your per-hour productivity doesn't fall through the floor. Focus, get the critical few done, and get out. E-mailing all weekend is no way to spend the little time you have on this planet. It's hip to focus on getting things done, but it's only possible once we remove the constant static and distraction. If you have trouble deciding what to do, just focus on not doing. Different means, same end.Profitability often requires better rules and speed, not more time. The financial goal of a start-up should be simple: profit in the least time with the least effort. Not more customers, not more revenue, not more offices or more employees. More profit. Based on my interviews with high-performing (using profit-per-employee metrics) CEOs in more than a dozen countries, here are the 11 basic tenets of the "Margin Manifesto" ... a return-to-basics call that gives permission to do the uncommon to achieve the uncommon: consistent profitability, or doubling of it, in three months or less. I review the following principles whenever facing operational overwhelmingness or declining/stagnating profits. Hope you find them useful. 1. Niche Is the New Big—The Lavish Dwarf Entertainment Rule Several years ago, an investment banker was jailed for trade violations. He was caught partly due to his lavish parties on yachts, often featuring hired dwarves. The owner of the dwarf rental company, Danny Black, was quoted in the Wall Street Journal as saying "Some people are just into lavish dwarf entertainment." Niche is the new big. But here's the secret: It's possible to niche market and mass sell. iPod commercials don't feature dancing 50-year-olds, they feature hip and fit 20- and 30-somethings, but everyone and his grandmother wants to feel youthful and hip, so they strap on Nanos and call themselves Apple converts. Who you portray in your marketing isn't necessarily the only demographic who buys your product—it's often the demographic that most people want to identify with or belong to. The target isn't the market. No one aspires to be the bland average, so don't water down messaging to appeal to everyone—it will end up appealing to no one. 2. Revisit Drucker—What Gets Measured Gets Managed Measure compulsively, for as Peter Drucker stated, What gets measured gets managed. Useful metrics to track, besides the usual operational stats, include CPO ("Cost-Per-Order," which includes advertising, fulfillment and expected returns, charge-backs, and bad debt), ad allowable (the maximum you can spend on an advertisement and expect to break even), MER (media efficiency ratio), and projected lifetime value (LV) given return rates and reorder percent. Consider applying direct response advertising metrics to your business. 3. Pricing Before Product—Plan Distribution First Is your pricing scalable? Many companies will sell direct-to-consumer by necessity in early stages, only to realize that their margins can't accommodate resellers and distributors when they come knocking. If you have a 40% profit margin and a distributor needs a 70% discount to sell into wholesale accounts, you're forever limited to direct-to-consumer ... unless you increase your pricing and margins. It's best to do this beforehand if possible—otherwise, you'll need to launch new or "premium" products—so plan distribution before setting pricing. Test assumptions and find hidden costs by interviewing those who have done it: Will you need to pay for co-op advertising, offer rebates for bulk purchases, or pay for shelf space or featured placement? I know one former CEO of a national brand who had to sell his company to one of the world's largest soft drink manufacturers before he could access front-of-store shelving in top retailers. Test your assumptions and do your homework before setting pricing. 4. Less Is More—Limiting Distribution to Increase Profit Is more distribution automatically better? No. Uncontrolled distribution leads to all manner of headache and profit-bleeding, most often related to rogue discounters. Reseller A lowers pricing to compete with online discounter B, and the price cutting continues until neither is making sufficient profit on the product and both stop reordering. This requires you to launch a new product, as price erosion is almost always irreversible. Avoid this scenario and consider partnering with one or two key distributors instead, using that exclusivity to negotiate better terms: less discounting, prepayment, preferred placement and marketing support, etc. From iPods to Rolex and Estée Lauder, sustainable high-profit brands usually begin with controlled distribution. Remember, more customers isn't the goal; more profit is. 5. Net-Zero—Create Demand vs. Offering Terms Focus on creating end-user demand so you can dictate terms. Often one trade publication advertisment, bought at discount remnant rates, will be enough to provide this leverage. Outside of science and law, most "rules" are just common practice. Just because everyone in your industry offers terms doesn't mean you have to, and offering terms is the most consistent ingredient in start-up failure. Cite start-up economics and the ever-so-useful "company policy" as reasons for prepayment and apologize, but don't make exceptions. Net-30 becomes net-60, which becomes net-120. Time is the most expensive asset a start-up has, and chasing delinquent accounts will prevent you from generating more sales. If customers are asking for your product, resellers and distributors will need to buy it. It's that simple. Put funds and time into strategic marketing and PR to tip the scales in your favor. 6. Repetition Is Usually Redundant—Good Advertising Works the First Time Use direct response advertising (call-to-action to a phone number or website) that is uniquely trackable—fully accountable advertising—instead of image advertising, unless others are pre-purchasing to offset the cost (e.g., "If you prepurchase 288 units, we'll feature your store/URL/phone exclusively in a full-page ad in..."). Don't listen to advertising salespeople who tell you that 3, 7, or 27 exposures are needed before someone will act on an advertisement. Well-designed and well-targeted advertising works the first time. If something works partially well (e.g., high response with low percentage conversion to sales, low response with high conversion, etc.), indicating that a strong ROI might be possible with small changes, tweak one controlled variable and microtest once more. Cancel anything that cannot be justified with a trackable ROI. 7. Limit Downside to Ensure Upside—Sacrifice Margin for Safety Don't manufacture product in large quantities to increase margin unless your product and marketing are tested and ready for rollout without changes. If a limited number of prototypes cost $10 per piece to manufacture and sell for $11 each, that's fine for the initial testing period, and essential for limiting downside. Sacrifice margin temporarily for the testing phase, if need be, and avoid potentially fatal upfront overcommitments. 8. Negotiate Late—Make Others Negotiate Against Themselves Never make a first offer when purchasing. Flinch after the first offer ("$3,000!" followed by pure silence, which uncomfortable salespeople fill by dropping the price once), let people negotiate against themselves ("Is that really the best you can offer?" elicits at least one additional drop in price), then "bracket." If they end up at $2,000 and you want to pay $1,500, offer $1,250. They'll counter with approximately $1,750, to which you respond: "I'll tell you what—let's just split the difference. I'll overnight FedEx you a check, and we can call it a day." The end result? Exactly what you wanted: $1,500. 9. Hyperactivity vs. Productivity—80/20 and Pareto's Law Being busy is not the same as being productive. Forget about the start-up overwork ethic that people wear as a badge of honor—get analytical. The 80/20 principle, also known as Pareto's Law, dictates that 80% of your desired outcomes are the result of 20% of your activities or inputs. Once per week, stop putting out fires for an afternoon and run the numbers to ensure you're placing effort in high-yield areas: What 20% of customers/products/ regions are producing 80% of the profit? What are the factors that could account for this? Invest in duplicating your few strong areas instead of fixing all of your weaknesses. 10. The Customer Is Not Always Right—"Fire" High-Maintenance Customers Not all customers are created equal. Apply the 80/20 principle to time consumption: What 20% of people are consuming 80% of your time? Put high-maintenance, lowprofit customers on autopilot—process orders but don't pursue them or check up on them—and "fire" high-maintenance, high-profit customers by sending a memo detailing how a change in business model requires a few new policies: how often and how to communicate, standardized pricing and order process, etc. Indicate that, for those clients whose needs are incompatible with these new policies, you are happy to introduce other providers. "But what if my largest customer consumes all of my time?" Recognize that (1) without time, you cannot scale your company (and, oftentimes, life) beyond that customer, and (2) people, even good people, will unknowingly abuse your time to the extent that you let them. Set good rules for all involved to minimize back-and-forth and meaningless communication.What if you never had to check e-mail again? If you could hire someone else to spend countless hours in your inbox instead of you? This isn't pure fantasy. For the last 12 months, I've experimented with removing myself from the inbox entirely by training other people to behave like me. Not to imitate me, but to think like me. Here's the upshot: I get more than 1,000 e-mails a day from various accounts.89 Rather than spending 6–8 hours per day checking e-mail, which I used to do, I can skip reading e-mail altogether for days or even weeks at a time ... all within 4–10 minutes a night. Let me explain the basics, followed by tips and exact templates for outsourcing your own inbox. 1. I have multiple e-mail addresses for specific types of e-mail (blog readers vs. media vs. friends/family, etc.). tim@ ... is the default I give to new acquaintances, which goes to my assistant. 2. 99% of e-mail falls into predetermined categories of inquiries with set questions or responses (my "rules" document is at the bottom of this post—feel free to steal, adapt, and use). My assistant(s) checks and clears the inbox at 11 A.M. and 3 P.M. pst. 3. For the 1% of e-mail that might require my input for next actions, I have a oncedaily phone call of 4–10 minutes at 4 P.M. pst with my assistant. 4. If I'm busy or traveling abroad, my assistant leaves the action items in numerical order on my voicemail, which I can respond to in a bullet-point e-mail. These days, I actually prefer the voice-mail option and find that it forces my assistant to be more prepared and more concise. Each night (or early the next morning), I'll listen to my assistant's voicemail via Skype and simultaneously write out the next actions (1. Bob: Tell him that ... 2. Jose in Peru: Ask him for ... 3. Speaking in NC: Confirm ..., etc.) in a Skype chat or quick e-mail. How long does the new system take? 4–10 minutes instead of 6–8 hours of filtering and repetitive responses. If you only have one e-mail account, I recommend using a desktop program like Outlook or Mail instead of a web-based program like Gmail for a simple reason: If you see new items in your inbox, you'll check them. Like they say in AA: If you don't want to slip, don't go where it's slippery. This is why I have a private personal account that I use for sending e-mail to my assistant and communicating with friends. It's almost always empty. E-mail is the last thing people let go of. Fortune 500 CEOs, best-selling authors, celebrities—I know dozens of top performers who delegate everything but e-mail, which they latch onto as something only they can do. "No one can check my e-mail for me" is the unquestioned assumption, or "I answer every e-mail I receive" is the unquestioned bragging right that keeps them in front of a computer for 8–12 hours at a stretch. It's not fun, and it keeps them from higher-impact or more rewarding activities. Get over yourself. I had to. Checking e-mail isn't some amazing skill that you alone possess. In fact, checking e-mail is like everything else: a process. How you evaluate and handle (delete vs. archive vs. forward vs. respond) e-mail is just a series of questions you ask yourself, whether consciously or subconsciously. I have a document called "Tim Ferriss Processing Rules," to which my assistants add rules when I send them a note via e-mail with "ADD TO RULES" in the subject. Over the course of a week or two with a virtual assistant (VA), you will end up with an externalized set of rules that reflect how your brain processes e-mail. It often shows you how haphazard your processing is. I've included my "rules" here to save you some time. A few tips: 1. Setting appointments and meetings takes a lot of time. Have your assistant set things up for you in Google Calendar. I input my own items via my Palm Z22 or iCal, then use Spanning Sync and Missing Sync for Palm OS to sync everything. On my überlight Sony VAIO, which I still use for travel, I use CompanionLink for Google Calendar. I suggest batching meetings or calls in one or two set days, with 15 minutes between appointments. Scattering them throughout the week at odd times just interrupts everything else. The Palm Z22 has been discarded, and I now use a 13-inch MacBook and BusySync to synchronize iCal with Google Calendar.) 2. If you jump in your assistant's inbox and answer anything, BCC them so they are aware that you handled it. 3. Expect small problems. Life is full of compromises, and it's necessary to let small bad things happen if you want to get huge good things done. There is no escape. Prevent all problems and get nothing done, or accept an allowable level of small problems and focus on the big things. Ready to jump in and test the holy grail? Here are the steps. 1. Determine exactly which accounts you will use and how you want them to respond to (or just categorize or purge) e-mail for you. 2. Find a virtual assistant. 3. Test for reliability before skill set. Have the top three candidates do something on tight deadline (24 hours) before hiring them and letting them in your inbox. 4. Use a probationary period of 2–4 weeks to test the waters and work out the problems. Again: There will be problems. It will take a good 3–8 weeks to get to real smooth sailing. 5. Design your ideal lifestyle and find something to do other than let your brain fester in the inbox. Fill the void.I work whenever I want (no boss) about 24–30 hours/week (including office hours and music-studio hours) and what I do now is only what I really love to do. I'm still step-by-step optimizing efficiency to reduce office hours (currently about 10 hours/week). My dream is to dissolve my office altogether, go paperless, and basically only have my laptop as an office. I eliminated all work that has gotten me down or was wearing me out (eliminated an extra workload of about 10 hours/week). I do not take on jobs (writing/producing music) unless I really love the project. I eliminated all complainers and haters (saves my stomach).

CHAPTER FIVE

profit creation

Ingrained belief has us sell first, then pay expenses, and let the profit take care of itself. Which it rarely does, because the profit is what's left over. An afterthought. Profit surely isn't baked into the daily operations. For many entrepreneurs profit is only considered after the fact. Sometimes monthly. Sometimes quarterly. And way too often, annually, when their accountant is preparing the tax returns. The old, been-around-forever, profitless formula is: Sales – Expenses = Profit The new, Profit First Formula is: Sales – Profit = Expenses The math in both formulas is the same. Logically, nothing has changed. But Profit First speaks to human behavior—it accounts for the regular Joes of the world, like me, who have a tendency to spend all of whatever is available to us. So in this regard, with the Profit First flip, everything has changed. Now you secure your profit first, and run your business on the remaining cash you have left. It comes down to this—do you want to treat your profitability like leftovers, knowing you may only find scraps or an empty plate? Or do you want to get your full, healthy share right up front? I don't know about you, but I want to get my due portion first. I have taught the Profit First system to small companies and big companies, to private companies and even public companies. It works for all of them. And it will work for you. My commitment to you is that, if you follow the Profit First system, your business will become permanently profitable from the moment of your next deposit. Since I began following the system, I have built two more businesses for myself that are now growing at a healthy rate, profitable right from the start. And the one business that managed to survive my Angel-ofDeath spending spree? We implemented Profit First and that business is now not only the leader of its niche; it also turns a profit every month. In the pages of this book, you will discover how to make your business permanently profitable. The Profit First system is simple—as I said, shockingly so. But don't confuse simple with easy. Understanding what I am about to reveal to you will be a no-brainer. Having the discipline to do it and follow through will be the challenge. I will ready you for both. Provided you take each action step I recommend, you will have transformed your business is now not only the leader of its niche; it also turns a profit every month. In the pages of this book, you will discover how to make your business permanently profitable. The Profit First system is simple—as I said, shockingly so. But don't confuse simple with easy. Understanding what I am about to reveal to you will be a no-brainer. Having the discipline to do it and follow through will be the challenge. I will ready you for both. Provided you take each action step I recommend, you will have transformed your business by the end of Chapter 5. Do I want you to read the rest of the book? Hell yes! In fact, if you want to fully realize your potential as a business leader and take your business where you know it was meant to go, you need to read the rest of the book. Consider Chapters 6 through 12 the intermediate and advanced courses in Profit First, in which you will learn all of the methods, tactics and tweaks that will ensure your cash cow continues to make your life easier, happier and more fulfilling. In essence, Chapters 1 through 5 will revive your business. Chapters 6 through 12 will revive you. Following the Profit First system will take courage and dedication; it will require you to set your own ego aside. The payoff is worth it, so worth it. If you will commit to fixing your business's financials once and for all, you'll never have to pull off a last-minute miracle to cover anything again. You'll never have to have your own "piggy bank" moment, as I did, or feel like a fool, as my friend Debbie did when she first realized the financial reality of her business. When you commit to following the simple but powerful Profit First system, you will finally reap the rewards of entrepreneurship, cashing in on your business—while still running it—over and over again, like clockwork. Today is the day you say enough is enough. Whether your business is experiencing occasional financial stress or total financial horror, today is the day we fix it. Today is the day your business becomes permanently profitable.What is the only way out we can see? Growth. It is the battle cry of nearly every entrepreneur and business leader. Grow! Grow! Grow! Bigger sales. Bigger customers. Bigger investors. The only problem is, it doesn't work. Growth is only half the equation. It is a critical half, but still only half. Have you ever seen the guys at the gym with the massive arms and heaving chests, the ones as big as oxen who also have toothpick legs? They're only working half the equation and have become unhealthy freaks as a result.

Sure, that guy can throw a monster punch, but God forbid he needs to step into it, or move a little. His puny legs will give out instantly; he'll curl up on the floor and cry like a baby. Most business owners try to grow their way out of their problems, hinging salvation on the next big sale or customer or investor, but the result is simply a bigger monster. (And the bigger your company gets, the more anxiety you deal with. If both are cash-eating monsters, a $300,000 company is much easier to manage than a $3,000,000 company. I know; I have survived operating both, and bigger.) This is constant growth without concern for health. And the day that big sale or customer or investor doesn't show, you will fall to the ground and curl up crying like a baby. If you think operating your business is closer to a horror story than to a fairy tale, you're not alone. Since I wrote my first book, HOW TO STAY FOCUSED , I've met thousands of entrepreneurs; and let me tell you, most are struggling to tame the beast that is their business. Many companies—even those that appear to have it all together, even the big guys who seem to dominate their industries—struggle to stay afloat.

Balancing profit-making with social value creation

Corporate businesses and investors are increasingly aware about the potential source of profit and rich institutional ecosystem that can be 'tapped' to facilitate engagement with Base of the Pyramid (BoP) markets in developing countries. To be successful by making a profit from these markets and combining this by making a positive impact on poor communities means adapting a specific business approach that is not replicable from formal economies. The literature shows that corporate businesses and investors who engage with the BoP must consider investing time and money in special partnerships with local stakeholders (preferably in informal economies), making use of innovative payment methods, and taking into account gender issues to increase impact, while accepting a lower return on investment (Ngoasong et al., 2015). Nowadays, business actors emphasise on engaging with the poor as agents rather than as passive consumers. The challenge of reaping these high-volume (4 billion people) and lowmargin opportunities, is not to create formal institutions, but to make informal arrangements 'legible' to capital with a view to incorporating them into new business systems. The emphasis is on acquiring 'native capability', understanding local business practices, mapping local markets and consumer behaviour, and building local partnerships (Leliveld &

Knorringa, 2018). Population dynamics show that the BoP market remains a growth market for decades to come. It will continue to increase in absolute numbers, the market will become more urban oriented, and there is a growing demand for frugal innovations and special services targeted at special needs of an increasing group of displaced people. However, to make any sense of the BoP market and its impacts (positive and negative) on local entrepreneurs, producers, manufacturers, middlemen and consumers, who operate mainly in informal economies, businesses that target the poor with services and products should be categorised by size, inclusiveness, social value creation and their engagement with the BoP. The literature mentions several challenges, for example that of serving rural communities (dealing with mistrust, high levels of illiteracy, high transportation costs, lack of skilled people), of receiving an earned income from engaging with the BoP, and of building sustainable partnerships with local actors. Further, there is a lack of access to finance particularly for smaller businesses, because of higher risks and costs, long term commitments, and lower return on investment. However, the potential of making a positive impact on local communities and their livelihoods is considerably higher. The literature shows that large business are not better in combining profit-making with positive impact generation for the poor in comparison with emerging and maturing businesses (Business Call for Action, 2014). From a management perspective there is a shift in thinking towards the idea that corporate businesses need access to informal markets through micro-enterprises. To help improve the distribution channels, businesses are making use of informal retail chains, micro-enterprises, and village-level entrepreneurs to increase their reach across remote areas and urban slums. There are different payment methods for services and products targeted at poor people (e.g. pay-asyou-go, special arrangements with micro-credit organisations, or to let a third party pay for products or services) that help them to generate an earned income. The success of partnerships depends on how relationships are grounded in social rather than legal contracts and requires a capability to understand and appreciate the benefits of the existing social infrastructure with the lack of Western-style institutions (Bendul et al., 2018). Corporate businesses prefer (because of the complexity of dealing with such environment) to work together with civil society actors and social entrepreneurs. 3 From a development perspective, there is evidence that BoP and shared value approaches are not lifting micro-business actors out of poverty and informal economies, but rather keeping them in poverty, as BoP strategies are based on copying from the informal economy, free-riding on informal community and economic networks, bypassing informal commercial intermediaries in favour of NGOs and social entrepreneurs, and ultimately shifting most of the risks and costs to the poor micro-enterprises, for example through franchising (Meagher, 2018). The literature also shows that doing business with the poor only makes sense if it looks through a gender lens (Vossenberg, 2018). Firstly, literature shows that the socioeconomic impact of female entrepreneurs on livelihoods is higher and that their specific challenges to succeed in markets (e.g. power structures) have been ignored in most BoP projects. Secondly, the literature on BoP markets and frugal innovations lack specific evidence for gender outcomes. The task is to deliberately examine markets and look for replicable innovations that can have empowering effects for marginalised women. 2. The market dynamics at the Base of the Pyramid The debate about businesses that provide services and products targeting the poor in local markets is referred to in the literature as the Base/Bottom of the Pyramid (BoP) discourse. It suggests that corporate business can make significant profits by serving the people at the base of the pyramid, those living on less than US$2 a day; an estimated 4 billion people worldwide (Prahalad & Hart, 2002). Together they have substantial purchasing power: the BoP constitutes a US$5 trillion global consumer market (Hammond et al., 2007). Although more than ten years old, these statistics are still widely used in literature to describe the potential of the BoP market. Such markets are often rural, poorly served, dominated by the informal economy, and, as a result, relatively inefficient and uncompetitive. In contrast to the wealthier mid-market population segment of 1.4 billion people that is largely urban, already well served, and extremely competitive. Asia has by far the largest BoP market (2.86 billion people with an aggregate income of US$3.47 trillion), followed by Latin America (360 million people with US$509 billion) and Africa (486 million people with US$429 billion). The majority of the income is spent on food (US$2.9 trillion), followed by energy (US$433 billion), housing (US$332 billion), transportation (US$179 billion) and health (US$158 billion). A relatively low part of the income is spent on water (US$20 billion) and one of the most rapidly growing sectors is in communication technology (Hammond et al, 2007). Population dynamics impact on future BoP markets. Three sub-trends are particularly relevant: population growth, urbanisation, and displacement because of political turmoil and (natural) calamities (Leliveld & Knorringa, 2018). ?

Projections forecast that the world population will continue to grow mainly in Low Income Countries for decades to come. After 2050 population growth will almost exclusively be driven by fertility levels in the world's least developed countries, mainly in sub-Saharan Africa (Dietz, 2017). The combined population of these countries, roughly one billion in 2017, is projected to increase by 33% between 2017 and 2030, and then to reach 1.9 billion persons in 2050 (UN, 2017). ? High levels of urbanisation are forecasted. Over half of the world's population (54%) now lives in urban areas, up from 30% in 1950. The world's population in 2050 is 4 projected to be 66% urban, of which 2.5 billion are projected to be urban poor with nearly 90% of the increase concentrated in Asia and Africa (UN, 2015). These two regions, which are projected to become 56% and 64% urban by mid-century, respectively, are still expected to be less urbanised than other regions of the world. ? The number of displacements has almost doubled since 2000. The number of refugees in 2016 are estimated at 22.5 million (UNHCR, 2017). In addition, 31.1 million people were internally displaced by conflict, violence, and disasters in 2016 of which 24.2 million by natural disasters and 6.9 million by conflict and violence (IDMC, 2017). With regard to violence and conflict-related displacements, sub-Saharan Africa overtook the Middle East as the region most affected. South and East Asia were the regions most affected when it comes to displacements caused by natural disasters. These population dynamics show that the BoP market will continue to increase in absolute numbers in the next decades, that this market will become more urban oriented, and that there is a growing demand for frugal innovations and special services to serve the needs of the increasing group of displaced people. India, Nigeria, China, Indonesia, and South Africa have been identified as the current top BoP markets as income inequality is expected to remain high (Euromonitor International, 2017). 3. A shift from top-down business strategies towards shared value strategies Traditionally, the BoP market would be referred to as the informal market where micro, small and medium scale local manufacturers, entrepreneurs, farmers and retailers provide all kinds of products and services targeting the poor population. However, at the start of the 2000s the BoP market (triggered by the awareness of its market potential) became associated with corporate business (Prahalad & Hart, 2002). The literature refers to this as the first generation (2002-2009) of businesses that see the BoP as purely consumers. Kolk et al. (2014) analysed this period and concludes that the literature was more practitioner oriented, concentrated on a few markets (e.g. China, India and Bangladesh) and a few companies (e.g. Unilever and Grameen Bank). Although the early BoP studies offer evidence (including some data on increased profits, jobs and numbers of customers) suggesting that corporate businesses can engage profitably with the BoP and create increased self-esteem and economic progress for people at the BoP, Kolk et al. (2014) show in their study that the vast majority of articles that view the poor primarily as consumers fail to identify rigorous measures of the real economic, social and environmental impact of these initiatives. The second generation (after 2009) of businesses that target the BoP is associated with the idea of alleviating poverty by generating business activities that engage with the lives of the poor (Amaral Dionisio, 2016). The idea behind this generation is based on the recognition that the poverty marketplace is as "vast and diverse as humanity itself" (Kotler & Lee, 2015, p.74). To make sense of this complex market and find specific solutions that would be beneficial for both business and society, corporate businesses need to establish local partnerships: collaborating with non-traditional partners, co-inventing custom solutions and building local capacity in order to get better expertise and relationships with local institutions. Singh et al. (2014, p.364) states that such multi-stakeholder partnerships do lay the foundations for co-creation of shared value on which new business models would be based. 5 The notion of reciprocity is central to the current BoP concept and the idea of mutual value creation is common in the second generation of BoP literature. According to Porter & Kramer (2011, p.64): "The solution lies in the principle of shared value, which involves creating economic value in a way that also creates value for society by addressing its needs and challenges". As such the basic principle regarding businesses targeting the poor with innovative products and services has shifted from "doing more with less" (Radjou et al., 2012) to "doing better with less" (Radjou & Prabhu, 2015), presenting it as a win–win socially responsible business proposition that combines high turnovers and profits with realising development goals. This discourse resonates with other common terms, such as 'inclusive business for the poor' (alternatively 'social business' or 'pro-poor business'), which addresses questions such as how to marry profits with social aims, assuming that business activities can contribute to the long-term goal of poverty alleviation by embedding the rural and urban poor into efficient value chains and market structures (Leliveld & Knorringa, 2018). The technology and innovation side of the discussion is labelled as "frugal innovation", which encompasses (re)designing products, services, systems, and business models in order to reduce complexity and total lifecycle costs, and enhance functionality, while providing high user value and affordable solutions for low-income customers (Leliveld & Knorringa, 2018). There is a recognition of valuing the developmental relevance of localised and embedded bottom-up innovations by usually poor individuals, entrepreneurs, households, and communities, that give agency and a competitive advantage to innovators and entrepreneurs in local communities and local (informal) economies, because they possess (often tacit) knowledge about the unique local circumstances, local preferences, and needs. Corporate businesses' challenge is, therefore, that it cannot just simply provide stripped-down versions of products to middle- and high-income consumers, but instead provide newly designed, and value and context sensitive products and services that are truly compatible with the circumstances of people living in poverty, including distribution and payment methods (Nakata & Weidner, 2012). By doing so, multinationals are increasingly penetrating informal economies in more remote and isolated communities with services and products. In addition, they increasingly interact with local NGOs and social entrepreneurs. 4. Categorising businesses that target the Base of the Pyramid Making sense of all the different types of businesses that serve the poor, the literature has started to categorise businesses in term of their size (e.g. employees, turn-over, profit, client base) or on the economic sectors in which they work (e.g. health, energy, agriculture, education). The literature also identifies ways businesses to do business with the BoP that can be categorised into three groups (Intellecap, 2016): ? Access-led businesses provide affordable products and services to poor communities. As such they engage with the low income populations as consumers and provide them with products and services. ? Ability-led businesses partner with the poor communities on a more equal basis, for example by buying or brokering a deal for their produce. As such they engage with the low income populations as producers or partners, and provide them with skills and market linkages to gain livelihoods and earn incomes. 6 ? Knowledge-led businesses improve the access to knowledge services of poor communities. As such they disseminate information or knowledge to increase awareness and bring about behavioural change amongst low income and underserved populations. The Intellecap study (2016) concludes that across East Africa, most sustainable and scalable models are ability-led businesses in the agrifood sector: ability agribusinesses. This is primarily because they provide support across all segments of the value chain and market the produce to customers from the middle and higher income brackets. Through interventions across segments, these enterprises are able to ensure quality as well as efficient and continuous supply to markets. Ability agribusinesses have, therefore, attracted considerable investor interest. Besides the agriculture sector, a number of scalable and sustainable models are observed in clean energy. These access enterprises provide clean energy solutions to low income populations, and are constrained on pricing and payments. Some of the most interesting innovations in payment models are seen in this sector, although many of the enterprises in this sector are still backed by grants.1 Some other literature adds the category of employment-led businesses (Nyssens, 2006), which create direct employment for people like the low-qualified unemployed youth or the disabled, who are increasingly excluded from the labour market in low income countries. The mission of this so called 'work integration social enterprises' (WISEs) is to integrate excluded members into work and society through a productive activity. Businesses targeting the BoP could also be categorised through targeting the BoP as core business or not (Business Call to Action, 2014): ? Large and established companies are established national or multinational companies that are introducing new business lines that buy from or sell to the BoP. The aim is to start a new and innovative part of the business that is intended to differentiate them from competitors, bring access to new markets, and position them in the long term. Because buying from or selling to the BoP is a new aspect of their business, there can be internal challenges, such as making a compelling business case or getting support and buy-in from different parts of the organisation. ? Emerging and maturing companies are small to medium enterprises (SMEs) located in Low- and Middle-Income Countries and High-Income Countries, whose original business idea focused on an opportunity at the BoP. They have premised their business model on buying from or selling to underserved markets. Their business lives or dies on finding a commercially viable model at the BoP. Business Call to Action (2014) concludes that there is often a misunderstanding that large and established companies are the most efficient and successful to combine profit-making with social impact due to greater financial resources. Emerging and maturing companies are doing both better and worse, meaning they have more initiatives reported as either progressing slowly or flourishing. Revenue analysis shows that emerging and maturing companies are strongly represented, when it comes to high revenue earnings.

Challenges of profit-making and doing good Corporate businesses that target the poor and marginalised people around the world have to look beyond the search for short-term profits. If they want to be sustainable, fair and socially responsible it could be difficult to keep costs low, which is necessary to serve the needs of poor people with products and services (and as a requirement to keep investors happy) (Ngoasong et al., 2015). The literature shows several challenges that can be clustered as follows (e.g. F&BKP, 2016; Bendul et al., 2018). ? Challenges of serving rural communities: As the majority of the BoP market is still in rural areas, there are specific constraints and challenges of working directly with rural communities as the main customers or stakeholders. Several examples have been mentioned in the literature: ? It is difficult to break down the negative misconceptions towards organisations extending assistance. Businesses have to deal with mistrust among many farmers who have in the past been victims of scams and have been exploited by middlemen who took advantage of weak rural market networks (Institute for Social Entrepreneurship in Asia, 2015; Griffin-EL & Darko, 2014; Darko & Koranteng, 2015). ? The high level of illiteracy amongst the poor, in particular in rural areas, is another obstacle. Businesses need to invest sufficient time in upskilling them to use their products and services. For example, they require more demonstrations, guidance and follow-up when offering services to farmers (Griffin-EL & Darko, 2014; Darko & Koranteng, 2015; Thompson & MacMillan, 2010). ? Reaching remote rural areas with their teams and equipment can be challenging, especially during rainy seasons. To reach remote rural areas while being revenue-generating and commercially viable can mean that businesses are forced to be selective and limited about where they can operate to a greater extent than grant-reliant NGOs (Griffin-EL & Darko, 2014; Darko & Koranteng, 2015). ? There are difficulties in identifying professionals who are equipped with both the necessary skills and knowledge and who share a vision of creating positive impact and transformation. Some of the most vulnerable populations reside in remote rural areas, and businesses struggle to find professionals willing to live in remote areas (Smith & Darko, 2014; Griffin-EL & Darko, 2014; Darko & Koranteng, 2015). ? Challenges of receiving an earned income: In particular, is it difficult to find the right payment model for poor communities as part of gaining an earned income from providing services and products. Some communities are used to receiving free services and inputs as delivered by public and aid organisations. As a consequence, there remains a dependency environment, which makes it more difficult to build the business case (Intellecap, 2016; Griffin-EL & Darko, 2014).

Challenges to access finance: For the emerging and maturing businesses, access to finance is another challenge. Although there is often a reasonable flow of early-stage grant capital, for many enterprises getting the first injection of capital can be difficult. In particular, there is a concentration of specific types of financial resources, which leads to resource gaps for certain sizes of enterprises and stages of growth. For example, one ODI study acknowledged that there are two stages at which entrepreneurs can identify such challenges (Griffin-EL & Darko, 2014). The first is the "Seed/ Blueprint" stage when social capital seems to play a role that has bias leaning towards less-well-connected entrepreneurs. The next growth phase at which entrepreneurs struggle is the "Operationalize/Grow" stage, when the business model has been proven but is not yet sustainable so it is risky for commercial investors, and capital needs are too high for many grant schemes. ? Challenges of building and maintaining partnerships: The last cluster of challenges relates to building and maintaining partnerships with stakeholders. Corporate businesses struggle to find ways to connect with local stakeholders to give them access to informal or remote markets. Smaller businesses question the value of engaging with corporations for funding and of their endorsement (Bendul et al., 2018). Pursuing corporate social investment seemed to be "too much work for too little gain", and that emerging businesses eventually end up compromising their mission and become increasingly dependent (Griffin-EL & Darko, 2014). 6. Developing payment methods for the poor Businesses must earn money in the market. As social business expert Tania Ellis wrote in her book "The new pioneers", businesses that target the poor people may not seek the highest profit; holding costs low is evident to survive in the markets (Ellis, 2010). However, such businesses have the disadvantage of serving customers who are mostly excluded, live in remote or deprived areas, and with limited capacity to pay. A longitudinal field experiment in rural Malawi showed that poor customers of a water purification product were more likely to remain using the product with a deeply discounted price, instead of paying the moderate price or take it for free (Christensen et al., 2014). Intellecap (2016) observed a shift in the way businesses in East Africa react to the challenges of affordability. Creating affordable products was synonymous to creating low-cost products with basic features. However, entrepreneurs "now focus on designing innovative pricing and payment solutions for full-feature products and services". They use sliding fee scales or special discounts for people of lesser means or introduce new payment models. Several payment models have been mentioned in the literature (e.g. F&BKP, 2016): ? Rental model: The lease or rental model is particularly popular in agriculture where businesses lease out processing facilities to farmers and train them to use the facility. For example, Baridi Stores uses such a model to solve one of the biggest challenges in Uganda: wastage of agricultural produce due to lack of affordable storage infrastructure. Post-harvest, the shelf life of produce is limited and hence farmers are forced to agree to unfavourable prices or allow wastage. Baridi Stores has since designed and developed solar powered storehouses exclusively for agricultural products. These storehouses are leased out to farmers for a rental fee to prevent food wastage, which simultaneously enables farmers to negotiate a better price for their produce. 9 ? Prepaid fee: The prepaid fee approach in the form of subscription payments is mostly used in ICT-enabled models that provide capacity building through mobile phones, for example, by creating market linkages or providing access to educational material. A traditional prepaid model requires the customer to purchase a particular amount of credit before services can be used. For customers, the prepaid model allows them to purchase services as and when cash is available, while for enterprises, the model allows them to eliminate the risk of payment defaults. For example, SokoNect in Kenya uses a technology-based platform to eliminate brokers in the agriculture value chain, thus enabling farmers to access markets directly. Farmers prepay a predetermined fee to use the platform. ? Pay-as-you-go: Another trend is the pay-as-you-go model which is also referred to as a progressive ownership model or rent-to-own model. Businesses use this model to provide rural asset financing for the low income population. In this model, a consumer pays an initial deposit for an asset and pays instalments on a regular basis. Once the instalments are paid to cover the balance cost, the consumer owns the product and can stop paying instalments. For example, Akili Holding in Kenya and Juhudi Kilimo co-invest this way with rural communities to provide them with tools and assistance. ? Small percentage from sales: Most businesses targeting the poor seek ways to earn a small commission on the sale of products on the market while offering multiple services and capacity building. For instance, Tanzania-based East Africa Fruits Farm leases out farmland to farmers who earn less than US$1 per day. It provides training and support to farmers to increase yield and procures the harvest for distribution. EA Fruits Farm then cleans, processes and packages the produce for distribution in retail outlets and for doorto-door delivery. The enterprise pays farmers at regular intervals of seven to ten days. Another example is Kigali Farms in Rwanda that provides inputs, training and support for producing mushrooms which it buys back for processing and export. ? Cooperate directly with microcredit organisations: Businesses also work together with microcredit organisations to increase the opportunity for the poor to buy a product. Some companies that provide solar powered energy solutions for off-grid communities offer products which can be bought with microfinance services. ? Making use of third parties: When there are too many difficulties with charging the beneficiaries themselves, businesses can earn income through third parties, like government agencies, NGOs and corporations that have a vested interest in an intended beneficiary group to pay for services or products for them. Governments can do this for collective goods and in the welfare for the poor, while corporations can pay for services that benefit their employees or suppliers (Khieng & Quak, 2013). Most beneficiaries share some of the costs through co-payments and deductibles. For example, Irelandbased Valid Nutrition works with local manufacturers in Malawi, Kenya and Ethiopia that produce their nutritious ready-to-eat food products. Undernourished people are their clients, however the main part of their paid customers are public institutes, large international aid donors and multilateral organisations. 7. Building partnerships In the management and business literature there is a growing interest and movement towards the idea that businesses need to move beyond thinking about scaling up to achieve organisational growth. McPhedran Waitzer & Paul (2011) stated the transition "from an enterprise 10 to an ecosystem" in which entrepreneurs have become part of strategic networks or alliances and adopt a broader, integral and more political approach to reach their goal. Davies & Simon (2013) underlined the importance to distinguish the concepts of scaling and diffusion. They wrote that scaling is only useful in thinking about the growth of the business, where diffusion tools, although primarily descriptive, could help to understand how to increase positive impact. For shared value, equal and sustainable partnerships between corporate businesses and local SMEs are important. Bloom & Skloot (2010) showed that local businesses that embrace social values could be interesting partners for the private sector, governments and civil society. For example, they are often pioneers in new technology or finding new usages for existing technology, which makes them attractive partners. Building partnerships could help such businesses to be more cost efficient and to deal with the many specific challenges of serving poor communities. To overcome high distribution and transportation costs, some SMEs partner with large corporate businesses that have existing channels to rapidly increase reach. For instance, One Degree Solar entered into a partnership with Coca-Cola to market its solar power kits Brightbox to kiosk owners selling Coca-Cola (F&BKP, 2016). From the perspective of corporate businesses, they need access to informal markets through micro-enterprises. To help improve the distribution channels, businesses are making use of informal retail chains, micro-enterprises, and village-level entrepreneurs to increase their reach across remote areas or urban slums. For example, SunnyMoney in Kenya distributes lamps through cooperatives as well as local shops and agents (Intellecap, 2016). Unilever works with women shopkeepers to sell their products in India (Amaral Dionisio, 2016). The success of partnerships depends on how relationships are grounded in social rather than legal contracts and requires a capability to understand and appreciate the benefits of the existing social infrastructure with the lack of Western-style institutions (Hart & London, 2005, p. 33). This requires a middle-ground between top-down and bottom-up approaches to innovation and economic development, facilitating the 'co-creation' of new products and new business ecosystems for the mutual benefit of formal as well as informal actors (Knorringa et al, 2016). In the telecommunications sector, Anderson et al (2010, p. 16) describe how non-traditional partnerships with informal actors were used to reduce transaction costs of setting up base stations in slums and rural areas by allowing multinational partners to benefit from local entrepreneurs' 'basic commercial acumen, entrepreneurial spirit, and a deep understanding of how to manage the local environment'. The BoP management literature celebrates the value of 'connectivity' between the formal and informal economies, which forms a basis for the formation of new 'business ecosystems' made up of a wide range of non-traditional business actors, including multinational firms, NGOs, universities, donors, government policy-makers and informal firms. Cozzens and Sutz (2012, p. 25–26) draw attention to the role of such partnerships in 'bridging formal and informal settings', stressing the need for such partnerships to '[b]e as close to the community as possible and [at] the same time assure linkages to wider networks able to provide support; add "formality" in all possible ways taking care to do this by fine tuning previous informal ways of doing things instead of ruling them out...'. However, as Hammond (2013) shows, small businesses struggle in building meaningful relationships especially with larger or more powerful organisations. For such partnerships to work, corporate businesses need a basis of trust, and they often give that trust through legal 11 contracts that define roles, milestones and obligations, while SMEs and micro-entrepreneurs in particular informal networks expecting a different kind of trust. NGOs and social entrepreneurs are often used to gain access to informal organisational infrastructure. 'Many locally embedded NGOs possess the resources and network relationships needed to create and manage links between multinationals and BOP markets. As such, NGOs can serve as effective alliance partners to MNEs ... for exploiting opportunities in BOP markets' (Webb et al, 2010, p. 568). However, little is known about the entrepreneurial opportunities this offers for domestic firms. On the one hand, there is an optimistic view that polycentric innovation can indeed lead to more chances for domestic firms; on the other hand, there is a critical view that points out possible crowding out or exploitation of (informal) domestic firms (Knorringa et al, 2016). Both views lack empirical evidence (Leliveld & Knorringa, 2018). Another stakeholder is the government. Partnerships with national governments can be very bureaucratic and time-intensive (Quak, 2017). To foster trust with poor communities, local governments sometimes assist businesses through validation of their products, however being involved in local power structures as an outsider could be very challenging for social entrepreneurs. To exchange lessons learned, peer-to-peer networks are necessary. However, such networks are limited in the rural context with most businesses concentrated in the largest urban areas (Institute for Social Entrepreneurship in Asia, 2015; Darko & Koranteng, 2015). For example, Jiro-VE, a business that provides solar lights to rural communities in Madagascar, is deliberately not partnering with the national government, because the political situation has been far from stable (Stamhuis, 2014). 8. Impact on the informal sector The literature that looks to the impact of businesses from a development perspective, is more critical on BoP and shared value approaches. Far from collaborating with informal economic systems and actors in search for mutual benefit, corporate businesses that target the poor tend to treat informal economies as a pool of workers and organisational resources to be tapped for the benefit of corporate actors (Meagher, 2018). This is particularly acute in sub-Saharan Africa, where

66% of those working outside of agriculture earn their living in a wide range of informal economic activities (ILO, 2013). Fressoli et al. (2014, p. 278) point out, 'inclusion is not an unproblematic, smooth endeavour; rather, in practice it can also involve uneven, unequal, incomplete and sometimes antagonistic processes and outcomes'. Moreover, informal economic systems generate opportunities for accumulation as well as basic livelihoods, shaping informal career paths in production, service and trading activities that can lead to middle-class incomes and even considerable wealth. BoP strategies are ignoring this wider informal ecosystem, making it less clear that they improve economic opportunities for informal workers, entrepreneurs and consumers (Meagher, 2018). Meagher identifies four mechanisms of adverse incorporation operating within frugal innovation and BoP models: ? Copying: The strategy of copying from the informal economy is widely encouraged by BoP initiatives, with particular reference to micro-packaging, 'leveraging' local knowledge and identifying market opportunities. These practices are more delicately referred to as 'adapting products and processes' by the UNDP (2008, p. 18) report 'Creating Value for All'. 12 ? Free-riding: Also referred to as 'leveraging soft networks', or 'leveraging the strengths of the poor', the idea is to reduce costs by free-riding on informal community or economic networks and institutions downward flow of benefits that is often checked by the use of formal contracts, bureaucratic complexities and other forms of corporate discipline to 'align incentives' and protect corporate profits For example, a high turnover of sales agents in BoP distributive networks indicates that benefits are often slow to trickle down. ? Bypassing nodes of accumulation: This means the sidelining of informal manufacturers and de-legitimation of informal commercial intermediaries, including informal wholesalers, brokers and money-lenders, who may absorb a higher share of profits into the informal economy. BoP strategies call for the replacement of informal intermediaries by NGOs or social enterprises to facilitate access to these otherwise difficult to reach markets. This serves to restructure value chains away from informal nodes of accumulation which redistribute profits into informal economic systems. NGOs are regarded as 'honest brokers' who facilitate economic inclusion of the poorest, while the informal commercial intermediaries are censured for 'monopolistic behaviour' (Dolan & Rajak, 2016). ? Shifting risk and costs: In addition to free-riding on informal marketing networks, BoP distribution channels that use micro-credit-based payment solutions and microfranchising arrangements force informal entrepreneurs to absorb marketing costs, turnover risks and interest payments within their very low margins. A number of studies have detailed how BoP programmes such as Care International's Rural Sales Programme, Grameen 'Phone Ladies', and Avon in South Africa and Brazil transfers risk onto poor women by requiring them to buy equipment or goods up front on credit, leaving them to cope with increasingly saturated markets, falling returns and in some cases the social opprobrium of transgressing cultural boundaries (Dolan and Roll, 2013). Delayed payment and financial pressures within low-income communities place increasing strains on social networks, eroding rather than strengthening local social capital. Ultimately, the objective is not to draw the poor out of informality, but to benefit from the cost advantages of keeping them informal. For example, a study on small-scale mobile money agents in Zambia suggests that the franchising relationship, although holding some entrepreneurial potential for agents, should be closely monitored to avoid adverse labour relations among tellers (Pesa, 2018). 9. Looking through a gender lens There has recently been an increasing interest in female entrepreneurship, specifically in developing countries. There are two reasons for this: an increase in interest in the role of entrepreneurship in the economic development process, and the insight that female-led enterprises can have a more significant impact on socioeconomic opportunities of households and communities (De Winter, 2014). In this light, supporting and expanding female entrepreneurship has become an objective to empower women and to reduce poverty in developing countries. The practice of entrepreneurship in itself marks a long-established traditional division of labour for women, due to gender identity in the market and a lack of available economic and political networks (Kleinrichert, 2012). However, the traditional business literature still tends to consider entrepreneurship as gender neutral. Feminist economists critically describe this as 'the imaginary 13 entrepreneur', who makes decisions unhindered by socioeconomic inequality or the unequal distribution of power and income, and free of family obligations or care responsibilities (Vossenberg, 2013). As a result, women entrepreneurs are often those left in the informal economy and running microenterprises, having lower returns and fewer employees than their male counterparts. However, for businesses that combine profit-making with social impact there are four women entrepreneurs for every five men (GEM, 2011).2 A study conducted by the Third Sector Research Centre (2012) found that women are more inclined to get involved in ventures with a social mission and that – unlike in 'regular' businesses – social ventures employed around twice as many women as men. This raises the question whether male-female differences and the challenges they involve do not apply in the case of enterprises that look for positive impacts (De Winter, 2014). By adopting a gender lens, the identification of the socioeconomic impact of female entrepreneurs on communities and their specific challenges in the market, is expanded to encompass how specific products and services that target 'the poor' also include women. Vossenberg (2018) shows that current literature on frugal innovations and specific products and services for the BoP markets mention development outcomes, but lack more specific evidence for gender outcomes. Therefore she comes to the conclusion that for advancing such research the task is to deliberately examine markets and look for replicable innovations that can have empowering effects for marginalised women. Such a 'means to an end' approach indicates that one needs to explicate what development outcomes such products and services value and seek to achieve. Doing this through a gender lens, automatically implies a shift from the current research emphasis on how products and innovation processes contribute to individual wealth accumulation to a focus on exploring empowerment and social and economic well-being outcomes in lives of marginalised women and gender equality.

Profit is the underlying goal for most business entities. But what does it mean to achieve profits in the economy and how such recurring success impacts our financial system? To understand consequences of this process, we have to have a look a bit into very simple accounting rules. Nothing complicated, just necessary basics: Every company that achieves profits has sales which are higher than its costs. Easy, why not?

What constitutes the sales part is not important for now, it is each businessman decision where he/she is going to make business.

What interests us is the costs side. Costs consist from wages, material, subcontractors and capital costs. It is simplified view but sufficient. Let´s have a closer look at particular costs. If the material is being priced, where is its price coming from? Raw materials, either natural or manufactured are delivered by companies that have employees of their own, are consuming their own subcontractor's services, material and trying to achieve profits. How the price of coal is determined? Corporation must pay its employees, subcontractors and determine a price that is higher than these costs so it can incorporate also some profit. The same applies for companies providing services, energies and capital as well. The price must be always higher than the sum of costs, including costs for capital.

We can describe it like this

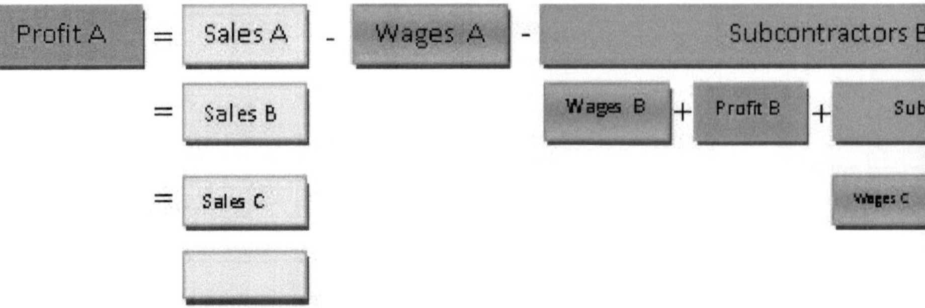

So we can see that all other costs are in fact transformed wage costs and profit. Under subcontracted costs we can understand the broadest category which includes material, services and capital. Costs of subcontract B consists from wages of company B, profit of B and subcontracted costs of other companies allocated for this subcontract. The same way costs of C are made from similar components and so on until the end of the pyramid.

Yes, even the price of capital is in reality determined by cost of labor (bank officials of all kind) and profit (as determined by difference between interest rates for customers and costs of capital from savings or interbank market)

The final effect is that the profit of any company is the difference between sales and wages of people participating on these sales in the broadest sense and profit margin of all subcontractors

Profit A = Sales A - Wages $(A + B_a + C_a + \ldots + Z_a)$ - Profit $(B_a + C_a +$

For company A to achieve profit it must be so that sales are greater than costs, which means that overall wages, cooperating on such production must be lower than sales.

And here is the catch!!! If this is the equation of a successful company, how can this production be realized? How can you sell the production when the buying power of all employees, participating on its making is lower than planned sales? If you total all wages paid in the production process associated with this particular production (not just direct wages but also wages of all subcontractors, apportioned to this and providing input like materials, services and machinery) they will be lower than planned sales by exactly planned profit.

The example:

Company A uses own workers and pays them 100$.
Apart from labor it buys material worth 30$ form company B and uses machinery produced by company C worth 40$ which is planned to be used over 4 years, so its costs are calculated as $1/4^{th}$ of 40$ = 10$ per year.

So total costs of A are: 100 + 30 + 10 = 140$

If they plan to achieve profit of 10%, A has to sell whatever they produce for 140 x 1,1=154$

Company B as supplier of material has to make profit as well and if we say the expected profit margin will be as well 10% their paid wages allocated on this delivery cannot be more then 30 / 1.1 = 27$. If they paid more in wages, they would not achieve their planned margin 10%.

Company C as producer of machinery of longer life span if planning profit has to take into account that the wages paid to their workers have to be calculated in line with expected turnover. So they cannot pay their workers more then 10 / 1.1 = 9$ per year if expected profit margin is again 10%. They will not sell new machine in this micro economy until the old one is fully depreciated and new one is needed by company A.

The resulting buying power distributed through wages is following:

AD (aggregate demand=buying power) = 100$ (A) + 27$(B) + 9$(C) = 136$

The aggregate supply of products of company A is:AS = 154$.
The difference between AS and AD is 18$, which consists from 14$ (profit A) + 3$ (profit B) + 1$ (profit C)

So the production of company A is going to have some problems being realized as there is simply not enough buying power distributed through wages as is expected to be achieved in sales. This simple example describes the problem with profit and its effects on diminished buying power. The higher the profit margin, the bigger the end difference between available demand and offered supply.

You will say, and correctly that sales are achieved mainly through customers which are not employees. Correct. But these people are employees of some other company as well - and their employer is guided by the same equation. He too wants to achieve profit. Therefore he too, logically sets his prices in a way that his planned sales are higher that collection of his own and transformed wages. Therefore, we can transform the equation of one company into one global equation, describing sum of all sales of all companies in economy:

Profit Sum(A..Z) = Sales Sum(A+...+Z) - Wage

Example:

We can add additional company D which produces some another product with 1000$ wages and plans profit at margin 20%, so is expecting sales of 1200$.

The available buying power distributed through these two companies is now

1000(D) + 136(A+B+C) = 1136$

The supply is represented by two set of productions valued at 154(A) + 1200(D) = 1354$

Even the second company added substantially more buying power into the system, its collective customers are not able to buy what is offered. The difference between AS(1354) and AD (1136) is again in the profit:

18$(A+B+C) + 200$(D) = 1354$ - 1136$

It could be that well paid employees of company D would buy all production of company A, but in that case there would be insufficient remaining demand(1136 – 136 = 1000$) to satisfy sales of company D. At least not with any profit. If all employees participating in production tree A+B+C would use their wages to complement buying power of employees D, they would be able to buy nearly 95% (1136 / 1200) of production D while maintaining its profit margin but company A would realize no sales at all and end up bankrupt.

The result is striking and surprising for some:

If all people had only employee's income and sales would be derived from this source only, it would not be possible to achieve it with planned profit as buying power distributed through companies as wages is lower than planned sales.

Profit = Sales (paid wages) + additional resources - Wag

Wages= buying power + additional resources - Wag

People are able to buy only as much, as they get through wages and other resources which we call additional. As wages are planned and paid lower as aggregate sales, these sales are not possible to achieve only from the volume of salaries. It is mathematically impossible. How can the system be functioning then? (Because it is functioning, or at least looks so).

Additional resources needed for profit creation

What are these additional resources? We shell discuss them in detail:

It is striking discovery, but in reality any profits in economy are achieved only through personal loans, consumption of savings, state transfers and consumption of profits in the form of personal profit spending or pensions.

Savings are from long point of view doubtful source of consumption. Firstly, their volume is finite, secondly the very fact that they exist means that in previous periods people did not realize all their wages into sales and therefore profit in the past was lower by exactly the amount of savings. However subjectively useful, savings are not sustainable source of economic growth, because their volume will eventually shrink to zero. If people would theoretically saved all what they earned in the form of wages and had no other income through loans or transfers, global profit in that year would be zero.

So we get to this:

All costs are in reality transformed wages and profits.

Profit, in order to be realized, needs apart from wages as primary distributed buying power additional sources to complement them to the level enabling it ´s creation. So profit in the long run and in global scale depends totally from volume of loans in the system, transfers and consumption of already created profit. Otherwise, there is no way to achieve it globally at all.

Private loans

As salaries are not enough to globally create profits, people, companies have to borrow. We all know it too well: mortgages, consumer loans of every kind, credit cards. The more we borrow and spend the higher sales we make and the higher the profits of companies.

The problem is that loans have to be repaid. While in the year, where loan is transformed to sales system receives more money into circulation, in subsequent years is the volume of money in economy shrinking by installments and interest. These money stop circulation in economy, they cannot generate further sales and they are returning to banks. The only way how they could get into circulation again would be through further loans. However, this is without further monetary policy manipulations impossible to maintain for eternity.

Imagine simple mortgage for 20 years with 4% p.a. interest. Do you know how much are you going to pay extra against the principal? It is 47%. Take the same mortgage for 30 years and the result is striking 73%!

The chart displays how much buying power the economy is losing in total if purchases are funded through loans. The methodology is simple, it compares all interest paid over full term of the loan against principal.

This extra money, which you pay on interests are costs of lost opportunity, they represent those sales, which you are never going to make because you decided for purchase on loan and the result is the permanent decimation of your buying power for decades to go. That is the way thousands of households are deciding every day and so accumulation of these decisions are creating the aggregate result of both positive side of loans on sales (momentarily increase of profits) as well as negative – sure degradation of sales (profits) in the future. Interests represent diminishing of monetary supply in circulation, which when not replenished will cause collapse of the whole financial system.

At the beginning of the cycle there is capital in the bank from profits from previous years. Under profits we here understand all its forms that are company profits, personal savings.

In the next step households will take out loans, which are transformed into consumption, sales and bring profits to companies. These profits are financed from old profit, which is now missing at the bank.

New profit comes back to banks, old capital represents uncovered money, which at the moment does not exist. If their owners, depositors wanted to withdraw them at that moment (together with new depositors who just deposited new profits) it would not be possible, bank do not have these money, and it will have them only if households will repay their loans. This is first, systemic risk of banking system generating new money and it is in the fact, that depositors believe that their money are at the bank safe but reality is that this money are not physically there. If all depositors would decide to withdraw together all their money any bank without help would immediately go bust. Every bank. Therefore there must be an option to refinance (either interbank or from central bank) which can supplement momentarily missing financial resources which will be coming back in future as repayments of issued loans.

Next comes the phase of repaying, households are reducing their common consumption by expenditures equaling installments and interest.

Profits of
companies are falling in line with reduced sales. Loss in private sector is the same as total volume of installments.

The more money is out of circulation, the more the sales are falling. More and more money are at the banks, because interests are causing the ebb of buying power. Uncovered capital at the banks is becoming covered (as a result of installments), that means money are back at the accounts for real. People are no longer willing to borrow, as their installments are maximal possible.

At the moment of full repayment of all loans is indebtedness of households zero, bank has on its accounts financial resources at full volume of original capital, new profit and paid interest.

However, that new money cannot be born out of nowhere. There is a law of preservation of matter and therefore this new money must be coming from real economy, where their withdrawal from circulation caused depletion of sales of another companies exactly by same amount that is new profit plus interest.

So there was a profit at the side of companies, bank got their interest but in global scale were this profits fully compensated by losses in different part of economy, through loss of sales.

From given analysis of loans as source of profits it is evident, that they cannot represent permanent and sustainable source of profits in capitalism. If the people are financing their needs through loans, it can and will increase of profits in certain companies, during repayments of interest there is profit created in the banks but at the global aggregate level it causes decrease of sales in another parts of economy, because buying power of all people was diminished by installments, which will not be showing as sales. Interest represent aggravating circumstance, by which the effect of arising global loss is multiplied and is greater than profit generated from sales on credit. We can feel it ourselves without any deep analysis. As soon as we take out a mortgage or any bigger personal loan our spending habits change dramatically: we reduce our standard spending and save more to cover those installments.

If somebody objects that loans can be repaid by new loans, even greater than old ones, so the answer is cruel reality that man can service only certain level of loans and that is given by his disposable income, diminished be necessary living costs. If individual already achieved this level of indebtedness, further increases are not possible. He would not have resources to repay and would go bancrupt.

Volume of profit coming from loans is therefore constant and given by total capacity of personal indebtedness multipied by number of people in the society.

It is necessary to keep in mind that such growth of profits is only temporary and highly cyclical and only seemingly substitutes missing buying power of people. What is at the beginning moving into profits is during the full repayment period source of losses, that are arising as unrealized sales from reason of permanent decimation of buying power caused by repayments of principal and interest.

If we have a society, where there is in circulation certain amount of money coming from wages (which by themselves are not sufficient to create profit) and we create additional buying power from loans during repayments we are going to get ourselves into situation that there will be not enough money in the economy to repay all the loans.

Simply, if there is in circulation for example 1 mil $ and to repay the loan and interest we need 1,4 mil this 0,4 mil does not exist and during repayments it will manifest itself by certain amount of loans not beeing repaid at all and individuals or companies will have to declare bankrupcy. During this bankrupcy the volume of capital in bank will be diminished by unpaid loans which means that savings from previous years will dissapear as well. Therefore profits achieved in the past and deposited at the banks are only illusory, their durability beeing seriously endengered by achieveing current profits again through loans. During repayments the whole system collapses (there is not enough money in circulation to repay all principals and interests) and profits are ereased.

What is the meaning of interest if it is causing such negative fall in global buying power followed by fall of global profits?

Classical theory teaches that interest is a reward for risk taking. Simple mathematics is proving that existence of interest at global scale is directly contributing to collapse of economy as a whole and as such is not repayable. Definitely not all of it, as there is no resources in the system for it. There are examples from history where certain nations considered interest as evil and was banned. Interest is causing ebb of capital from economy and its concentration in the banks which are trying to lend more and more. The more they are successful, the more money is being withdrawn from circulation and the whole economy is falling into recession. The recession would start even during repayments of principals, but interest is reinforcing it massively.

It is no wonder that first steps of central banks in recessions are lowering the interest rates and massive financial injection in the form of ultra cheap loans into retail banking houses. Without that the banks would go bust soon because there is not enough money in the circulation to repay all loans with interest. Their deposits would remain uncovered and depositors would wake up into very rough morning discovering that their cash machine withdrawals would not be realized.

Therefore uncovered old and new profits (deposits) are temporarily covered by loans from central banks. Is it a permanent fix? Do the banks have the chance to repay back this money? No, they don´t. If this central bank loans were to be repaid (principal and interest), there would have to be somewhere in the real economy money to be able to return into retail banks. But these don´t exist, as this was the reason of failing to repay the original loans at the first place. The only thing commercial banks can hope for is that they will manage to provide new loans with even higher interest and gradually repay the central bank loans. However this procedure is causing further reduction of money supply in the real economy and further deepening of recession. This new loans will not be repaid and the system is coming to a grinding halt.

Subsidies into commercial banks in the form of loans from central banks do not increase purchasing power of people, only temporarily cover missing resources at commercial banks. There is no further consumption, the people do not have their buying power restored. The only thing they are presented is an option for new loan. But to be able to get a loan of 1000$ is definitely not the same as getting a pay rise of 1000$ monthly. During recession there is huge unemployment, uncertainty, salaries are not rising and so there is no will to borrow. Everyday experience are foreclosures, people we knew lost their house or apartment because they were not able to afford monthly installments. In such circumstances consumers are not willing or able to fund their consumption through loans and so the wheel of capitalism is stopping. To try to revive the economy through new loans is therefore self-destructing policy which leads only to unsustainable growth.

The only weak option with loan fuelled economy is connected with inflation. If inflation is higher than interest rates, that is the only way how to get more money into the system. But if inflation is not matched with equally rising wages, then the effect of rising prices is simply the increasing of profit margin and that is having the worst impact on available buying power as described later in the model. There are three possible outcomes regarding inflation and wages:

Interest rate < Inflation (products & services) > wages growth

The loans are getting more money into economy but the effect of that is negated by wages not keeping the pace with inflation. After a time, the people would not be able to buy through loans what they used to buy before as their wages will not be sufficient to obtain the loan itself. This method is therefore not a long term solution and leads to overall decline in buying power as a result of loans.

Interest rate < Inflation (products & services) = wages growth

If wages are rising at the same rate as inflation, we might say that this is a win-win situation. Loans are delivering additional resources into economy as inflation above the interest rates and equally rising wages are providing needed supplement to distributed wages. But the problem here is that inflation needs to be permanent and constantly above consumer interest rates, and that is rarely the case. In today´s environment, it would need to be at the level above 4-5% for mortgages and 8-10% for consumer loans, so average some 6-7%! That is not so desirable and would bring with itself scores of other problems like diminishing the value of pension funds, thus ruining future pensioners and their buying power.That could very well offset all the gains of inflation connected with loans as means of adding buying power into the system. It is important not to forget that it would need also wages to rise at the same speed. So it would be necessary to forget about current practises of productivity rising above wages, which is an unfavourable notion with many CEOs. But if you agree that inflation is the only option and you want to go that route then why complicate it by first injecting money into economy through bank loans(which is diminishing buying power during repayments), then hope and orchestrate inflation and make it permanent by adding further and further monetary additions to keep it going ? Because if you are willing to „print money" you can as well supplement missing buying power directly through monetary stimulus to the government who redistributes it between people through various programs (see next chapters). By using direct monetary stimulus the size of it will be considerably smaller (no need to be above the interest rate to offset the effect of loans) and no need for inflation! The monetary supplement stimulus might provide inflation potential but only a potential, which does not necessarily have to grow into fully blown inflation (see chapter Collectors vs. Inflators). To sum up, to really supplement buying power through loans is more complicated and risky business than anybody might think at the first glance. To make it work requires also highly coordinated inflation of defined parameters, which is too dangerous and unpredictable road to go.

Interest rate < Inflation (products & services) < wages growth

That would work for the loans but not for businesses. Increases of wages over productivity are short term fix to bring balance to unfair distribution of GDP if such need would be but cannot continue forever as businesses would go bust.

The reasons, why the banks are not letting it sink into their collective consciousness, or they do not have to is because there is this further element of additional resources which is significantly supplementing the missing purchasing power. Without it, they would very soon see the consequences, as was evident in the first great depression in the thirties. After that, introduction of New Deal, more active role of the state, rising of state debt started supplementing the missing purchasing power and the need to analyze their own success became more and more distant and its sources considered as a matter of fact.

Transfers.

As the loans do not represent source of buying power that can be permanently transformed into sales and profits because of effect of interest, which is decimating buying power until the very collapse of economy let´s try to have a look if transfers can deliver something better.

During transfers missing purchasing power is replaced by additional sources coming from state and consequently redistributed between citizens through various programs.

Financial resources, from which state is financing transfers, are:

The proportion of particular parts can be highly variable, depending from macroeconomic policy the government chooses.

There is a bitter debate raging about the role of the state, the need to reduce the spending and cut costs, especially during the recession as state budgets are getting hit by lower taxes. This theory is trying to explain that state expenditures are indeed absolutely necessary even in good times and if such additional resources are not added into the economy on a regular basis, it starts to deteriorate. It is difficult to grasp that knowledge as natural instinct of every businessman and even ordinary citizen is to start saving if things are not going well. But what works for micro economy does not apply for macro economy as well. This distinction is absolutely essential, and ability to get through that common ordinary man thinking is key to any success of nation or state. At that top level, methods and strategies used by companies competing between each other are no longer valid. The role of a government of a country is not to win over its businesses, but to provide a framework in which they can prosper. At that position, things like monetary aggregate comes into play and profits are no longer achieved because of good business ideas but because there was money added into economy which allowed for some to become millionaires and keep that profits.

Taxes

In case, those sources of transfers are taxes, what is happening is partial exhausting already created profit:

Planned sales are higher than wages, and therefore they are not achievable at global scale without loans or transfers. If we take some part from profit and use it to finance such additional resources, we are getting buying power higher than wages paid to employees. Resulting are higher sales, which are still not at the level of planned sales as there is still some profit retained by which amount are planned sales lower against achievable, that is potential buying power.

Effect of taxes is evident, it immediately increases buying power but it is still not enough to full planned sales. The reason is simple, planned sales are higher by untaxed profit and so the wages are still not adequate to provide full needed buying power. At global scale the transfers from profit alone cannot be used permanently to stimulate economic activity as higher and higher taxes are increasing the buying power but at the same time they are lowering profit to zero. In such extreme case are taxes 100%, sales are at the level of wages and taxes (there is full realization of planned sales) but the profit is 0.

While the effect of interest and consequent lowering of profits because of falling sales isn´t so obvious (indeed, companies are neither aware of it and are not thinking about the fact that sales gained through loans will have certain global consequences) transfers from profit by way of taxes are much easily understood and companies are fighting them ferociously. Therefore always, if there is a new government which plans higher taxation, the stock markets are aiming south. It is obvious, when adhering to taxing strategy there is direct fall in profits but sales are rising. Therefore, the effect of taxing will slow down creation of profit but will increase sales and economy turnover.

Not even taxes by themselves will create sustainable source of economic growth and profit making. If they were to be at the level that would guarantee realization of full planned sales it would mean 100% taxation, which would be not very motivational for the companies. If they are at lower level, planned sales are not achieved exactly by missing part of the profit, which remains untaxed. At the global level, it is impossible to achieve profits through taxes long term.

As taxes are not sufficient to replace missing buying power, states are often resorting to loans, which are then used as source for transfers.

Together with taxes they are used to replace full missing buying power and the system looks balanced. But it is only temporary fix, because even the state will have to repay is debts one day and than there will be the same boomerang effect as with individual loans to ordinary people. Difference is that loans taken by the state are not preceived so critically by people as their own personal loans. They don´t have to make monthly installments towards it – at least this is what majority of people thinks. In reality they do, and they do it in the forms of increased taxes or lack of public services which are being cut in effort to repay the state debt. But because the states are rarely repaying principal and interest, for politicians it is very tempting path. When the debt is maturing, it is revolved with new debt. In reality, the states would have enormous problems repaying existing debts without somebody lending them again. This is clearly visible at current situation in Europe. Despite the fact,majority of states are still accumulating more and more debt.

Where are the resources financing the state coming from ?

It is easy,companies that made a profit and don´t know what to do with it are eager to provide it to the state.

In essence it is the same as if state collected 100% taxes. Difference is that this is voluntary, even that voluntary nature is bit fictitious. If the companies would decide not to buy state debt, their profits would stay at the banks and they would invest them the same way. If nor companies neither banks would be willing to finance the state, they would very soon discover that it is going to have serious consequences. The difference can be seen in Greece, Spain whose citizens are no longer willing to finance the state debt compared with Japan, where there is still this will and trust.(despite higher debt to GDP ratio)

Third option is to finance transfers through additional printing of money, quantitative easing. State, central bank issues further currency into circulation and gives it to the state (commercial banks) to spend. Devilish thought.

But it is also one of the means how to finance state transfers which can bring profits creation without backward cycles of recession which are arising during repayments of loans and allows persisting of profits without them having to be taxed as is the case with transfers financed through taxes.

It is not necessary to raise taxes to complement buying power from taxed profits. There is no increasing indebtedness of the state, which will become a serious problem sooner or later.

There are no economical cycles to fight against as there is no diminishing of sales stemming from repayments of personal loans. Profit creation is possible, as buying power consisting from wages and additional resources (transfers financed from monetary stimulus) is adequate to realize all planned sales and consequently profits.

This profit is of the same volume as the size of monetary stimulus.

However, such model of profit making has its serious faults as well:

Profit is created only from monetary stimulus, redistributed through transfers. Every new profit requires new money printing and so the profit itself is just illusionary, it is only new inflationary money whose purchasing power is lower and lower. If companies and individuals would try to realize all profits they would recognize that inflation would follow. The only reason why there is no serious inflation is that multimillionaires and billionaires really do not need and don´t spend their fortunes at once. The wealth is conserved at bank accounts, its buying power untested and trust maintains its value.

In reality these three options are used together and the government is using at least two of them (taxes and state loans) regularly and if situation is not good, monetary stimulus comes to play as well.

Choices of supplementing the missing demand can be easily described as 4 doors, behind which there lie different policy options, all with their benefits and consequences.

Taxes – obviously very unpopular choice. No politician wants to go that route and even if he does, the results achievable through this option are not optimal. After all, there are so many loopholes and half-legal ways to avoid higher taxation that total amount generated from planned higher taxes is rarely the same as actually collected. That quite misses the point and also brings with it the stigma of tax riser who at the end of day did not deliver on his promises, because the target goal is not fulfilled. The ultimate economic problem is that until taxes would not be 100% (and this is not politically feasible at all) , that option alone would not deliver the missing buying power in full and so the economy would not be growing just by that.

Monetary easing – is often seen as measure of last defense. After all, if we have to print the money that is the admittance that we are not able to effectively tax the saved profits and that means that we are having two bags of identical money: one sitting idle at bank accounts (or hidden in mattresses, old socks...), not revolving in real economy and as a consequence we have to print replacements, the duplicates which we try to incorporate into the real economy cycle of consumption, production. It brings the inevitable fears of inflation, as if we go about this route too often and for too long, there might be reasonable founded question what would one be able to buy for all this money if it all started to circulate in real economy at once.

Private debt – is a form of state policy as well. It simply means to do nothing and wait as private individuals will indebt themselves as they will have no other choice to survive. From our theory it is known that salaries are not enough to buy all what is produced and as profits are most easily achieved by pricing goods and services at AA level (level which requires households to take out loans to satisfy their basic needs, see later in chapter 5.1 Forced debt during consumption) it will happen sooner than later. But this avenue is dark and short as capacity of individual debt is rather limited and repayments represent built in recession factor of lost opportunity sales, magnified by interest being repaid. Once the individuals reach their debt limit, that road to profits is closed for good.

State debt – and this leaves us to the final source of profits in the economy, one used by everyone. It is easy, simple, hardly anybody complains. Companies are not hurt, indeed financing of state debt provides opportunity for investing free funds. General public have no understanding of the concept at all. It is not their debt (at least this is how the majority of people perceive it) and so they don´t have to worry about missing their installments. It does not incorporate such obvious heavy monetary tricks as money printing, so there is this feeling that money mass is maintained intact without inflation fears. Politicians are not reluctant to use it as all parties participate at the same game and all use the same tool. Infrequent voices to reduce the debt or lower the rate of annual deficits are not admitted and in reality there is no way it could have been done without starting serious recession, which would demolish the whole system. Nobody tried it so far and as we see from most recent developments, those who are embarking on this suicidal road are already reaping the expected „benefits“ of recession, deflation and wide spread economy collapse.

The state debt, its existence and ever growing size is necessary and unavoidable partner of capitalistic economy based on achieving profits, where these profits are not spent in full.

All profits ever achieved are financed by this debt through providing additional buying power which enables to create them.

The state debt is impossible to repay without further monetary action. Every attempt to do so would mean throwing economy into recession and continuous reduction of this debt would only deepen it. Repayment of state debt means not only stopping the flow of additional buying power which creates new profits, it erases the previous profits achieved. It is happening through reduction of money in circulation and this is reducing the overall business activity. More and more businesses are not achieving their planned profits (as there is no source of demand to fuel it) and failing companies and personal bankruptcies are causing the banks to record and write off more and more bad loans which will never be repaid. When bank goes bust, money lost during its bankruptcy is money accumulated from previous profits.

So far we have been discussing sources for state transfers. Now let´s have a look how these transfers can get money between real people and complement their buying power (that is the point). There are many options:

Structural projects as building of roads, railroads, hospitals ... green energy projects, hydropower plants, ebb power plants, hydrogen economy infrastructure and many more. That way the governments can build useful infrastructure and also stimulate demand. It is good if the need for such projects is evident. The problem is that these specific projects are aimed at specific areas (industries) and therefore their redistributing ability (their ability to complement missing buying power between wide layers of society) is rather limited. Income from them has only specific professions participating at these projects and complementing buying power is spreading further indirectly through further purchases that can or don´t have to be realized. Also this consumption is geographically limited to area of project and so its multiplication effects are not working at broader geographical scale. Large part of invested capital ends up at the hands of companies as profit (which is hindering factor of strengthening buying power) and there is the risk of corruption and overpayment of government projects, which is not doing good name for this kind of stimulus. Of course, in areas where infrastructural developments are obviously needed, there is nothing to wait for.

Family support. It is universal tool how to support buying power. It is working across the board through hands of many individuals, who know best how to spend their money and therefore there is no risk of deforming the market through moving of resources from needed industries to governmentally chosen ones, as is the case of infrastructural projects. (Having said that it is not a conclusion that government is not to realize infrastructural projects at all! The point is to realize that it is better to give the money Directly to the people to spend at what they need than having to invent artificial infrastructural government spending if none is evidently needed.) Additional buying power which families will gain through child supplements and similar benefits will be used accordingly to natural needs of consumers and will contribute to sales and profits in standard industries. At present developed industrial countries are facing falling fertility rates and aging of their populations. There are less and less children born which is causing deepening problems in pension systems around the globe. Some nations are desperately trying to replace their missing labor force with immigration. Transfers in the form of family benefits structured as progressive support based on number of children can be of great help in fighting this problem. It is easy and effective way how to encourage families to have more children and also provide for their increased living costs associated with upbringing of higher number of kids which is definitely not insignificant. The same way it is boosting the buying power of whole society. It is just as well as upbringing the kids' takes real effort and society should reward those who are doing it properly. Last, but also most important aspect of this policy is to ensure that this family supplements are not paid as means of easy money for families that do not care about their children and their education properly.

One of the views on pensions is such that their individual amount depends from how much person saved during his active life and consequently that is how much he is going to get when he retires. That is the principle of merit. This way of securing individuals for their golden age is useful, promotes individual efforts to work and achieve as much as possible during his active life. It is OK if majority of people that worked hard will get from their pension system adequate result. If pension funds are seriously diminished as a result of depression, or continuous system suffers a fall in contributions during prolonged unemployment what happens is that buying power of future generation of pensioners is seriously crippled as well. And this is having serious effect on further economy growth during following decades. And this brings us to the second view on pensions and that is as an extremely important source of buying power and profit creation.

If we allow that through fall of value of shares, bonds the value of pension funds is permanently diminished and we will not take steps to supplement it, we are in fact arranging for decline in economy due to definitely diminished buying power of pensioners. And we are speaking about multimillion army of consumers with enormous potential.

Pensions are outstandingly important society wide factor because they represent further missing part of sales, which is contributing to profit creation as such.

Therefore supplementing the pensions as one kind of state transfers is an ideal way how to stimulate economic growth. If it is not realized, stagnation of whole industries of production and services follows, which would otherwise be prospering and providing jobs for millions. It is also morally correct as people who worked hard all their life, paid taxes should not be crippled because of recession caused by wrong macroeconomic government policies and embedded system faults which are directly causing these recessions to happen. Furthermore, inaction in this area is causing further deterioration in economy as a whole because of fall in buying power of pensioners.

Without regard to the type of pension system from time to time there is a recession or trend (unfavorable demographic developments, fall in births, rise in age) which causes a situation in which real pensions are much lower than calculated.

Expected scenario: Recession causes fall of value of funds or lower pension contributions:

Represents shortage of buying power due to fall of pensions that will be causing permanent fall in companies' profits.

The question is, whether government should only accept the fact and take only preservative action or to take more proactive approach.

In continuous system there is the problem of unfavorable demographic development (the ratio between economically active persons and pensioners is going down) which is often advised to be solved by postponing the retirement age. As there is less and less workers per pensioner it seems the solution is retire later, so the pension amounts would be preserved.

In capital system it is very similar, when recession hits and value of pension funds go down its members are forced to work longer and save more years because their accumulated capital is not enough for adequate pension.

In both cases, where the solution is postponing the retirement age there are however serious side effects of such fix.

Maybe it is not commonly known (and advocates of prolonging working time pretend that the issue does not exist) but in a society there is only certain volume of useful work that needs to be done and requires employment. With growth of productivity that needed amount of work is continuously declining. Mechanization, computerization are bringing huge increases in productivity, the question is how these savings are passed to the people. During medieval ages people worked six days per week, often twelve hours daily. Nobody even dreamed about paid holidays. Today working time is usually five days, seven or eight hours daily, we are resting by the sea for 4-6 weeks.

Every year in society there are millions of jobs created as older people start their long awaited and earned pension. These jobs are gradually filled through intercompany rotation: senior employees are replacing pensioners, junior employees are being promoted to senior positions and graduates are getting their first jobs. However, if this natural circulation stops because senior employees are forced to postpone pension (whatever the reason) there is a consequence. Younger people are not able to find a job, because there is simply no work there. The circle of life had stopped. Every year by which pension age is prolonged the unemployment increases by 1-1,5% (depending from number of people in a grade). This is a terrible increase and it is a permanent one. If there will be no corresponding decrease of working time in one of subsequent grades, the unemployment will not decrease. There is extremely dangerous long-term unemployment arising, which is ruining people's lives and bringing whole “lost generations”.

Long term unemployment is also creating downward pressure at wages, which is consequently causing the decrease of overall pensions (in continuous systems directly, through fall in pension contributions, in capital system indirectly through fall of profits because of diminished buying power – the same applies for continuous system as well) and so the situation is deteriorating even further. There is a downward spiral starting, where falling pensions are forcing people to work longer, which is causing unemployment, pressing wages down and further diminishes future pensions.

Standard situation is described above. However, if recession hits and potential pensioners are postponing leaving, there is an overhang of supply of labor against demand for labor.

Therefore solving the unemployment stemming from recession is also in solving the financial situation of future pensioners and active management of labor market. Lowering of supply of labor by allowing people to go to pension (who are reluctant to do so because of financial strains) also lowers general unemployment.

Fall in pensions for whatever reason does not constitute fall in resources, which would pensioners be normally consuming, if there would be no fall in pensions. These capacities, natural resources, services, human work bind to them are still waiting to be used.

There is no reason why should this sector of economy fall and consequently deepen the recession. What happened is inadequate allocation of financial resources which were lowered by processes and factors which have no influence at availability of these capacities of real economy.

If we understood the principles of profit creation, its dependence from enough buying power we should not tolerate its fall without any action. As fall of values of pension portfolios in capital system depends directly from inadequate volume of state transfers (the profit exists from major part only as a result of transfers, fall in transfers causes fall in profits) the government is responsible for the fall of pensions as well, because it did not adequately support buying power and so caused fall of companies profits. Therefore, it is government duty to correct what it messed up and simultaneously supplement missing buying power of pensioners in the form of subsidies to temporarily lowered pensions.

In today times it is a habit to listen from politicians, that because of underfunding of pension systems the present workers will have to postpone their retirement, as there is no money and so in order for workers to ensure their decent pension they will have to work a bit longer. And therefore they are slowly, quietly approving laws which are making this a reality and are postponing the start of pension.

It sounds logically, simple and sound – as you have saved not enough money, you will have to save a bit more.

But it is a great lie, demagogy and unemployment which is steadily growing (and mostly among young people) is its direct consequence.

Imagine a mini economy, in which there is 1 company producing cakes. This company employs 12 people and its production is enough to satisfy needs of 220 people (120 employees, 50 children and 50 pensioners)

How the financial system which enables is functioning is not important at this moment.

Simply, there is a distributional mechanism which enables that every member of society gets his fair share.

After a time, new technological progress occurs which enables this company to substitute 20 employees with machines and produce instead of 220pc, say 250 cakes.

How the situation looks now ?

The result is quite worrying: the company produced more, but in reality this surplus has no market as the buying power decreased by 20 customers, who became unemployed and additional production which arose as a result of automation has no customers at all.

If before the automation the pension system (whatever type it is) was getting contributions from 120 people, now it is just 100 – so it is logically underfunded by 20%.

But this deficit in pension system is just FINANCIAL, and has to do solely with the way financial resources are distributed.

The REAL, RESOURCES based economy produced the same, even bigger amount of goods as before and therefore it is possible for people to go to pension at the previous age or even sooner !

What needs to be done for this scenario to materialize is to recalibrate the FINANCIAL economy, so as the redistribution of financial resources is adequate to the new production capacities of REAL economy.

Because in reality there is no problem, people in this society did nothing wrong. Quite the opposite – through technological advancement they reached higher level of production, which provides the basis for higher consumption. But it is just a potential and to make it transform into reality there is needed a change in financial flows, otherwise there will be, due to technological advancement quite opposite, illogical situation, where citizens will suffer.

While in the previous situation the company was getting 220 financial units (50+120 employees and their children, 50 pensioners) and was producing 220 units of production, now it is in a situation where it gets 200 financial units (50+100 employees, children and 50 pensioners) and is producing 250 production units – and this represents a loss against previous variant.

What logically follows is reduction of production, as there are no customers for it:

The result of unmanaged technological progress is an increase of unemployment and a finding, that built production capacities (not so a small investments) were in reality quite useless. There comes a desinvestment, which is even bigger as previous increase of production capacity and accompanying factor is growing unemployment. This reduction of REAL production potential is real threat to society as a whole, as it is really diminishing the amount of goods the economy will be able to provide in the future. It is not just an optical illusion, which arises as a result of wrongly calibrated financial system.

(we can see it on a daily basis, whether it is a case of automobile producers, steel makers or other industrial factories which are shedding thousands of employees, or cities going bust, which were once a pride of the nation and home of millions)

Of course, such approach is a total stupidity.

And imagine, that reaction to such problem is prolonging the amount of working time available through postponing the retirement age ! It is not enough that there is unemployment rising in the society, which is signaling the surplus of available labour (due to the rising automation), but we are going to increase this available working time even more !

Because postponing the pension age is exactly this, increasing the available working time on individuals and society as a whole. In reality, our problem is quite the opposite and requires quite the opposite solution: to decrease the available working time, which is not needed to be so high due to the technological advancement and to redistribute the financial resources so that everybody would get the fair share from increased production capacity of our economy.

So the postponing of retirement age is stupidity squared !!!

(and indeed leads to deepening of existing problems, drifting further away from real solution)

Imagine a hypothetical society in a distant future, where all the work is done by robots. Robots are working in factories, robots are serving in restaurants, providing all sorts of services... But this production is not for free. There is still a private ownership of production means and therefore their owners are asking money for their production.

Who will give it to them ? And where they will take them from ?

The buying power comes from wages, and entirely. The pensions are just transformed wages and savings are just wages not consumed so far.

As all work is done by robots, who are not taking any salary, citizens who have no income has no buying power and are not able to buy not even basic necessities.

Such a society would soon go bust, because after extinguishing the savings which would be flowing in just one direction (towards owners of robots) no more transactions could occur – simply there would be no money for it, and technological advancement of such world would soon show itself as quite useless.

The only way how such a world could survive would be 100% taxation, which would be regularly taking away all sales going to robots´s owners and redistributing them back between citizens.

100% taxation is inevitable, because with lower (say 90%) the citizens would get only 90% resources back to revitalize their buying power which would mean only 90% future sales. In further year it would be only 90% from 90%, so 81% and so on, so rather easily understood recession of such overrobotized world.

Such society is so far highly utopistic and represent pure communism, which corresponds to the level of taxation. But with such level of technological advancement it would be the only possible economical system.

The second extreme is some prehistoric society, where there are no production tools and so all people have to work to survive (to really produce, what their society needs). As work of everyone is essentially inevitable for survival and all have to consume rather equal amounts of goods (food) to survive, everybody will get share of common production (food = wage) and taxation is 0%. If there would be any taxation, some members of such society would not get their full share and they would perish by hunger. As everybody´s work is essential for survival of society as a whole, there is no taxation and everybody uses his full wage (share) to maintain his life.

Our present position is somewhere in the middle. Production is partially automated, and is moving more and more to the right of the chart. During last 20-30 years there has been an enormous technological progress, mainly because of computerization and automation in production. That means shifting of profits towards owners of production means. If such shift is not matched with higher taxation, there comes an automated decrease of sales and fall of economic system into recession, as buying power was reduced due to technological progress and its revival to previous level is not happening.

The rise of capital share on society product (so clearly visible during last 20-30 years) is inevitable asking for higher taxation, which will shift part of profits (and so buying power) back towards employees. Otherwise the increased production capacity of our economy will come in vain and temporary substitute of regular buying power (wages) by personal debt will inevitably lead to bust. Personal debts are not a sustainable form of aggregate demand.

So if you are hearing argument of the Right, that taxes were lower in the past and now they are too high and so to start the economy we have to lower them again, you can understand why this reasoning is wrong.
Those, asking for lower taxes often go in their reasoning back to the medieval times, where they quote 10% taxation as that time prevailing tax to landlords and comparing it with today´s 25-30%.

Of course! This historical increase of taxation is an inevitable reaction to technological progress, which is more and more removing the need for human work. Production remains (increases) but the number of people working towards its achieving is continuously falling. Therefore we need higher and higher redistribution, so that production output would get to previous number of members of society.

(if the Right is not asking for removal of certain number of citizens by war, which would of course clearly depict its agenda for potential voters. And not to mention that even such barbaric solution would not bring equilibrium to economic system. Why to build an industry if its builders will get only destruction and its production capacity will remain useless ?)

The another argument, you may come across is the following: technological progress, and unemployment that comes with it is OK, those who are against it are idiots and the society always managed to cope with this problem and moved to higher level. They will tell you about demolishing of machinery in GB during industrial revolution and they will point out to the indisputable progress and higher living standards of today.

It is a matter of course that technological progress is OK, and this theory never disputed it. Technological progress increases production capacity of REAL, resources based economy as an only possible way to provide higher consumption to the people.

But these critics will never tell you, HOW the society actually managed to cope with this problem !!!

Before industrial revolution people commonly worked 10-12 hours per day, 6 days in week, children labor was a matter of fact and nobody from common employees even dreamed about paid vacation.

After the industrial revolution, and as a mean to solve problems related with unemployment the situation of employees changed dramatically:

What happened:

Shortening of working time to 10, later just 8 hours per day

Ban on child labor

Shortening of working week to 5 days

Introduction of paid vacation and increasing its duration

Introduction of paid pension

Continuously shortening of weekly working time

So, all measures logically aimed at shortening of working time (as the need of human labor is continuously decreasing) and parallel increasing of taxation (in order to pass the increase in productivity on all members of society, not just owners of production means)

Without these measures the society would quickly deteriorate into chaos, revolutions and civil wars.

So which way shell we go now?

Will it be the way of enlightenment, further passing of benefits of increased productivity towards the people in the form of decreasing the working time ?

We can choose from: to further lower daily working time, more weeks off, sooner pension

Of course, it is historically inevitable and in line with technological progress to further increase the rate of taxation, which will enable the FINANCIAL side, redistribution which will enable consumption for all.

Or will it be the path of barbarity?

Increase of unemployment, not utilizing and destruction of already existing production capacities or even worse – war?

And all of this just because we are not able to understand the necessity of redistribution, accompanying the technological progress?

Situation in Europe seems as if we forgot all the knowledge accumulated during the 30. of previous century and we are going to repeat all the cruel mistakes again and again.

Postponing the retirement age is definitely one of wrong ways, which will lead only to further suffering and decline.

Is it an accident or direct cause that recession arose through excessive mortgage indebtedness?

During previous 10 years house prices were rising more than inflation. People were happy from the property boom, there was surety that house is the best investment and its value is steadily raising. This gave them feeling of safety and supported their buying spree. This feeling was however based on irrational basis.

If a family has one child, parents can say that increase in value of family house represents future inheritance, which is compensating higher price that this child will have to pay for his own home. It is however only weak remedy for total higher living costs. There is also the risk that value of property will go down and so the proceeds from sale of parent's house will be lower than the price of his own new home. Main problem in this model is the fact that with only one child human society is destined to extinction. To maintain stable population, there is a need to have at least 2,1 children that is minimum two kids. So even with ideal economy developments, where house prices would be rising without interruption there would be no long term profit from that as society as a whole would be walking towards extinction.

If family have two children, when property prices are rising the value of family home is rising as well but during its sale and division of inheritance between two kids the proceeds per child are not enough to offset the increased price of new home that each child had to pay (offset is only 50%) and so the total balance of wider family is negative. Children have worse financial situation than their parents, because their buying power is smaller than their parents (due to higher mortgage installments).

With three and more children the situation is even worse.

Rise of property prices is very illusionary benefit. In reality it causes diminishing of buying power and it is binding it to bricks and mortar for decades.

So are the efforts to revive the economy by restarting the growth of property prices. This kind of thinking is evidence of not understanding of principles of causes of recession and how these sources are manifesting in the real life. To try and measure revival, green shots by increasing property prices is utterly counterproductive. That's how the recession started.

The recession came because through consecutive rising of house prices there was also corresponding increase of mortgage installments and so the aggregate demand was diminished. Year by year. That decrease in buying power was temporarily replaced by loans (often backed by mortgage) but repayments of these loans were decreasing the buying power even more.

Every year in which the prices of property were rising more than inflation (and with it the salaries) the volume of permanent buying power, which does not have to be financed by loans, was decreasing.

The solution of the problem is the solution of its source and also its consequences. Through partial debt relief that is transfer financed from monetary stimulus or taxes the state will pay certain part of mortgages. The final effect is immediate and permanent increase of buying power of citizens, as decrease of mortgage installments is also permanent.

This method can be used to improve financial situation in certain geographical location. It is possible to lower mortgage indebtedness in certain states, counties which are hit by the recession the most and so stimulate these areas which need it most.

If somebody starts thinking why we should repay somebody's mortgages, just because they were not able to calculate that they will not be able to repay them the answer is the following:

Millions of people lost their jobs and roof above their heads without any fault of their own. Financial recession, caused by greedy and stupid banks ruined thousands of businesses and how is the problem being addressed today?

The very same banks that caused this are being bailed out, FED is providing them billions of cheap loans to survive and in spite of all this it is not working. Why pour the finances to the banks, where effect is only in strengthening the balance sheets, but is not contributing to missing demand? If bank gets cheap money, the only thing it can do with them is to lend them again

But during situation where our neighbors are losing jobs and houses the willingness to borrow is rather low. Even if people started to borrow, what they cannot repay back, we would be back to the square one. Cheap credit is getting only to speculators who are investing them to shares thus causing their prices to go up. The yield goes down, investors will be asking increase in profits which will cause pressure to inflation. With general decline of buying power the rise in inflation will cause further deterioration of living standards.

Instead of pouring money to banks it is suitable to put them to the second side of the equation – to mortgage saddled citizens. That will decrease their monthly installments and boost their buying power. Through partial debt relief the balance sheets of the banks will be equally strengthened, the similar way as through direct cheap loans from FED. But the final effect to growth is incomparable. It is also immoral to give extra loans to banks, which caused the crisis and not to provide them to people directly, as only people can start the economy moving again. Partial repayment of mortgages is the same as providing the ultra cheap loans to citizens.

Correct approach should be to decrease indebtedness of citizens directly:

All these types of transfers (structural projects, family support, pensions support, debt relief) have similar effect – they are stimulating the economy as they are generating buying power of citizens which is causing increase of sales and ability to achieve the planned sales. Without their existence there is no possibility to achieve profit long term.

Limits of supply side stimulus.

It is important to again address the fact that some banks are being bailed out and some are not. This is viewed by wide public as highly unfair practice, one that is clearly stinking by oligarchic manners. If you are too big to fail, you can do any kind of stupid and risky deals and in the event things go wrong the taxpayers are left with the bill. Of course, if short term profits materialized OK, there would be no adequate profit sharing with public. We economists understand the need to preserve the functional banking system and the risk of massive systemic failure of it in case of inaction during such domino failures. But public does not. And also small banks that went under just because their clients were not able to pay their obligations because they lost their jobs en masse in the aftermath of financial meltdown caused by too big to fail feel that double meter was used. And what about the thousands and thousands of small businesses? Why they had not been bailed as well? Why secondary victims of financial crisis are left to the wolves and primary culprits are being saved? Sure, sure, too big to fail.

But in this case we are not speaking about capitalism, or democracy. What we have in here is pure corporate fascism. Some entities are getting preferential treatment because their size. This was case not just for banks, but also automakers and other financial companies like AIG. Without regard of success of such bailouts we must think about the future. The very democracy here is at risk. The issue is not how many jobs were saved by the measures taken, but the very fact that such measures were seen as inevitable to prevent total meltdown.

Because if the governments took such steps and they were truly necessary, then similar alleviations should had been provided fairly to all market participants. That would be fair, that would be democratic. And if we agree that government should provide relief to market participants to overcome the worst recession in modern history, that there is a reasonable point in logic that government should rather provide preventive aid to all market participants based on equal approach in order to prevent the crisis than consequent "firefighting" and more costly efforts.

What are we speaking about?

The post crisis bank saving measures by FED and other central banks around the world through pouring huge liquidity into banks and quantitative easing is in fact still help to the supply side only. And that in highly developed economies with mature markets might simply not be good enough.

Imagine a neighborhood, where there is high unemployment, low salaries, simply a poor neighborhood. And there is a place, perfectly suitable for a restaurant. Because there is this perfect spot and there seems to be a need for such establishment, as there is no other restaurant nearby, there comes this savvy entrepreneur and applies for a loan with the bank. He gets it and builds a wonderful place. But as the neighborhood is really short of excessive buying power, the restaurant is not prospering and eventually goes bust. Bank takes a hit and has to write off this loan. But during the time the restaurant was still struggling it was paying wages to its employees who in turn were able to spend and so was supporting the mini economy of their neighborhood.

After a time, another entrepreneur comes there and says: What an opportunity!

And so he goes the same route as his predecessor with similar results, and another bank suffers the loss. This scenario can repeat in many forms, scales and geographic locations, but the common ground is based on fact that there was a monetary stimulus provided to the economy in the form of business loan which generated employment, wages and from it stemming consequent additional buying power which contributed to profit making in particular area. But as the corresponding buying power which was expected to support the original business venture is not adequate and sustainable, it collapses and causes a loss of capital in the banking sector. The byproduct of such buying power injections are profits at some other businesses that benefited from increased overall demand, fuelled by wages of failed companies.

This is the nature of supply side of monetary stimulus. It provides wages, coming from bank capital, which are lasting for the duration of venture built with such bank capital. After the venture goes bust, bank capital takes a hit. Monetary stimulus provides new, cheap capital to the banks to start lending again, but it is not addressing the reasons why the venture collapsed and so caused the need for additional monetary stimulus.

Without the corresponding boost of demand, which would be permanently matching the new supply created, such new venture (supply entity) has no chance to survive or can survive only at the expense of another supply entity. The examples are plentiful: Nokia, Blackberry surrenders to Apple, Sony and Panasonic are being beaten by Samsung... It is a dog eat dog world. It is a wonderful mechanism which brings about innovations and technological progress as only new and better, cheaper products are getting chance to survive. But is not answering the problem of increased or just sustainable consumption at mature, concentrated markets. After some time there is no one willing to build that "restaurant" business again as there is already wide spread knowledge that it will simply not succeed. It does not matter how good the offering will be, there are simply no customers there with enough money to support it.

Banks are not willing to lend, as they are also fully aware of the fact of missing demand and regardless how pro-business they are, there is no sense of throwing money into black hole. This is the point in time, where supply side stimulus of cheap central banks money is not going to do any good to the economy as all participants are already in understanding that the problem is at the Demand side.

And if this is the case, then the preventive role of the government is to boost the overall demand of its citizens by any of above mentioned methods. There is no point of permanently boosting the supply side only to see how ineffective these efforts are. Dog eat dog world is good in rapidly developing countries where new inventions are everyday reality. With mature markets, and massive unemployment there is a space for live and let live approach, which is facilitated by supporting the aggregate demand. The entrepreneurs should be given a chance to be rewarded for their risk taking by supporting the sustainable demand.

Which side to support, whether supply (through cheap credit) or demand (by supplementing demand) is easy to decide by level of unemployment and production capacities utilization. If unemployment is high and factories are not working at 100%, then demand side needs help. If unemployment is OK and economy is not significantly beyond its production potential then supply side should be given green to go.

It is necessary to distinguish profit and economic growth. As our models are saying that without additional resources it is not possible to achieve profits long term, it does not apply to economic growth. Economic growth is possible to achieve even without making the profits. The growth in productivity enables increases in real life living standards, but must be fully passed towards buying power of people.

The relationship between profit and productivity documents the following scheme:

Let´s imagine a cooperative, where 10 people are baking breads. Their monthly production is 10 pieces and to ensure justice in distribution of duties and rewards they all agreed, that wage will be 1$ for each and price of finished product 1$ as well. So everybody who works his part will get salary which will enable him to buy exactly one bread and cooperative will achieve full sales. Sales are equal to costs, there is no profit planned.

This is an example where there is full realization of production, all that was produced will be sold. There are no losses from overproduction but no profit either. As redistributed buying power is of the same volume as planned sales, no additional resources are needed to achieve these sales.

Now let´s add category of profit.

There comes this smart guy with entrepreneurial skills and he says to our bakers: you have it very nice here, but you are working rather inefficiently. Sell this cooperative to me, I will introduce capitalism here which will be making profits and together we shall be working more efficiently. We shall be producing twice as many breads and you will be getting the same wage as today, that is 1$.

Sounds like a good proposition, does it not? Productivity will rise twofold, wages will stay the same so there should be mutual satisfaction and bakers should be better off. And so they agree and introduce capitalism. But capitalism asks for some profits, does it not?

Let´s say that by changing the character of economic system our businessman really manages to achieve better productivity, brings new technologies, improves organisation of work and production really increases twofold as he promised.

But how can be in this improved way of doing business achieved profit, how big it is going to be?

This depends from setting the unit selling price. The entrepreneur has four generic choices to make:

A) The price will stay the same, that is 1$ per bread. In this case bakers will gain the same as before introduction of profits, they will be able to buy the same amount for their salaries, their buying powere will be not diminished and as set selling price per unit remains the same their needs will be satisfied at the same level.

The problem is what to do with the remaining 10 unsold breads. As our market represents 10$ (total buying power), there will be no more sales as there are no more buyers, that would be possessing additional buying power. 10 additionally produced breads will rot as there is nobody needing them. This represents problem of capitalism that is known as overproduction. We can see it every day. Hypermarkets are dumping tons of food every day because there is nobody to buy it, while there are countries where people are dying from hunger.

Such business result would please no businessman. If he were to achieve growth in productivity and managed to produce twice as many and achieved no profit he would be really unhappy. The additional production of 10 breads representing hypothetical profit of 10$ would never be realized, as there would be no additional buying power to make it so. The result of business in this case would be zero and consequently there would be pointless wasting of natural resources as to produce twice as many breads he would have to use twice as much ingredients.

Another subvariant (in case of durable goods) is that this unsold production will remain in the warehouse. Here comes the increase of balance sheet and anticipation of future sales in next period. However, as there is no more buyers in our little simulated economy, respectively all employess already spent all their wages we cannot expect from them any further sales in the next period. Their buying power will be restored only with next wages which anticipates also next round of production which is not going to happen. The already produced goods are still at the warehouse, there are no buyers and so instead of further production and wages what follows are layoffs. Production for warehouse is not a solution of this price variant.

The only salvation for businessman who sets price at his employees buying power level is to sell his overproduction in another economy, where there is additional buying power. This leads to expansion, globalization and colonial practises. The efforts to gain new markets is another of build in genes of capitalism, desperately trying to achieve profits. But this effort is at the global level not sustainable longterm. What is trying to achieve businessman in country X, is identical to businessmann in country Y. I shell describe this situation further in the chapter of international trade.

If there is no external economy where this overproduction could be realized, there must come to play the phenomenon of additional resources as transfers and loans. That way the buying power of citizens gets a boost temporarily but it is really only temporary fix which does not enable long term profit creation. Option, where missing buying power is replaced by loans looks like this:

In the first step the consumers will borrow 10$ and so will manage to make planned sales 20$.

In the second step the company will again produce 20 breads but buying power is no longer supplemented by loan. Indeed, it is the contrary. After its repayment at the amount of 10$ + interest (say 10% = 1$) the buying power will decrease to negative numbers. Employees are not only unable to buy any product (all their wages are used to repay the loans) but they are at the minus caused by their inability to repay interest. Payed salaries, which are at full used to repay the loans represent a net loss for the enterpreneur, which he is at this stage not aware of. His planned sales will not be realized at all. Sales from previous year financed through loan will come back as boomerang in the form of totally decimated buying power.

Therefore the final bilance looks like this:

In total the enterpreneur gained nothing as with this strategy the profit achieved in the first year is fully offset with the loss, coming from paid wages in second year which are not transformed to buying power as these are in full used to repay the loans. As paid wages were at the level of 10$, the interest will not be repaid at all, there are no financial resources in the system for that. Bank will suffer a loss, which will manifest itself as write off of profits deposited by enterpreneur in the previous year.

This model is showing that to achieve profit by financing consumption through loans is not possible, it is allowing only for cyclical boost in buying power which is subsequently followed by its decline and this decline is greater by amount allocated to interest.

B) At price between 0,5-1 we are speaking about partial passing of productivity gains to employees. The result would be similar to 1$ in the fact that actually making profit without loan is not possible, only employees would benefit a little more. With price 0.7$ they are able to buy some 14.3 breads but 4$ in additional resources is still missing.

C) If the enterpreneur would set the price at 0,5$ per unit of production, the planned sales would be at the level of available buying power but he would not achieve any profit.

This option is in full benefiting employees (full passing of productivity gains towards employees) but with zero profit for enterpreneur.

D) By setting price below production costs, say 0,4$ it is obvious that the result would be a loss and the employees would have theoretically saved 2$ from their available buying power but the saving would remain really only theoretical as their wages would not be paid at full. The business with sales of 8$ would not be in the position to pay wages of 10$.

As options C and D bring no profit to enterpreneurs, they will not be used.

There are serious doubts about profitability of option A(or B). If there is no other market where overproduction could be placed to achieve profit is possible only through increased consumption of existing consumers and only through their incurring private debt. However, it is questionable why should the existing customers voluntarily take on debt to buy twice as many goods as they were consuming till now. As their needs were satisfied so far, to rely that these will double at the cost of additional debt is not exactly the safest strategy.

Therefor to existing options A,B,C,D we have to add variant AA, which guaratees profit by setting the price the way so that common(used to) consumption can be achieved only through additinal debt. That means the unit selling price will be higher then 1$.

This option has great advantage against original A option where profit is possible (through additional debt) but we cannot be sure that people will take on this debt as their basic needs were already satisfied.

AA represents ultra capitalistic premise of unsatisfied needs which forces employees to take on debt so that they could satisfy their basic needs.

As this need is really strong there is objective feeling of lack and the people are forced to indebt themselves and the debt is a way how to achieve profit (even just short time). Entrepreneur does not care that it is only short time profit, what counts that there is some profit. Situation with option AA looks like this:

This is the simplified AA wher we anticipate sales without regard where they would be coming from. It is obvious that emplyees in that economy will be able to spend only 10$. Given that their normal consumption is 10pieces having value 10 x 1,1= 11$, they have strong motivation to take on loan 0.1$ per person(cumulatively 1$). By comparing wage 1$ with loan 0,1$ it does not look as such a bad proposition as interest(at whatever actual amount) will not represent a big part of their wage and installment looks managabe as well.

Fully split AA looks like this:

Here we clearly see 2 sources of sales:

Coming from internal economy, where we are expecting profit 1$, stemming from standard buying power 10$ represented by common wages and loan of 1$, supplementing buyingpower to the level of common needs (10$).

Is expected from external environment, where there are no further production costs and therefore the profit is at the level of sales. In reality this profit is a bit lower because of marketing, distribution costs but these represent only a fraction from sales.

What are the conclusions from the model ?

Capitalistic way of doing business which is aimed at achieveing profits can lead and leads to increased productivity, there is no doubt about it.

Fact that productivity raises is not a guarantee of actually achieving profit. If all increases in productivity are fully passed to employess as option C shows (change 1 $ to 0.5$), there will be no profit achieved.

By zero passing of productivity gains to citizens there is no profit but only overproduction, which represents a wasting of natural resources and is being dumped (price 1$ unchanged – option A)

If citizens will try to use this rise of productivity in this variant it is possible only through loans, which is not sustainable long term. During repayments there is a significant decline of satisfaction of common needs (expansion, recession) and the interest is not paid at all. During recession the profits created in previous years are erased, as cost of production which is produced is not covered by sales as wages are used solely to repay previous higher consumption.

Even those enterpreneurs which will set their prices without passing productivity gains on employess (variant A) will quickly discover that they have problems with overproduction and so there is a strong pressure to set the prices even higher until they reach level which is at least partially compensating unsure profits from external environment. The prices are higher and higher until they reach level AA, where there is not possible to satisfy even basic needs without loans. So the citizens are forced to take on loans and some profit is guaranteed. The overproduction remains and it can or is not placed outside of domestic economy.

In capitalism, in order to achieve profits the prices are eventually set in a way where citizens have very little benefit from increases of productivity gains. The only sure method to achieve profits is to set them higher and higher so as their level is even negating the increased productivity. The accompanying factor is overproduction, which needs placement and that can happen either in domestic economy (which is possible only through loans) or in external economy where (if the placement is a success) huge profits are generated.

At least that looks like the plan. But international trade chapter will show us that even that is just a dead end illusion.

The question of overproduction which is often raised in discussions is clearly answered.

If somebody argues that problem is in overproduction and there are excessive capacities build which are generating too many goods which the companies are not able to place which eventually leads to unemplyment the answer is: Yes, it is the overproduction. But, it is not the excessive capacities !!!

Every level of production is generating the overproduction !

The overproduction is the reason of agregate demand always lacking behind agregate supply because of category of profit, which is causing the AD never to be able to fully cover AS.

Because of this, there is a need of additional resources to supplement AD(loans) and the prices are desperately being set the way which stimulates taking on loans.

Imagine the second country Y, where there is similar process underway. Instead of breads they are producing orange juice and price and wage parameters are the same. Both countries are producing same amount of their respective products, they set prices at their employess buying power, achieve overproduction of 50% and they start to solve the problem of placing it in the neighbouring country.

Optimal variant – no profit, full passing of increased productivity to consumer

In this optimal variant of international trade we see similar results as from individual production when all profits from increased productivity are fully passed to consumers. In this case is international trade sure benefit to all as growth in productivity and specialization is enabling bigger and more versatile consumption as would be achieved in particular economies without specialization and trade. The problem is the finding that there is no profit there at all with this optimal solution.

It is really the same as if there were 2 companies within one country and their consumers would trade their products between themselves. This system without profit is sustainable long term; the nations can trade together forever as long as they have enough natural resources for their specific production.

To realize all produced goods (services) there is no need of any additional resources, no need to take on debt, no need to tax profits and consequently redistribute through transfers. There is no need for monetary stimulus, the citizens of both countries wield with enough buying power to realize all domestic as well as imported production.

There is no trade deficit which would be causing outflows of monetary mass from one of the economies and no exchange rate discrepancies. It is an ideal win-win situation.

But let´s add the factor of profit:

Variant with profit, as usual – no full passing of increased productivity to consumer

In this case we are getting to the situation as in the variant A) of individual company.

It is the ending of an equation, where entrepreneur trying to achieve profit is thinking of placing his overproduction in external economy as domestic consumers due to amount of redistributed salaries do not have adequate buying power for realization of all his production

The problem is that also companies in his target export country are trying to realize their production through the same strategy and so the result is increased variety of supply but still insufficient demand.

With international trade there is this additional factor of uncertainty how will the consumers decide:
Will they be consuming domestic production and import will be ignored? Will it be import, which will be favored? What will be the distribution ratio between domestic production and imports?
Will there be increase in consumption at all and will the consumers be willing to finance it through loans?

If consumers will decline to finance increased supply through loans, the result will be 0 profits in global scale. Total buying power 20$ is enough to realize sales in the same amount 20$(each nation 10$), what will cover just production costs. When consumption is distributed evenly between domestic and import products or both nations will decline imports totally businesses will gain nothing at all from that export strategy.

If increased supply is tempting enough and citizens are trapped in additional loans, there is expansion through indebtedness which will bring temporary profits but during its repayments there comes recession which will erase profits from previous years and consumption falls below minimal desired level.

Specialty in international trade is the possibility to partially of fully subdue one economy by another. So far we have been thinking with assumption that consumption will be more or less equally divided between domestic production and imports, or that imports will be equally ignored. These variants are not influencing the overall structure of economy of participating countries. But imagine the situation when citizens of one country will decide to absolutely favor certain imports before its own production:

Company A can fully place part of its production in domestic economy, where there is enough buying power due to paid wages and tries to sell the rest in country B.

Company B in country B has similar intentions but because of preference of its consumers he fails and gets nothing from A and nothing from B as well, as his domestic consumers decides to prefer imports before their own goods. As he paid 10$ during production as wages, his loss is -10$. Consumers in country B (unfaithful) at the beginning see no problem at all, they used their financial resources to buy what they wanted (from country

A) and they are happy from their freedom of choice. The reasons for such preference could have many sources:

Subjectively perceived or objective higher quality of goods from A

Lower price (often only marginally lower price can influence the purchasing decisions)

Here it is important to notice that lower price can be achieved through two different ways:

Either through wages reduction or through increase in production volumes and from it stemming economies of scale. This is often forgotten especially in today´s Europe problems where advice to some countries in problems is: You have to increase your competitiveness ! and it is meant as : Reduce your labor costs !

But in reality the success of some Northern Europe countries is not based on wage reductions but more on volume increases and consequent exports to Southern Europe as is evident in multibillion trade imbalances forming between these two groups. So becoming more competitive does not necessarily mean to cut labor costs, indeed those who provide such advice are profiting from exactly the opposite! As explained with AA variant of unsatisfied needs if domestic consumers are using just a little bit of loans the price of exported goods can be as low as desired and set to defeat any pricing of competitors in target country. The little profit in domestic country is guaranteed and majority of profits is generated through exports at whatever price. The point in this knowledge is such that getting lower prices of your production is generally not a result of wage level, but volume. But such strategy cannot be adapted by all. Doubling the production capacity of both trade partners would lead only to double supply, not double demand as well!

Difference in marketing quality

Ownership (influence over) distributions channels

This factor is really important. To get your goods to shelves today is herculean task and if there is exceptional relation between producers and distributors, these can get exclusivity at given territory. If they gain dominance at particular market, they gain all its buying power.

Without regard of reasons of preference occurring in the next step consumers in B will discover that domestic producers that were giving them jobs and salaries(used to buy goods from A) are bust and they are jobless. Now they cannot buy domestic goods even if they wanted as their domestic production base was destroyed, jobs and skills were lost. Their only hope how to satisfy their needs is to take on further debt (as their buying power is zero)

anks permanently finance consumption in country B? How could this model be functioning long term when it is evident that country B without industry and wages has no chance to repay its loans which it is using to buy imports from A? How are the banks in A going to accept that B is repaying its loans only through another loans and its indebtedness is ever growing?

These are all correct questions and there are no logical answers for them why it should work. This simplified model is leaving nobody at doubts that such trade is most dubious and unsustainable.

But it is happening!!! And it is happening as you are reading this book.

Country A is China, country B is USA.

USA since 80ies has opened its markets to Chinese goods and now the China is exporting billions of USD. As a consequence the whole industries of USA were ruined and millions of jobs were lost. At the beginning it looked as a profit, preferences which lead American consumers to choose Chinese goods were obviously the price. However, as unemployment was rising, so was the indebtedness (which was partially covering the potential of even higher unemployment and huge losses). China was also the lender. And it is still lending. If it stopped, the huge deficit of USA would be unable to refinance and the whole system would collapse.

There would be huge increase in unemployment in China, fall in profits of production businesses exporting to USA as well as fall of Chinese banks. Their loans are already not repayable, they are just being revolved. If the circle was to stop, it would be obvious that USA is not able to repay this debt and they would follow the path of Greece (without straightforwardly printing the money to cover the debt, as USA has that option. What kind of effect it would have on the value of its currency and inflation however remains a question)

In Europe countries A are Germany, Netherlands, Belgium – European exporters (the North) and countries B are Greece, Italy, Spain, Portugal and France (the main EU importers). The problem here is the same. A is exporting to B, which have no money to pay with, their domestic industry is falling due to these excessive imports and their finances are maintained only through mega loans provided by countries A.

So economic model, which is unstable and unsustainable is in fact widely used and its failures are visible on everyday problems which are getting bigger and bigger. The huge imbalances are just inflating to ever bigger proportions, lack of real missing power is being replaced just with loans which are revolving to eternity (?).

Politicians established this system on behalf of their industrial groups which were already not able to achieve profits in their domestic economies.

But this system will not last forever as growth on debt is only temporary and backward cycle of recession erases all already achieved profits. It seems that industry somehow got the message and so it is trying to make profits abroad. But these external profits are not sustainable either and will collapse because of the basic problem which is fall in buying power as a result of achieving profit as such. Every unspent profit is destroying buying power and if it is not substituted by transfers coming from state, it gradually diminishes until it falls to a level where the whole system comes to downward spiral of recession.

Expectations, that trade balances will level over time and state budget deficits will decline and so the unemployment and financial problems will be solved are vain. The only situation when this could have been achieved would be with zero profit at global scale. And this zero profit in international trade could become positive again only through loans and transfers. However, this is a thing which the industry is not able to recognize, or the equilibrium seems too distant in time to matter.

And the time bombs are ticking.

This brings whole new serious dangers to play:

If in domestic economy certain number of businesses and banks goes bust, it is an internal problem of that economy. Foreign countries bear no loss and it is none of their business. However, if country of type B declares bankruptcy it can lead to serious consequences. There are much bigger sums of money at play and subsequent threat of banks going bust in partner country as well as an substantial increase in unemployment stemming from fall of whole sectors of industries, which lost their foreign markets can lead to international incidents in the forms of wars (Give us back our money !!!, It is your fault !!! can have devastating consequences).

If the growth is achieved through monetary stimulus in domestic economy, excessive money printing can cause inflation in this country. However, if international trade is being financed through printing press, countries of type A can have serious objections that their savings are being devalued and the consequences could be similar.

So the globalization brings additional risks as model of unsustainable profit making will come to an dead end eventually in one of its forms and participating nations could see it as result of unfair approach of counterparty and ask for damages of revenge for lost time and resources invested in production (which ended unpaid) through war conflicts.

But in reality it is nobody's fault and it never will be anybody's fault. The profit is not achievable long term nor through international trade, neither in local economy. Globalization just postpones the inevitable and adds additional clouding of matters in the way of accusing somebody else. The principle: your shirt is closer then coat works well and to steal from "those" foreigners is always considered somehow more acceptable then to steal from your own people. But the parties are not aware that the global outcome will still be the same. It may last longer, but the end crush will hurt even more. (If you are banging your own head against the wall, you can be sure that it is not going to hurt as much as if your enemy would be doing you the service).

CHAPTER SIX

MAKE A PROFIT

You hear some success stories about new businesses instantly making tons of money, but the reality is often much different. It usually takes years for new companies to discover how to make a profit – and that's if they're able to stay open at all. If you've recently started a business, you've hopefully planned for this delay in income; however, you're also eager to start bringing in more money. After all, this is one of the reasons why you've decided to become an entrepreneur in the first place.A profitable business doesn't just happen. So how do businesses make money? You'll need the right knowledge, strategies and tools – and you'll need a plan. Commit to constant and never-ending improvement, and you can learn how to make a profit in business.

HOW TO MAKE A PROFIT IN BUSINESS

Businesses large and small have the same goal: reliable profits. Those just starting out have a few extra considerations as they build the foundation required to grow their business sustainably.

1. UNDERSTAND FINANCIALS

Before you can answer that question, you need to understand what it really means to make a profit. The money you bring into your company is considered revenue – and you don't get to put all of that in the bank. Once you pay for costs including payroll, taxes, supplies and other expenses, what's left over is your profit margin. This is the real number that will determine if you stay in business, experience explosive growth or have to close your doors.

You also need a basic knowledge of financial terms and the ability to read financial statements. You wouldn't fly a plane without knowing how to read the gauges – and the same applies to business. You can't tell if you're winning or losing if you don't understand the controls. Being able to read a balance sheet, income statement and cash flow statement means you'll be able to participate fully in conversations about how to make a profit.

2. CREATE A BUSINESS MAP

You won't be able to get where you're going if you don't have a map to get there. Every successful business starts with a plan – or even better, a business map. A business map is more than a way to get from point A to point B. It incorporates different scenarios so that you're ready for anything, then connects it all back to your overarching company vision.

Your business map will include a plan for how to make a profit. What can you do today, this week or this month to start improving your quality of profit ratio? Working with a business coach can also be an invaluable tool in this stage as they've helped countless others create a plan that is sustainable and scalable.

3. SET REALISTIC GOALS

With any new venture, it's easy to start thinking about the end goal. Today, you're opening your business; tomorrow, you want to make $10 million. If you think this way – in terms of creating a profitable business through massive growth from the get-go – you'll miss out on opportunities along the way and quickly become overwhelmed.

Instead, think in terms of incremental growth. Set SMART goals – Specific, Measurable, Achievable, Realistic and anchored within a Time Frame – and focus on improving your processes and systems and steadily increasing profits over time. Everything in life that's worthwhile takes work. Don't be distracted by "quick fixes" or get caught up in a competitive race. Focus on long-term growth and what's right for your business.

4. IDENTIFY WHAT'S HOLDING YOU BACK

As you're wondering how to make a profit, you must take an objective look at your entire organization. What's currently preventing you from making the money you know you're capable of earning? Is it a lack of viable leadership skills? Is it a problem with your sales team? Have you not spent enough time getting the word out about your brand?

The problem could also be something within you: Are you emotionally holding on to something that's limiting your company's growth? Have you held on to limiting beliefs? Once you've identified what is holding you back from your plan to increase profit, you can seek out the personal or professional tools needed to break through your barriers.

5. HIRE RIGHT

Tony always says to focus on your strengths, and hire for your weaknesses. Identify your own personal strengths and learn how to leverage them in leadership. Then identify your weaknesses and determine who you need to hire to fill those gaps. Perhaps you need an accountant or bookkeeper, or an incredible sales team.

You also want to hire raving fan employees. Who supports you 100%? Who not only knows the company inside and out, but can also rally the troops and bring in new customers? When you assemble a team of people who are excited to work for your brand and spread the message, it becomes much easier to be successful.

Finally, think about how you can better retain your existing employees. Do you need to hire fresh talent? Do you need to offer more benefits or make changes to the company culture? Do you need to invest more in your employees' well-being? Find the right mix of leadership, inspiration and incentives, and you'll find the key to how to make a profit in business.

6. ADD REAL VALUE FOR YOUR CUSTOMERS

How do businesses make money? The most important answer is that they always add real value for their customers. The bottom line for how to make a profit isn't actually a number – it's the value customers perceive in the business' product. When someone finds a product that fills a need they can't find anywhere else, they fall in love.

How do you truly add value your ideal customer can't ignore? Prioritize your market research to understand your customer's lifestyle and taste. By inhabiting your customer's mind and preferences, you're able to create compelling innovations customized to your market. As you innovate, track how your buyer responds so you can adjust your strategy as needed.

7. FOCUS ON STRATEGIC INNOVATION

There aren't many companies who can say they honestly offer their customers something brand new. Those that do are true disruptors, but that doesn't mean you have to be that type of company to increase profit. At this point, successful businesses expand on existing ideas, but they do it in a way that's useful and appealing to their customers. In other words, they strategically innovate. To do this, you need to identify who your customer really is and why they need your product or service.

An example of a strategic innovator is Netflix. Before the streaming service came along, people were happy to rent tapes at Blockbuster. Netflix saw how they could capitalize on this need for home entertainment, and found a way to make movies even more accessible for their target audience.

Netflix not only found a way to make a profit, but also a way to change the entire entertainment industry. If you're able to do this, you'll be leagues ahead of your competitors and can expect your profit margins to rise accordingly.

8. LEVERAGE YOUR CONNECTIONS

Running a profitable business requires far more than just number-crunching and managerial savvy. Like most of life, business success hinges on many factors, and building connections is one of them. Look at your network not as a collection of individuals, but as a collection of strategic alliances.

Build relationships with complementary businesses in your industry, and consider partnering with them for referrals. By learning to leverage your connections, you increase your scope and ability to make a profit.

9. CUSTOMIZE YOUR CUSTOMER ENGAGEMENT STRATEGIES

Understanding how to make a profit means taking a close look at how you're engaging your target market. There is no one-size-fits-all sales or marketing strategy, and you must customize yours to fit your product and clientele.

Given modern technology and the popularity of social media, for many products, outreach is about immediacy. Engage your target market digitally through your website and social media so they can easily access and learn about your product. You might consider adding interactive tools like webinars and demos to attract customers.

To make a profit, think outside the box about your product. You might need to cross-sell (provide new products or services that complement your existing ones, like a gym selling supplements), or adopt a sales model that creates returning customers (e.g. monthly service plans or bulk discounts). Whatever approach you take, measure your results to determine what tactics are working and which ones aren't.

10. TAKE MASSIVE ACTION

Once you've figured out what's holding you back, how to grow and how to strategically innovate, it's time to get to work and make your plan for how to make a profit. Create a timeline and develop a series of steps you and your team will take to increase profit margin.

Then make a massive action plan that will help you jumpstart growth and increase profit at your business. Maybe this involves creating a new department, launching a new marketing campaign or undergoing leadership training so you're better equipped to lead your company. Whatever you need to do, make sure it's included in your plan and that you have concrete, achievable goals for your company.

11. TRACK YOUR PROGRESS

Just because you've created an action plan doesn't mean your choices are set in stone. Monitor your results as your plan progresses. Have you figured out how to make a profit in a sustainable way? Set times that you'll check in with your team and reevaluate your progress. Maybe this is a monthly thing, or perhaps you check in every three or six months to monitor growth.

Tracking your progress allows you to evaluate what's working and what isn't, refine your strategies for making a profit and gather feedback from your employees. If you're consistently missing your goals, is it because they aren't realistic? Or because you're focusing on the wrong areas? If you're achieving your goals easily, you can ramp up your goal-setting – and your profits.

Printed by Libri Plureos GmbH in Hamburg,
Germany